W9-BDY-606

IN TWO VOLUMES
VOLUME ONE

John L. Stephens

Incidents of Travel in Yucatan

127 ENGRAVINGS
by
FREDERICK CATHERWOOD

EDICIONES

INCIDENTS OF TRAVEL IN YUCATAN
John L. Stephens.
(tomo I)

© Producción Editorial Dante, S.A.
  Calle 59 # 472
  Mérida, Yucatán, México.

Queda hecho el depósito que marca la ley
I.S.B.N. 968-7232-36-6

Ilustraciones: Frederick Catherwood.
Diseño de portada: Carlos Cámara.

IMPRESO EN MEXICO
PRINTED IN MEXICO

PREFACE

In his "Incidents of Travel in Central America, Chiapas, and Yucatan," the author intimated his intention to make a more thorough exploration of the ruins of the latter country. That intention has since been carried into effect, and the following pages are the result. They describe, as the author has reason to believe, the most extensive journey ever made by a stranger in that peninsula, and contain the account of visits to forty-four ruined cities, or places in which remains or vestiges of ancient population were found. The existence of most of these ruins was entirely unknown to the residents of the capital;—but few had ever been visited by white inhabitants;—they were desolate, and overgrown with trees. For a brief space the stillness that reigned around them was broken, and they were again left to solitude and silence. Time and the elements are hastening them to utter destruction. In a few generations, great edifices, their façades covered with sculptured ornaments, already cracked and yawning, must fall, and become mere shapeless mounds. It has been the fortune of the author to step between them and the entire destruction to which they are destined; and it is his hope to snatch from oblivion these perishing, but still gigantic memorials of a mysterious people. The descriptions are accompanied by full illustrations from Daguerreotype views and drawings taken on the spot by Mr. Catherwood, and the engravings were executed under his personal superintendence.

CONTENTS

CHAPTER I

CHAPTER II

CHAPTER III

CHAPTER IV

CHAPTER V

CHAPTER VI

CHAPTER VII

CHAPTER VIII

Contents

CHAPTER IX

CHAPTER X

CHAPTER XI

CHAPTER XII

Contents

CHAPTER XVI

CHAPTER XVII

APPENDIX

LIST OF ILLUSTRATIONS

List of Illustrations

CHAPTER I

The reader of my "Incidents of Travel in Central America, Chiapas, and Yucatan," may remember that the researches of Mr. Catherwood and myself in the last-mentioned country were abruptly terminated by the illness of the former. During our short sojourn in Yucatan, we received vague, but, at the same time, reliable intelligence of the existence of numerous and extensive cities, desolate and in ruins, which induced us to believe that the country presented a greater field for antiquarian research and discoveries than any we had yet visited. Under these circumstances, it was a severe hardship that we were compelled to leave it, and our only consolation in doing so was the hope of being able to return, prepared to make a thorough exploration of this unknown and mysterious region. In about a year we found ourselves in a condition to do so; and on Monday, the ninth of October, we put to sea on board the bark Tennessee, Scholefield master, for Sisal, the port from which we had sailed on our return to the United States.

The Tennessee was a down-Easter of two hundred and sixty tons burden, turned out apparently from one of those great factories where ships are built by the mile and chopped off to order, but stout, strong, well manned and equipped.

Her cargo was assorted for the Yucatan market, and consisted of a heavy stratum of iron at the bottom; midway were miscellanies, among which were cotton, muskets, and two hundred barrels of turpentine; and on top, within reach of the hatches, were six hundred kegs of gunpowder.

We had a valuable addition to our party in Dr. Cabot, of Boston, who accompanied us as an amateur, particularly as an ornithologist. Besides him, our only fellow-passenger was Mr. Camerden, who went out as supercargo.

The first morning out we woke with an extraordinary odour of turpentine, giving us apprehensions that a barrel had sprung a leak, which, by means of the cotton, might use up our gunpowder before it came to the hands of its consignee. This odour, however, was traced to a marking-pot, which quieted our apprehensions.

On the evening of the fourth day we had a severe thunder-storm. This was an old acquaintance of ours in the tropics, but one which at that time we were not disposed to welcome very cordially. Peals of thunder broke and crashed close over our heads, lightning flashed across the dark vault of the heavens, lighting up the surface of the water, and making fearfully visible our little vessel, tossing and pitching, a mere speck in immensity; and at times an angry ray darted toward the horizon, as if expressly to ignite our gunpowder. We discussed, though rather disjointedly, the doctrine of conductors and non-conductors, and advised the captain to put a few links of a chain cable round the mainmast, and carry the end of it over the side. We had some consolation in thinking that six hundred kegs were no worse than sixty, and that six would do our business; but, in fact, at the moment, we were very much of opinion that lightning and gunpowder were the only dangers of the sea. The night, however, wore through, and morning brought with it the usual, and, unhappily, almost the only change in those who go down to the sea in ships—forgetfulness of past danger.

On the evening of the seventeenth we passed, with a gentle breeze, the narrow passage known as the Hole in the Wall, and before morning we were lying broadside to the wind, and almost flying before it. The gale was terrific; nothing could stand upright to windward, and the sea was portentous. The captain sat under the quarter rail, watching the compass, and turning anxiously to the misty quarter of the heavens from which the winds seemed let loose. At breakfast large drops of sweat stood on his forehead; and though at first unwilling to admit it even to himself, we discovered that we were really in danger. We were driving, as fast as the wind could send us, upon the range of sunken rocks known as Abaco reef. Directly under our lee was the worst part of the whole reef, marked on the chart "Dangerous rocky-shore." Unless the gale abated or the wind hauled, in eight or ten hours we must strike. I must confess I saw but little hope of a change, and this rocky reef was but a few feet under water, and twenty miles distant from terra firma. If the vessel struck, she must go to pieces; nothing made by man's hands could stand against the fury of the sea, and every moment we were nearer destruction. We sat with the chart before us, looking at it as a sentenced convict might look at an advertisement of the time fixed for his execution. The sunken rocks seemed to stand out horribly on the paper; and though every glance at the sea told us that with daylight no human strength could prevail against it, it added to our uncomfortable feelings to know that it would be nearly night when the crisis arrived. We had but one consolation—there were no women or children on board. All were able-bodied men, capable of doing all that men could do in a struggle for life. But, fortunately for the reader of these pages, to say nothing of the relief to ourselves, at one o'clock the wind veered; we got on a little canvass; the good ship struggled for her life; by degrees she turned her back upon danger, and at night we were again on our way rejoicing.

On the twenty-seventh we furled sails off the port of Sisal. Five vessels were at anchor, an extraordinary circumstance for Sisal, and fortunate for us, because otherwise, as our captain had never been there before, though carefully looking for it, we might not have been able to find it. Our anchorage ground was on the open coast, two or three miles from land, at which distance it was necessary to keep, lest we should be driven ashore in case of a norther. Captain Scholefield, in fact, before he had discharged his cargo, was obliged to slip his cables and put to sea, and did not get back to his anchorage ground in nine days.

It was only four o'clock in the afternoon, but, by the regulations of the port, no passenger could land until the vessel had been visited by the health and custom-house officers. We looked out till dark, and long after the moon rose, but no notice whatever was taken of us, and, with no very amiable feelings toward the lazy officials, we turned in again on board.

In the morning, when we went on deck, we saw anchored under our stern the brig Lucinda, in which we had thought of taking passage; she had sailed from New-York four days after we did, and arrived during the night.

Very soon we saw coming off toward us the separate canoas of the health and custom-house officers. We were boarded by a very little man with a very big mustache, who was seasick before he mounted the deck, and in a few minutes betook himself to a berth. The preliminaries, however, were soon settled, and we went ashore. All disposition we might have had to complain the night before ceased on landing. Our former visit was not forgotten. The account of it had been translated and published, and, as soon as the object of our return was known, every facility was given us, and all our trunks, boxes, and multifarious luggage were passed without examination by the custom-house officers.

The little town of Sisal had not increased either in houses or inhabitants, and did not present any additional inducements to remain in it. The same afternoon we sent off our luggage in a carreta for Merida, and the next morning started in calezas ourselves.

From the suburbs of the town the plain was inundated, and for more than a mile our horses were above their knees in water. When we passed before, this ground was dry, parched, and cracking open. It was now the last of the rainy season, and the great body of water, without any stream by which to pass off, was drying up under a scorching sun, to leave the earth infected with malaria.

We had arrived in the fulness of tropical vegetation; the stunted trees along the road were in their deepest green, and Dr. Cabot opened to us a new source of interest and beauty. In order to begin business at once, he rode in the first caleza alone, and before he had gone far, we saw the barrel of his gun protrude on one side, and a bird fall. He had seen at Sisal, egretes, pelicans, and ducks which were rare in collections at home, and an oscillated wild turkey, which alone he thought worth the voyage to that place; and now, our attention being particularly directed to the subject, in some places the shrubs and bushes seemed brilliant with the plumage and vocal with the notes of birds. On the road he saw four different species which are entirely unknown in the United States, and six others which are found only in Louisiana and Florida, of most of which he procured specimens.

We stopped at Huncuma during the heat of the day; at dark reached Merida, and once more rode up to the house of Doña Micaela. Coming directly from home, we were not so much excited as when we reached it after a toilsome and comfortless journey in Central America; but even now it would ill become me to depreciate it, for the donna had read the account of my former visit to Merida, and she said, with an emphasis that covered all the rest, that the dates of arrival and departure as therein mentioned corresponded exactly with the entries in her book.

We had arrived at Merida at an opportune moment. As on

the occasion of our first visit, it was again a season of fiesta. The fête of San Cristoval, an observance of nine days, was then drawing to its close, and that evening a grand *function* was to be performed in the church dedicated to that saint. We had no time to lose, and, after a hasty supper, under the guidance of an Indian lad belonging to the house, we set out for the church. Very soon we were in the main street leading to it, along which, as it seemed, the whole population of Merida was moving to the fête. In every house a lantern hung from the balconied windows, or a long candle stood under a glass shade, to light them on their way. At the head of the street was a large plaza, on one side of which stood the church, with its great front brilliantly illuminated, and on the platform and steps, and all the open square before it, was a great moving mass of men, women, and children, mostly Indians, dressed in white.

We worked our way up to the door, and found the church within a blaze of light. Two rows of high candlesticks, with wax candles eight or ten feet high, extended the whole length from the door to the altar. On each side hung innumerable lamps, dotting the whole space from the floor to the ceiling; and back at the extreme end, standing on an elevated platform, was an altar thirty feet high, rich with silver ornaments and vases of flowers, and hung with innumerable lamps brilliantly burning. Priests in glittering vestments were officiating before it, music was swelling through the corridor and arches, and the floor of the immense church was covered with women on their knees, dressed in white, with white shawls over their heads. Through the entire body of the church not a man was to be seen. Near us was a bevy of young girls, beautifully dressed, with dark eyes, and their hair adorned with flowers, sustaining, though I was now a year older and colder, my previous impressions of the beauty of the ladies of Merida.

The chant died away, and as the women rose from their knees, their appearance was like the lifting of a white cloud, or spirits of air rising to a purer world; but, as they turned toward the door, the horizon became dusky with Indian faces, and half way up a spot rose above the rest, black as a thunder-cloud. The whole front ranks were Indians, except a towering African, whose face, in the cloud of white around, shone like the last touch of Day and Martin's best.

We waited till the last passed out, and, leaving the empty church blazing with light, with rockets, fireworks, drums, and

19

violins all working away together on the steps, we followed the crowd.

Turning along the left side of the plaza, we entered an illuminated street, at the foot of which, and across it, hung a gigantic cross, also brilliantly illuminated, and apparently stopping the way. Coming as we did directly from the church, it seemed to have some immediate connexion with the ceremonies we had just beheld; but the crowd stopped short of the cross, opposite a large house, also brilliantly illuminated. The door of this house, like that of the church, was open to all who chose to enter, or rather, at ʰhat moment, to all who could force their way through. Waiting the motion of the mass before us, and pressed by those behind, slowly, and with great labour, we worked our way into the sala. This was a large room extending along the whole front of the house, hot to suffocation, and crowded, or rather jammed, with men and women, or gentlemen and ladies, or by whatever other names they may be pleased to be called, clamorous and noisy as Bedlam let loose. For some time it was impossible for us to form any idea of what was going on. By degrees we were carried lengthwise through the sala, at every step getting elbowed, stamped upon, and occasionally the rim of a straw hat across the nose, or the puff of a paper cigar in the eyes. Very soon our faces were trickling with tears, which there was no friendly hand to wipe away, our own being pinned down to our sides.

On each side of the sala was a rude table, occupying its whole length, made of two rough boards, and supporting candles stuck in little tin receivers, about two feet apart. Along the tables were benches of the same rough materials, with men and women, whites, Mestizoes, and Indians, all sitting together, as close as the solidity and resistance of human flesh would permit, and seemingly closer than was sufferable. Every person at the table had before him or her a paper about a foot square, covered with figures in rows, and a small pile of grains of corn, and by its side a thumping stick some eighteen inches long, and one in diameter; while, amid all the noise, hubbub, and confusion, the eyes of all at the tables were bent constantly upon the papers before them. In that hot place, they seemed like a host of necromancers and witches, some of the latter young and extremely pretty, practising the black art.

By degrees we were passed out into the corridor, and here we were brought to a dead stand. Within arm's length was an imp of a boy, apparently the ringleader in this nocturnal orgy, who stood on a platform, rattling a bag of balls, and whose un-intermitted screeching, singsong cries had throughout risen shrill and distinct above every other sound. At that moment the noise and uproar were carried to the highest. The whole house seemed rising against the boy, and he, single-handed, or rather single-tongued, was doing battle with the whole, sending forth a clear stream of vocal power, which for a while bore its way triumphantly through the whole troubled waters, till, finding himself overpowered by the immense majority, with a tone that set the whole mass in a roar, and showed his democratic princi-ples, he cried out, "Vox populi est vox Dei!" and submitted.

Along the corridor, and in the whole area of the patio, or courtyard, were tables, and benches, and papers, and grains of corn, and ponderous sticks, the same as in the sala, and men and women sitting as close together. The passages were choked up, and over the heads of those sitting at the tables, all within reach were bending their eyes earnestly upon the mysterious papers. They were grayheads, boys and girls, and little children; fathers and mothers; husbands and wives; masters and servants; men high in office, muleteers, and bull-fighters; señoras and señoritas, with jewels around their necks and roses in their hair, and Indian women, worth only the slight covering they had on; beauty and deformity; the best and the vilest in Merida; per-haps, in all, two thousand persons; and this great multitude, many of whom we had seen but a few minutes before on their knees in the church, and among them the fair bevy of girls who had stood by us on the steps, were now assembled in a public gambling-house! a beautiful spectacle for a stranger the first night of his arrival in the capital!

But the devil is not so black as he is painted. I do not mean to offer any apology for gambling, in Yucatan, as in all the rest of Mexico, the bane and scourge of all ranks of society; but Me-rida is, in a small way, a city of my love, and I would fain raise this great mass of people from the gulf into which I have just plunged them: at least, I would lift their heads a little above water.

The game which they were engaged in playing is called La Loteria, or the Lottery. It is a favourite amusement throughout all the Mexican provinces, and extends to every village in Yuca-tan. It is authorized by the government, and, as was formerly the case to a pernicious extent with the lotteries in our own country, is used as an instrument to raise money, either for the use of the government itself, or for other purposes which are considered deserving. The principle of the game, or the scheme, consists of different combinations of numbers, from one to ninety, which are written on papers, nine rows on each side, with five figures in each row. As ninety figures admit of combinations to an almost indefinite extent, any number of papers can be issued, each containing a different series of combinations. These papers are stamped by the government, and sold at a real, or twelve and a half cents each. Every player purchases one of these papers, and fastens it to the table before him with a wafer. A purse is then made up, each player putting in a certain sum, which is collected by a boy in a hat. The boy with the bag of balls then announces, or rather sings out, the amount of the purse, and rattling his bag of balls, draws out one, and sings the number drawn. Every player marks on his paper with a grain of corn the number called off, and the one who is first able to mark five numbers in a row wins the purse. This he announces by rapping on the table with the stick, and standing up in his place. The boy sings over again the numbers drawn, and if, on comparison, all is found right, delivers the purse. The game is then ended, and another begins. Sometimes mistakes occur, and it was a mistake that led to the extraordinary clamour and confusion we had found on reaching the neighbourhood of the boy.

The amount played for will give some idea of the character of the game. Before commencing, the boy called out that the stake should in no case exceed two reals. This, however, was considered too high, and it was fixed by general consent at a medio, or six and a quarter cents. The largest amount proclaimed by the boy was twenty-seven dollars and three reals, which, divided among four hundred and thirty-eight players, did not make very heavy gambling. In fact, an old gentleman near whom I was standing told me it was a small affair, and not worth learning; but he added that there was a place in the neighbourhood where they played monté for doubloons. The whole amount circulated during the evening fell far short of what is often exchanged at a small party in a private drawing-room at home, and among those who would not relish the imputation of being accounted gamblers. In fact, it is perhaps but just to say that this great concourse of people was not brought together by the spirit of gambling. The people of Merida are fond of amusements, and in the absence of theatres and other public entertainments, the loteria is a great gathering-place, where persons of all ages and classes go to meet acquaintances. Rich and poor, great and small, meet under the same roof on a footing of perfect equality; good feeling is cultivated among all without any forgetting their place. Whole families go thither together; young people procure seats near each other, and play at more desperate games than the loteria, where hearts, or at least hands, are at stake, and perhaps that night some bold player, in losing his medios, drew a richer prize than the large purse of twenty-seven dollars and three reals. In fact, the loteria is considered merely an accessory to the pleasures of social intercourse; and, instead of gaming, it might be called a grand *conversacione,* but not very select; at least such was our conclusion; and there was something to make us rather uncharitable, for the place was hot enough to justify an application to it of the name bestowed in common parlance on the gambling-houses of London and Paris.

At about eleven o'clock we left. On our way down the street we passed the open door of a house in which were tables piled with gold and silver, and men around playing what, in the opinion of my old adviser of the loteria, was a game worth learning. We returned to the house, and found, what in our haste to be at the fiesta we had paid no attention to, that Doña Micaela could give us but one room, and that a small one, and near the door. As we expected to remain some days in Merida, we determined the next morning to take a house and go to housekeeping. While arranging ourselves for the night, we heard a loud, unnatural noise at the door, and, going out, found rolling over the pavement the Cerberus of the mansion, an old Indian miserably deformed, with his legs drawn up, his back down, his neck and head thrust forward, and his eyes starting from their sockets; he was entertaining himself with an outrageous soliloquy in the Maya tongue, and at our appearance he pitched his voice higher than before. Signs and threats had no effect. Secure in his deformity, he seemed to feel a malicious pleasure that he had it in his power to annoy us. We gave up, and while he continued rolling out tremendous Maya, we fell asleep. So passed our first night in Merida.

CHAPTER II

Early the next morning the carreta arrived
with our luggage, and, to avoid the trouble of loading and un-
loading, we directed it to remain at the door, and set out
immediately to look for a house. We had not much time, and,
consequently, but little choice; but, with the help of Doña
Micaela, in half an hour we found one that answered our purpose. We returned and started the carreta; an Indian followed,
carrying on his head a table, and on the top of it a washhand-
basin; another with three chairs, all Doña Micaela's, and we
closed the procession.

Our house was in the street of the Flamingo. Like most of
the houses in Merida, it was built of stone, and had one story;
the front was about thirty feet, and had a sala covering the
whole, about twenty feet in depth. The ceiling was perhaps
eighteen feet high, and the walls had wooden knobs for fasten-
ing hammocks. Behind the sala was a broad corridor, opening
on a courtyard, at one side of which was a sleeping-room,
and at the back of that a comeder or eating-room. The floors
were all of hard cement. The courtyard was about thirty feet
square, with high stone walls, and a well in the centre. Next,
running across the lot, was a kitchen, with a sleeping-room for
servants, and back of that another courtyard, forty feet deep,
with stone walls fifteen feet high; and in order that my inquiring fellow-citizens may form some idea of the comparative
value of real estate in Merida and New York, I mention that
the rent was four dollars per month, which for three persons

we did not consider extravagant. We had our own travelling beds, the table, washhand-basin, and chairs set up, and before breakfast our house was furnished.

In the mean time the fiesta of San Cristoval was going on. Grand mass was over, and the next ceremony in order was a *corrida de toros,* or bull-fight, to commence at ten o'clock.

The Plaza de Toros, or, in English, the bull-ring, was in the square of the church of San Cristoval. The enclosure or place for spectators occupied nearly the whole of the square, a strange and very original structure, which in its principles would astonish a European architect. It was a gigantic circular scaffold, perhaps fifteen hundred feet in circumference, capable of containing four or five thousand persons, erected and held together without the use of a single nail, being made of rude poles, just as they were cut in the woods, and tied together with withes. The interior was enclosed by long poles, crossing and interlacing each other, leaving only an opening for the door, and was divided in like manner by poles into boxes. The whole formed a gigantic frame of rustic lattice-work, admirably adapted for that hot climate, as it admitted a free circulation of air. The top was covered with an arbour made of the leaves of the American palm. The whole structure was simple and curious. Every Indian could assist in building it, and when the fiesta was over it could be torn down, and the materials used for firewood.

The corrida had begun when we arrived on the ground, and the place was already thronged. There was a great choice of seats, as one side was exposed to the full blaze of the sun. Over the doors were written Palco No. 1, Palco No. 2, &c., and each box had a separate proprietor, who stood in the doorway, with a little rickety step-ladder of three or four steps, inviting customers. One of them undertook to provide for us, and for two reals apiece we were conducted to front seats. It was, if possible, hotter than at the loteria, and in the movement and confusion of passing us to our seats, the great scaffold trembled, and seemed actually swaying to and fro under its living load.

The spectators were of all classes, colours, and ages, from gray heads to children asleep in their mother's arms; and next to me was a half-blooded maternal head of a family, with the key of her house in her hand, her children tucked in between the legs of her neighbours, or under their chairs. At the feet of those sitting on the front seats was a row of boys and girls, with their little heads poked through the railing, and all around hung down a variegated fringe-work of black and white legs. Opposite, and on the top of the scaffold, was a band of music, the leader of which wore a shining black mask, caricaturing a negro.

A bull was in the ring, two barbed darts trimmed with blue and yellow paper were hanging from his flanks, and his neck was pierced with wounds, from which ran down streams of blood. The picadores stood aloof with bloody spears in their hands; a mounted dragoon was master of ceremonies, and there were, besides, eight or ten vaqueros, or cattletenders, from the neighbouring haciendas, hard riders, and brought up to deal with cattle that run wild in the woods. These were dressed in pink-coloured shirt and trousers, and wore small hats of straw platted thick, with low round crowns, and narrow brims turned up at the side. Their saddles had large leathern flaps, covering half the body of the horse, and each had a lazo, or coil of rope, in his hand, and a pair of enormous iron spurs, perhaps six inches long, and weighing two or three pounds, which, contrasted with their small horses, gave a sort of Bombastes Furioso character to their appearance. By the order of the dragoon, these vaqueros, striking their coils of rope against the large flaps of their saddles, started the bull, and, chasing him round the ring, with a few throws of the lazo caught him by the horns and dragged him to a post at one side of the ring, where, riding off with the rope, they hauled his head down to the ground close against the post. Keeping it down in that position, some of the others passed a rope twice round his body just behind the fore legs, and, securing it on the back, passed it under his tail, and returning it, crossed it with the coils around his body. Two or three men on each side then hauled upon the rope, which cut into and compressed the bull's chest, and by its tightness under the tail almost lifted his hind legs from off the ground. This was to excite and madden him. The poor animal bellowed, threw himself on the ground, and kicked and struggled to get rid of the brutal tie. From the place where we sat we had in full view the front of the church of San Cristoval, and over the door we read in large characters, "*Hic est domus Dei—hic est portus cœli.*" "This is the house of God—this is the gate of heaven."

But they had yet another goad for the bull. Watching narrowly that the ropes around his horns did not get loose, they fixed upon his back the figure of a soldier in a cocked hat, seated in a saddle. This excited a great laugh among the spectators. We learned that both the saddle and the figure of the soldier were made of wood, paper, and gunpowder, composing a formidable piece of fireworks. When this was fairly secured, all fell back, and the picadores, mounted, and with their spears poised, took their places in the ring. The band, perhaps in compliment to us, and to remind us of home, struck up the beautiful *national* melody of "Jim Crow." A villanous-looking fellow set off large and furiously-whizzing rockets within a few feet of the bull; another fired in the heel the figure of the soldier on his back; the spectators shouted, the rope was slipped, and the bull let loose.

His first dash was perfectly furious. Bounding forward and throwing up his hind legs, maddened by the shouts of the crowd, and the whizzing and explosion, fire and smoke of the engine of torture on his back, he dashed blindly at every picador, receiving thrust after thrust with the spear, until, amid the loud laughter and shouts of the spectators, the powder burned out, and the poor beast, with gaping wounds, and blood streaming from them, turned and ran, bellowed for escape at the gate of entrance, and then crawled around the wall of the ring, looking up to the spectators, and with imploring eyes seemed pleading to the mild faces of the women for mercy.

In a few minutes he was lazoed and dragged off, and he had hardly disappeared when another was led in, the manner of whose introduction seemed more barbarous and brutal than any of the torments inflicted on the former. It was by a rope two or three hundred feet long, passed through the fleshy part of the bull's nose, and secured at both ends to the vaquero's saddle. In this way he was hauled through the streets and into the ring. Another vaquero followed, with a lazo over the horns, to hold the bull back, and keep him from rushing upon his leader. In the centre of the ring the leader loosed one end of the rope, and, riding on, dragged it trailing on the ground its whole length, perhaps a hundred yards, through the bull's nose, leaving a crust of dirt on one side as it came out bloody on the other. The bull, held back by the rope over his horns, stood with his neck outstretched; and when the end of the rope passed through, he licked his gory nose, pawed the ground, and bellowed.

He was then lazoed, dragged up to the post, girt with the rope around his body like the other, and then, amid bursts of music, rockets, and shouts, again let loose. The chulos went at him, flaring before him with the left hand red and yellow ponchas, and holding in the right darts containing fireworks, and ornamented with yellow paper cut into slips. These they thrust into his neck and flanks. The current of air accelerated the ignition of the fire; and when the fireworks exploded, the paper still rattled about his ears. The picadores then mounted their horses; but, after a few thrusts of the spear, the bull flinched, and the spectators, indignant that he did not show more fight, cried out, *"Saca esa vaca!"* "Take out that *cow!"*

The next was hauled on in the same way by a rope through the nose. He was girt with the rope, tortured with darts, speared by the picadores on horseback, and, as he did not show good fight, they dismounted and attacked him on foot. This is considered the most dangerous contest both for man and beast. The picadores formed in front of him, each with a black or yellow poncha in his left hand, and poising his spear with the right. They stood with their legs extended and knees bent, so as to keep a firm foothold, changing position by a spring forward or backward, on one side or the other, to meet the movement of the bull's head. The object was to strike between the horns into the back of the neck. Two or three struck him fairly with a cutting, heavy sound, and drew out their spears reeking with blood. One man misdirected his blow; the bull threw up his neck with the long handle of the spear standing upright in it, and rushing upon the picador, hurled him to the ground, and passed over his body, seeming to strike him with all four of his hoofs. The man never moved, but lay on his back, with his arms outstretched, apparently dead. The bull moved on with the handle of the spear still standing up in his neck, a terror to all in the ring. The vaqueros went in pursuit of him with the lazos, and, chasing him round, the spear fell out, and they caught him. In the mean time, the fallen man was picked up by some of his companions, and carried off, doubled up, and apparently cured forever of bull-fighting. We heard afterward that he only had some of his ribs broken.

He was hardly out of sight when the accident was forgotten; the bull was again assaulted, worried out, and dragged off. Others followed, making eight in all. At twelve o'clock the church bells rang and the fight ended, but, as we were dispersing, we were reminded that another would begin at four o'clock in the afternoon.

At four we were again in our places. Our special reason for following up this sport so closely was because we were advised that in the morning common people only attended, but that in the afternoon all the *gente decente,* or upper classes, of Merida would be present. I am happy to say, however, that this was not true, and the only sensible difference that we noticed was, that it was more crowded and hotter, and that the price of admission was double.

This was the last corrida of the fiesta, and some of the best bulls had been kept in reserve. The first that was dragged on was received with acclamations, as having distinguished himself before during the fiesta; but he bore an ugly mark for a favourite of the people, having been dragged by the nose till the cartilage was completely torn out by the rope.

The next would have been worthy of the best bull-fights of Old Spain, when the cavalier, at the glance of his lady's eye, leaped into the ring to play the matador with his sword. He was a large black bull, without any particular marks of ferocity about him; but a man who sat in our box, and for whose judgment I had conceived a great respect, lighted a new straw cigar, and pronounced him *"muy bravo."* There was no bellowing, blustering, or bravado about him, but he showed a calmness and self-possession which indicated a consciousness of strength. The picadores attacked him on horseback, and, like the Noir Faineant, or Sluggish Knight, in the lists at Ashby, for a time he contented himself with merely repelling the attacks of his assailants; but suddenly, as if a little vexed, he laid his head low, looked up at the spears pointed at his neck, and, shutting his eyes, rushed upon a picador on one side, struck his horse in the belly with his horns, lifted him off his feet, and brought horse and rider headlong to the ground. The horse fell upon the rider, rolled completely over him, with his heels in the air, and rose with one of the rider's feet entangled in the stirrup. For an instant he stood like a breathing statue, with nostrils wide and ears thrown back, wild with fright; and then, catching sight of the bull, he sprang clear of the ground, and dashed off at full speed around the ring, dragging after him the luckless picador. Around he went, senseless and helpless, his whole body grimed with dirt, and with no more life in it, apparently, than in a mere log of wood. At every bound it seemed as if the horse must strike his hind hoofs into his forehead. A cold shudder ran through the spectators. The man was a favourite; he had friends and relatives present, and everybody knew his name. A deep murmur of *"El Pobre"* burst from every bosom. I felt actually lifted from my seat, and the president of the Life and Trust would not have given a policy upon him for any premium. The picadores looked on aghast; the bull was roaming loose in the ring, perhaps the only indifferent spectator. My own feelings were roused against his companions, who, after what seemed an age of the rack, keeping a special good lookout upon the bull, at length started in pursuit with lazos, caught the horse around the neck, and brought him up headlong. The picadores extricated their fallen companion, and carried him out. His face was so begrimed with dirt that not a feature was visible; but, as he was borne across the ring, he opened his eyes, and they seemed starting from his head with terror.

He was hardly out of the ring when a hoarse cry ran through the spectators, *"a pie! a pie!"* "on foot! on foot!" The picadores dismounted and attacked the bull fiercely on foot, flourishing their ponchas. Almost at the first thrust he rushed upon one of his adversaries, tumbled him down, passed over his body and walked on without even turning round to look at him. He too was picked up and carried off.

The attack was renewed, and the bull became roused. In a few moments he brought another picador to the ground, and, carried on by his own impetus, passed over the body, but, with a violent effort, recovered himself, and turned short round upon his prostrate prey, glared over him for a moment with a low bellow, almost a howl, and, raising his fore feet a little from the ground, so as to give full force to the blow, thrust both horns into the stomach of the fallen picador. Happily, the points were sawed off; and, furious at not being able to gore and toss him, he got one horn under the picador's sash, lifted him, and dashed him back violently upon the ground. Accustomed as the spectators were to scenes of this kind, there was a universal burst of horror. Not a man moved to save him. It would, perhaps, be unjust to brand them as cowards, for, brutal and degrading as their tie was, they doubtless had a feeling of companionship; but, at all events, not a man attempted to save him, and the bull, after glaring over him, smelling and pawing him for a moment, to all, a moment of intense excitement, turned away and left him.

This man, too, was carried off. The sympathy of the spectators had for a while kept them hushed; but, as soon as the man was out of sight, all their pent-up feelings broke out in indignation against the bull, and there was a universal cry, in which the soft tones of women mingled with the hoarse voices of the men, *"Matálo! matálo!"* "Kill him! kill him!" The picadores stood aghast. Three of their companions had been struck down and carried off the field; the bull, pierced in several places, with blood streaming from him, but fresh as when he began, and fiercer, was roaming round the ring, and they held back, evidently afraid to attack him. The spectators showered upon them the opprobrious name of *"cobardes! cobardes!"* "cowards! cowards!" The dragoon enforced obedience to their voice, and, fortifying themselves with a strong draught of agua ardiente, they once more faced the bull, poised their spears before him, but with faint hands and trembling hearts, and finally, without a single thrust, amid the contemptuous shouts of the crowd, fell back, and left the bull master of the field.

Others were let in, and it was almost dark when the last fight ended. With the last bull the ring was opened to the boys, who, amid roars of laughter, pulled, hauled, and hustled him till he could hardly stand, and, amid the solemn tones of the vesper bell, the bull-fight in honour of San Cristoval ended.

Modern laws, we are told, have done much to abate the danger and ferocity of bull-fights. The horns of the bull are sawed off, so that he cannot gore, and spears are not allowed of more than a certain length, so that the bull cannot be killed by a direct blow; but, in my opinion, it would be really better for effect upon moral character that a bullfight should be, as it once was, a battle for life between man and beast, for then it was an exhibition of skill and daring, around which were sometimes thrown the graces of chivalry. The danger to which the man exposed himself, to a certain extent atoned for the barbarities inflicted on the bull. Here for eight days bulls with blunted horns had been stabbed, mangled, and tortured; many, no doubt, died of their wounds, or were killed because they could not recover; and that day we had seen four men struck down and carried off, two of whom had narrowly escaped with their lives, if, indeed, they ever recovered. After the immediate excitement of the danger, the men were less objects of commiseration than the beasts, but the whole showed the still bloody effects of this modified system of bull-fighting. Men go into all places without shame, though not without reproach, but I am happy in being able to say that none of what are called the higher classes of the ladies of Merida were present. Still there were many whose young and gentle faces did not convey the idea that they could find pleasure in scenes of blood, even though but the blood of brutes.

In the evening we took another hot-bath at the loteria, and the next day was Sunday, the last day of the fiesta, which opened in the morning with grand mass in the church of San

Cristoval. The great church, the paintings and altars, the burning of incense, the music, the imposing ceremonies of the altar, and the kneeling figures, inspired, as they always do, if not a religious, at least a solemn feeling; and, as on the occasion of grand mass in the Cathedral on my first visit to Merida, among the kneeling figures of the women my eyes rested upon one with a black mantle over her head, a prayer-book in her hand, and an Indian woman by her side, whose face exhibited a purity and intellectual softness which it was easy for the imagination to invest with all those attributes that make woman perfect. Whether she was maid, wife, or widow, I never learned.

At four o'clock in the afternoon we set out for the procession and paseo. The intense heat of the day was over, there was shade in the streets, and a fresh evening breeze. The streets through which the procession was to pass were adorned with branches, and at the corners were large collections of them, forming groves of green. The balconies of the windows were hung with silk curtains and banners, and in the doorways and along the walks sat rows of ladies simply but beautifully dressed, without hats, their hair adorned with flowers, and their necks with jewels. Near the church of San Cristoval we were arrested by the crowd, and waited till the procession came up.

It was headed by three priests, all richly dressed, one supporting a large silver cross ten feet high, and each of the others bearing a tall silver candlestick. They were followed by an Indian band, a motley group, the leaders of which were three Indians, one supporting the head and another the foot of a large violoncello. Next came a party of Indians, bearing on their shoulders a barrow supporting a large silver cross. At the foot of the cross sat the figure of Mary Magdalen, large as life, dressed in red. Over her head was a blue silk mantilla, with a broad gold border, and across her lap the figure of the dead Christ. The barrow was ornamented with large glass shades, under which candles were burning, and garlands and wreaths of flowers. This constituted the whole of the ceremonial part of the procession, and it was followed by a large concourse of Indians, men and women, dressed in white, all carrying in their hands long lighted candles.

When the crowd had passed by we strolled to the Alameda. This is the great place of promenade and paseo in Merida. It consists of a broad paved avenue, with a line of stone seats on each side, and beyond, on both sides, are carriage roads, shaded by rows of trees. In full sight, and giving a picturesque beauty to the scene, rises the Castillo, a ruined fortress, with battlements of dark gray stone, and the spires of the old Franciscan church rising inside, romantic in its appearance, and identified with the history of the Spanish conquest. Regularly every Sunday there is a paseo around the castle and along the Alameda, and this day, on account of the fête, it was one of the best and gayest of the year.

The most striking feature, the life and beauty of the paseo, were the calesas. Except one or two gigs, and a black, square box-wagon, which occasionally shame the paseo, the calesa is the only wheeled carriage in Merida. The body is somewhat like that of an oldfashioned gig, only much larger, and resting on the shaft a little in front of the wheels. It is painted red, with light and fancifully coloured curtains for the sun, drawn by one horse, with a boy riding him—simple, fanciful, and peculiar to Yucatan. Each calesa had two, and sometimes three ladies, in the latter case the prettiest sitting in the middle and a little in front, all without hats or veils, but their hair beautifully arranged and trimmed with flowers. Though exposed to the gaze of thousands, they had no boldness of manner or appearance, but, on the contrary, an air of modesty and simplicity, and all had a mild and gentle expression. Indeed, as they rode alone and unattended through the great mass of pedestrians, it seemed as if their very gentleness was a protection and shield from insult. We sat down on one of the stone benches in the Alameda, with the young, and gay, and beautiful of Merida. Strangers had not been there to laugh at and break up their good old customs. It was a little nook almost unknown to the rest of the world, and independent of it, enjoying what is so rarely found in this equalizing age, a sort of primitive or Knickerbocker state. The great charm was the air of contentment that reigned over the whole. If the young ladies in the calesas had occupied the most brilliant equipages in Hyde Park, they could not have seemed happier; and in their way, not less attractive were the great crowds of Mestizas and Indian women, some of the former being extremely pretty, and all having the same mild and gentle expression; they wore a picturesque costume of white, with a red border around the neck and skirt, and of that extraordinary cleanness which I had remarked as the characteristic of the poorest in Merida. For an hour, one continued stream of calesas, with ladies, and Mestizas, and Indian women, passed us without any noise, or confusion, or tumult, but in all there was such an air of quiet enjoyment that we felt sad as night came on;

and, as the sun sank behind the ruins of the castillo, we thought that there were few places in the world where it went down upon a prettier or happier scene.

The crowning ceremonies of the fiesta were a display of fireworks in the square of the church, followed by a concert and ball. The former was for the people, the latter for a select few. This, by-the-way, could hardly be considered very select, as, upon the application of our landlady, all our household received tickets.

The entertainment was given by an association of young men called *La Sociedad Philharmonica*. It was the second of a series proposed to be given on alternate Sundays, and already those who look coldly upon the efforts of enterprising young men were predicting that it would not hold out long, which prediction was unfortunately verified. It was given in a house situated on a street running off from the Plaza, one of the few in the city that had two stories, and which would be considered respectable among what are called palazzos in Italy. The entrance was into an entresol paved with stone, and the ascent by a broad flight of stone steps. The concert room was the sala. At one end was a platform, with instruments for the performers and amateurs, and two rows of chairs were arranged in parallel lines, opposite each other, the whole length of the room. When we entered, one row was occupied entirely by ladies, while that opposite was vacant. We approached it, but, fortunately, before exposing our ignorance of Merida etiquette, it occurred to us that these also were intended for ladies, and we moved on to a corner which afforded a longitudinal view of one line and an oblique view of the other. As different parties arrived, after leaving shawls, &c., at the door, a gentleman entered, leading the lady by the hand, which seemed much more graceful and gallant than our fashion of hitching her on his arm, particularly when there were two ladies. Leading her to a seat, he left her, and retired to the corridor, or the embrasure of a window. This continued till the whole line of chairs was filled up, and we were crowded out of our corner for our betters, so that the room presented a *coup d'œil* of ladies only. Here they sat, not to be touched, handled, or spoken to, but only to be looked at, which, long before the concert was over, some were tired of doing, and I think I am safe in saying that the faces of some of the ladies lighted up when the concert was done, and the gentlemen were invited to take partners for a waltz.

For the first time in my life, I saw beauty in a waltz. It

was not the furious whirl of the French waltz, stirring up the blood, making men perspire and young ladies look red, but a slow, gentle, and graceful movement, apparently inducing a languid, dreaming, and delightful state of being. The music, too, instead of bursting with a deafening crash, stole on the ear so gently, that, though every note was heard clearly and distinctly, it made no noise; and as the feet of the dancers fell to the gentle cadence, it seemed as if the imagination was only touched by the sound. Every face wore an expression of pure and refined enjoyment—an enjoyment derived rather from sentiment than from excited animal spirits. There were not the show and glitter of the ballroom in Europe or at home, but there were beauty of personal appearance, taste in dress, and propriety and simplicity of manners. At eleven o'clock the ball broke up; and if the loteria was objectionable, and the bull-fight brutal, the paseo and baglio redeemed them, and left on our minds a pleasing impression of the fête of San Cristoval.

One fiesta was hardly ended when another began. On Monday was the great fête of Todos Santos. Grand mass was said in all the churches, and in every family prayers were offered up for the souls of the dead; and, besides the usual ceremonies of the Catholic Church throughout the world, there is one peculiar to Yucatan, derived from the customs of the Indians, and called Mukbipoyo. On this day every Indian, according to his means, purchases and burns a certain number of consecrated candles, in honour of his deceased relatives, and in memory of each member of his family who has died within the year. Besides this, they bake in the earth a pie consisting of a paste of Indian corn, stuffed with pork and fowls, and seasoned with chili, and during the day every good Yucateco eats nothing but this. In the interior, where the Indians are less civilized, they religiously place a portion of this composition out of doors, under a tree, or in some retired place, for their deceased friends to eat, and they say that the portion thus set apart is always eaten, which induces the belief that the dead may be enticed back by appealing to the same appetites which govern when living; but this is sometimes accounted for by malicious and skeptical persons, who say that in every neighborhood there are other Indians, poorer than those who can afford to regale their deceased relatives, and these consider it no sin, in a matter of this kind, to step between the living and the dead.

We have reason to remember this fête from one untoward circumstance. A friendly neighbour, who, besides visiting us frequently with his wife and daughter, was in the habit of sending us fruit and dulces more than we could eat, this day, on the top of a large, undisposed-of present, sent us a huge piece of mukbipoyo. It was as hard as an oak plank, and as thick as six of them; and having already overtasked ourselves to reduce the pile on the table, when this came, in a fit of desperation we took it out into the courtyard and buried it. There it would have remained till this day but for a malicious dog which accompanied them on their next visit; he passed into the courtyard, rooted it up, and, while we were pointing to the empty platters as our acknowledgment of their kindness, this villanous dog sneaked through the sala and out at the front door with the pie in his mouth, apparently grown bigger since it was buried.

The fêtes were now ended, and we were not sorry, for now, for the first time, we had a prospect of having our clothes washed. Ever since our arrival, our linen, &c., accumulated during the voyage, had stood in gaping bundles, imploring us to do something for them, but during the continuance of the fiestas not a lavandera in Merida could be found to take in washing.

CHAPTER III

I trust the reader has not forgotten our old
friend Don Simon Peon, to whom, of course, our first visit
was made. We were received by himself and his mother, the Doña
Joaquina, with the same kindness as on the former occasion,
and in a greater degree. They immediately offered all in their
power to further the objects of our visit, and to the last day of
our residence in the country we continued to feel the benefit of
their friendly assistance. For the present, the sala of the Doña
Joaquina was every evening the rendezvous of her large and
respectable family connexion; there we were in the habit of
visiting at all times, and had reason to believe that we were
always welcome guests.

Among the first of Don Simon's good offices was a presenta-
tion to the governor of the state. This gentleman, by reason of
the peculiar political position of Yucatan, occupied at that time
a prominent and important position; but, before introducing
him to the reader, it may not be amiss to give a brief account of
the country of which he is the official head.

It may be remembered that Columbus, in his first three
voyages, did not reach the Continent of America. On his fourth,
final, and ill-fated expedition, "after sixty days of tempestuous
weather, without seeing sun or stars," he discovered a small
island, called by the Indians Guanaja, supposed to be that now
laid down on some maps as the island of Bonaca. While on
shore at this island, we saw coming from the west a canoe of
large size, filled with Indians, who appeared to be a more

civilized people than any the Spaniards had yet encountered. In return to the inquiries of the Spaniards for gold, they pointed toward the west, and endeavoured to persuade them to steer in that direction.

"Well would it have been for Columbus," says Mr. Irving, "had he followed their advice. Within a day or two he would have arrived at Yucatan; the discovery of Mexico and the other opulent countries of New Spain would have necessarily followed. The Southern Ocean would have been disclosed to him, and a succession of splendid discoveries would have shed fresh glory on his declining age, instead of its sinking amid gloom, neglect, and disappointment."

Four years afterward, in the year 1506, Juan Dias de Solis, in company with Vincent Yañez Pinzon, one of the companions of Columbus on his last voyage, held the same course to the island of Guanaja, and then, steering to the west, discovered the east coast of the province now known by the name of Yucatan, and sailed along it some distance, without, however, prosecuting the discovery.

On the eighth of February, 1517, Francisco Hernandez de Cordova, a rich hidalgo of Cuba, with three vessels of good burden and one hundred and ten soldiers, set sail from the port now known as St. Jago de Cuba, on a voyage of discovery. Doubling St. Anton, now called Cape St. Antonio, and sailing at hazard toward the west, at the end of twenty-one days they saw land which had never been seen before by Europeans.

On the fourth of March, while making arrangements to land, they saw coming to the ships five large canoes, with oars and sails, some of them containing fifty Indians; and on signals of invitation being made, above thirty came on board the captain's vessel. The next day the chief returned with twelve large canoes and numerous Indians, and invited the Spaniards to his town, promising them food, and whatever was necessary. The words he used were *Conèx cotoch,* which, in the language of the Indians of the present day, means, "Come to our town." Not understanding the meaning, and supposing it was the name of the place, the Spaniards called it Point or Cape Cotoche, which name it still bears.

The Spaniards accepted the invitation, but, seeing the shore lined with Indians, landed in their own boats, and carried with them fifteen crossbows and ten muskets.

After halting a little while, they set out, the chief leading the way; and, passing by a thick wood, at a signal from the chief a great body of Indians in ambush rushed out, poured upon them a shower of arrows, which at the first discharge wounded fifteen, and then fell upon them with their lances; but the swords, crossbows, and firearms of the Spaniards struck them with such terror that they fled precipitately leaving seventeen of their number slain.

The Spaniards returned to their ships, and continued toward the west, always keeping in sight of land. In fifteen days they discovered a large town, with an inlet which seemed to be a river. They went ashore for water, and were about returning, when some fifty Indians came toward them, dressed in good mantas of cotton, and invited them to their town. After some hesitation, the Spaniards went with them, and arrived at some large stone houses like those they had seen at Cape Cotoche, on the walls of which were figures of serpents and other idols. These were their temples, and about one of the altars were drops of fresh blood, which they afterward learned was the blood of Indians, sacrificed for the destruction of the strangers.

Hostile preparations of a formidable character were soon apparent, and the Spaniards, fearing to encounter such a multitude, retired to the shore, and embarked with their water-casks. This place was called Kimpech, and at this day it is known by the name of Campeachy.

Continuing westwardly, they came opposite a town about a league from the coast, which was called Potonchan or Champoton. Being again in distress for water, they went ashore all together, and well armed. They found some wells, filled their casks, and were about putting them into the boats, when large bodies of warlike Indians came upon them from the town, armed with bows and arrows, lances, shields, double-handed swords, slings, and stones, their faces painted white, black, and red, and their heads adorned with plumes of feathers. The Spaniards were unable to embark their water-casks, and, as it was now nearly night, they determined to remain on shore. At daylight great bodies of warriors, with colours flying, advanced upon them from all sides. The fight lasted more than half an hour; fifty Spaniards were killed; and Cordova, seeing that it was impossible to drive back such a multitude, formed the rest into a compact body and cut his way to the boats. The Indians followed close at their heels, even pursuing them into the water. In the confusion, so many of the Spaniards ran to the boats together that they came near sinking them; but, hanging to the boats, half wading and half swimming, they reached the small vessel, which came up to their assistance. Fifty-seven of their companions were killed, and five more died of their wounds. There was but one soldier who escaped unwounded; all the rest had two, three, or four, and the captain, Hernandez de Cordova, had twelve arrow wounds. In the old Spanish charts this place is called the Bay "de Mala Pelea," or "of the bad fight."

This great disaster determined them to return to Cuba. So many sailors were wounded that they could not man the three vessels, in consequence of which they burned the smaller one, and, dividing the crew between the other two, set sail. To add to their calamity, they had been obliged to leave behind their water-casks, and they came to such extremities with thirst, that their tongues and lips cracked open. On the coast of Florida they procured water, and when it was brought alongside one soldier threw himself from the ship into the boat, and, seizing an earthen jar, drank till he swelled and died.

After this the vessel of the captain sprung a leak, but by great exertions at the pumps they kept her from sinking, and brought her into Puerto Carenas, which is now the port of Havana. Three more soldiers died of their wounds; the rest dispersed, and the captain, Hernandez de Cordova, died ten days after his arrival. Such was the disastrous end of the first expedition to Yucatan.

In the same year, 1517, another expedition was set on foot. Four vessels were fitted out, two hundred and forty companions enrolled themselves, and Juan de Grijalva, "a hopeful young man and well-behaved," was named captain-in-chief.

On the sixth of April, 1518, the armament sailed from the port of Matanzas for Yucatan. Doubling Cape San Antonio, and forced by the currents farther down than its predecessor, they discovered the Island of Cozumel.

Crossing over, and sailing along the coast, they came in sight of Potonchan, and entered the Bay of Mala Pelea, memorable for the disastrous repulse of the Spaniards. The Indians, exulting in their former victory, charged upon them before they landed, and fought them in the water; but the Spaniards made such slaughter that the Indians fled and abandoned the town. The victory, however, cost them dear. Three soldiers were killed, more than seventy wounded, and Juan de Grijalva was hurt by three arrows, one of which knocked out two of his teeth.

Embarking again, and continuing toward the west, in three days they saw the mouth of a very broad river, which, as Yucatan was then supposed to be an island, they thought to be its boundary, and called the Boca de Terminos. At Tobasco they first heard the famous name of Mexico; and after sailing on to Culua, now known as San Juan de Ulloa, the fortress of Vera Cruz, and some distance beyond along the coast, Grijalva returned to Cuba to add new fuel to the fire of adventure and discovery.

Another expedition was got up on a grand scale. Ten ships were fitted out, and it is creditable to the fame of Juan de Grijalva that all his old companions wished him for their chief; but, by a concurrence of circumstances, this office was conferred upon Hernando Cortez, then alcalde of Santiago de Cuba, a man comparatively unknown, but destined to be distinguished among the daring soldiers of that day as the Great Captain, and to build up a name almost overshadowing that of the discoverer of America.

The full particulars of all these expeditions form part and parcel of the history of Yucatan; but to present them in detail would occupy too large a portion of this work; and, besides, they form part of the great chain of events which led to the conquest of Mexico, the history of which, by the gifted author of Ferdinand and Isabella, it is hoped, will soon adorn the annals of literature.

Among the principal captains in the expeditions both of Grijalva and Cortez was Don Francisco Montejo, a gentleman of Seville. After the arrival of Cortez in Mexico, and while he was prosecuting his conquests in the interior, twice it was considered necessary to send commissioners to Spain, and on both occasions Don Francisco Montejo was nominated, the first time with one other, and the last time alone. On his second visit, besides receiving a confirmation of former grants and privileges, and a new coat of arms, as an acknowledgment of his distinguished services rendered to the crown in the expeditions of Grijalva and Cortez, he obtained from the king a grant for the pacification and conquest of the islands (as it is expressed) of Yucatan and Cozumel, which countries, amid the stirring scenes and golden prospects of the conquest of Mexico, had been entirely overlooked.

This grant bears date the eighth day of December, 1526, and, among other things, stipulated,

That the said Don Francisco de Montejo should have license and power to conquer and people the said islands of Yucatan and Cozumel:

That he should set out within one year from the date of the instrument:

That he should be governor and captain-general for life:

That he should be adelantado for life, and on his death the office should descend to his heirs and successors forever.

Ten square leagues of land and four per cent. of all the profit or advantage to be derived from all the lands discovered and peopled were given to himself, his heirs and successors forever.

Those who should join the expedition under him were for the first three years to pay only the one tenth part of the gold of the mines, the fourth year a ninth part, and the per centage should go on increasing till it reached a fifth part.

They should be exempted from export duty upon the articles they carried with them, provided they were not taken for barter or sale.

They were allowed portions of land, and, after living on them four years complete, were to be at liberty to sell them and use them as their own.

Also to take rebellious Indians for slaves, and to take and buy Indians held by the caciques as slaves, under the regulations of the council of the Indies. The tithes or tenth parts were granted to be expended in churches and ornaments, and things necessary for divine worship.

The last provision, which may seem rather illiberal, if not libellous, was, that no lawyers or attorneys should go into those lands from the kingdom of Spain, nor from any other part, on account of the litigation and controversies that would follow them.

Don Francisco Montejo, now adelantado, is described as "of the middle stature, of a cheerful countenance, and gay disposition. At the time of his arrival here (in Mexico) he was about thirty-five years of age. He was fitter for business than war, and of a liberal turn, expending more than he received;" in which latter qualification for a great enterprise he could perhaps find his match at the present day.

The adelantado incurred great expenses in the purchase of arms, ammunition, horses, and provisions; and, selling an estate, which yielded him two thousand ducats of rent, he fitted out four vessels at his own expense, and embarked in them four hundred Spaniards, under an agreement for a certain share of the advantages of the expedition.

In the year 1527 (the month is not known) the armament

sailed from Seville, and, touching at the islands for supplies, it was remarked, as a circumstance of bad omen, that the adelantado had not on board two priests, which, under a general provision, every captain, officer, or subject who had license to discover and people islands or terra firma within the limits of the King of Spain, was bound to carry with him.

The fleet stopped at the island of Cozumel, where the adelantado had great difficulty in communicating with the Indians from want of an interpreter. Taking on board one of them as a guide, the fleet crossed over to the continent, and came to anchor off the coast. All the Spaniards went on shore, and, as the first act, with the solemnities usual in the new conquests, took formal possession of the country in the name of the king. Gonzalo Nieto planted the royal standard, and cried out, in a loud voice, "España! España! viva España!"

Leaving the sailors on board to take care of the vessel, the Spaniards landed their arms, ammunition, horses, and provisions, and, remaining here a few days to rest, from the excessive heat some became sick. The Indians knew that the Spaniards had established themselves in New Spain, and were determined to resist this invasion with all their strength; but, for the moment, they avoided any hostile demonstrations.

As yet the adelantado had only touched along the coast, and knew nothing of the interior. Experiencing great difficulty from the want of an interpreter, he commenced his march along the coast under the guidance of the Indian from Cozumel. The country was well peopled, and, without committing any violence upon the inhabitants, or suffering any injury from them, the Spaniards proceeded from town to town until they arrived at Conil. At this place, the Indians being apparently friendly, the Spaniards were thrown off their guard; and on one occasion, an Indian, who came to pay a visit, snatched a hanger from a little negro slave, and attempted to kill the adelantado. The latter drew his sword to defend himself, but the soldiers rushed forward and killed the Indian on the spot.

The adelantado now determined to march from Conil to the province of Choaca, and from this time they began to experience the dreadful hardships they were doomed to suffer in subduing Yucatan. There were no roads; the country was stony, and overgrown with thick woods. Fatigued with the difficulties of their march, the heat, and want of water, they arrived at Choaca, and found it deserted: the inhabitants had gone to join other Indians who were gathering for war. No one appeared to whom they could give notice of their pacific intentions, and the tidings that an Indian had been killed had gone before them.

Setting out again, still under the guidance of the Cozumel Indian, they reached a town named Aké. Here they found themselves confronted by a great multitude of Indians, who had lain in ambush, concealed in the woods.

These Indians were armed with quivers of arrows, sticks burned at the ends, lances pointed with sharp flints, and two-handed swords of very hard wood. They had flutes, and large sea-shells for trumpets, and turtle-shells which they struck with deers' horns. Their bodies were naked, except around the loins, and stained all over with earth of different colours, and they wore stone rings in their ears and noses.

The Spaniards were astonished at seeing such strange figures, and the noise that they made with the turtle-shells and horns, accompanied by a shout of voices, seemed to make the hills quake. The adelantado encouraged the Spaniards by relating his experience of war with the Indians, and a fearful battle commenced, which lasted all that day. Night came to put an end to the slaughter, but the Indians remained on the ground. The Spaniards had time to rest and bind up their wounds, but kept watch all night, with the dismal prospect of being destroyed on the next day.

At daylight the battle began again, and continued fiercely till midday, when the Indians began to give way. The Spaniards, encouraged by hope of victory, pressed them till they turned and fled, hiding themselves in the woods; but, ignorant of the ground, and worn out with constant fighting, the victors could only make themselves masters of the field. In this battle more than twelve hundred Indians were killed.

In the beginning of the year 1528, the adelantado determined again, by slow marches, to reconnoiter the country; and, having discovered the warlike character of the inhabitants, to avoid as much as possible all conflict with them. With this resolution, they set out from Aké in the direction of Chichen Itza, where, by kindness and conciliation, they got together some Indians, and built houses of wood and poles covered with palm leaves.

Here the adelantado made one unfortunate and fatal movement. Disheartened by not seeing any signs of gold, and learning from the Indians that the glittering metal was to be found in the province of Ba Khalal, the adelantado determined to send the Captain Davila to found in that province a town of Spaniards. Davila set out with fifty foot-soldiers and sixteen horsemen, and from the time of this separation difficulties and dangers accumulated upon both. All efforts to communicate with each other proved abortive. After many battles, perils, and sufferings, those in Chichen Itza saw themselves reduced to the wretched alternative of dying by hunger or by the hands of the Indians. An immense multitude of the latter having assembled for their destruction, the Spaniards left their fortifications, and went out on the plain to meet them. The most severe battle ever known in wars with the Indians took place. Great slaughter was made among them, but a hundred and fifty Spaniards were killed; nearly all the rest were wounded, and, worn down with fatigue, the survivors retreated to the fortifications. The Indians did not follow them, or, worn out as they were, they would have perished miserably to a man. At night the Spaniards escaped. From the meager and unsatisfactory notices of these events that have come down to us, it is not known with accuracy by what route they reached the coast; but the next that we hear of them is at Campeachy.

The fortunes of Davila were no better. Arrived at the province of Ba Khalal, he sent a message to the Lord of Chemecal to inquire about gold, and requesting a supply of provisions; the fierce answer of the cacique was, that he would send fowls on spears, and Indian corn on arrows. With forty men and five horses left, Davila struggled back to the coast, and, two years after their unfortunate separation, he joined the adelantado in Campeachy.

Their courage was still unbroken. Roused by the arrival of Davila, the adelantado determined to make another attempt to penetrate the country. For this purpose he again sent off Davila with fifty men, himself remaining in Campeachy with but forty soldiers and ten horsemen. As soon as the Indians discovered his small force, an immense multitude gathered round the camp. Hearing a tumult, the adelantado went out on horseback, and, riding toward a group assembled on a little hill, cried out, endeavouring to pacify them; but the Indians, turning in the direction of the voice, and recognising the adelantado, surrounded him, laid hands upon the reins of his horse, and tried to wrest from him his lance. The adelantado spurred his horse, and extricated himself for a moment, but so many Indians came up that they held his horse fast by the feet, took away his lance, and endeavoured to carry him off alive, intending, as they afterward said, to sacrifice him to their gods. Blas Gonzales was the only soldier near him, who, seeing his danger, threw himself on horseback, cleared a way through the Indians with his lance, and, with others who came up at the moment, rescued the adelantado. Both himself and the brave Gonzales were severely wounded, and the horse of the latter died of his wounds.

About this time the fame of the discovery of Peru reached these unlucky conquerors, and, taking advantage of the opportunity afforded by their proximity to the coast, many of the soldiers deserted. To follow up the conquest of Yucatan, it was indispensable to recruit his forces, and for this purpose the adelantado determined on going to New Spain.

He had previously sent information to the king of his misfortunes, and the king had despatched a royal parchment to the audiencia of Mexico, setting forth the services of the adelantado, the labours and losses he had sustained, and charging them to give him assistance in all that related to the conquest of Yucatan. With this favour and his rents in New Spain, he got together some soldiers, and bought vessels, arms, and other munitions of war, to prosecute his conquest. Unluckily, as Tobasco belonged to his government, and the Indians of that province, who had been subdued by Cortez, had revolted, he considered it advisable first to reduce them. The vessels sailed from Vera Cruz, and, stopping at Tobasco with a portion of his recruits, he sent on the vessels with the rest, under the command of his son, to prosecute the conquest in Yucatan.

But the adelantado found it much more difficult than he expected to reduce the Indians of Tobasco; and while he was engaged in it, the Spaniards in Campeachy, instead of being able to penetrate into the country, were undergoing great sufferings. The Indians cut off their supplies of provisions, and, being short of sustenance, nearly all became ill. They were obliged to make constant sorties to procure food, and it was necessary to let the horses go loose, though at the risk of their being killed. They were reduced so low that but five soldiers remained to watch over and provide for the rest. Finding it impossible to hold out any longer, they determined to abandon the place. Gonzales Nieto, who first planted the royal standard on the shores of Yucatan, was the last to leave it, and in the year 1535 not a single Spaniard remained in the country.

It was now notorious that the adelantado had not fulfilled the order to carry with him priests, and, by many of the daring but devout spirits of that day, his want of success in Yucatan was ascribed to this cause. The viceroy of Mexico, in the exercise of the discretion allowed under a rescript from the queen, determined forthwith to send priests, who should conquer the country by converting the Indians to Christianity.

The venerable Franciscan friar, Jacobo de Festera, although superior and prelate of the rich province of Mexico, zealous, says the historian, for the conversion of souls, and desirous to reduce the whole world to the knowledge of the true God, offered himself for this spiritual conquest, expecting many hardships, and doubtful of the result. Four persons of the same order were assigned as his companions; and, attended by some friendly Mexicans who had been converted to Christianity, on the eighth of March they arrived at Champoton, famed for the "mala pelea," or bad fight, of the Spaniards.

The Mexicans went before them to give notice of their coming, and to say that they came in the spirit of peace, few in number, and without arms, caring only for the salvation of souls, and to make known to the people the true God, whom they ought to worship. The lords of Champoton received the Mexican messengers amicably, and, satisfied that they could run but little risk, allowed the missionaries to enter their country. Regardless of the concerns of this world, says the historian, and irreproachable in their lives, they prevailed upon the Indians to listen to their preaching, and in a few days enjoyed the fruit of their labours. This fruit, he adds, "was not so great as if they had had interpreters familiar with the idiom; but the divine grace and the earnestness of these ministers were so powerful that, after forty days' communication, the lords brought voluntarily all their idols, and delivered them to the priests to be burned;" and, as the best proof of their sincerity, they brought their children, whom, says the Bishop Las Casas, they cherished more than the light of their eyes, to be indoctrinated and taught. Every day they became more attached to the padres, built them houses to live in, and a temple for worship; and one thing occurred which had never happened before. Twelve or fifteen lords, with great territories and many vassals, with the consent of their people, voluntarily acknowledged the dominion of the King of Castile. This agreement, under their signs and attested by the monks, the bishop says he had in his possession.

At this time, when, from such great beginnings, the conversion of the whole kingdom of Yucatan seemed almost certain, there happened (to use, as near as possible, the language of the historian) the greatest disaster that the devil, greedy of souls, could desire. Eighteen horsemen and twelve foot-soldiers, fugitives from New Spain, entered the country from some quarter, bringing with them loads of idols, which they had carried off from other provinces. The captain called to him a lord of that part of the country by which he entered, and told him to take the idols and distribute them throughout the country, selling each one for an Indian man or woman to serve as a slave, and adding, that if the lord refused to do so, he would immediately make war upon them. The lord commanded his vassals to take these idols and worship them, and in return to give him Indian men and women to be delivered to the Spaniards. The Indians, from fear and respect to the command of their lord, obeyed. Whoever had two children gave one, and whoever had three gave two.

In the mean time, seeing that, after they had given up their gods to be burned, these Spaniards brought others to sell, the whole country broke out in indignation against the monks, whom they accused of deceiving them. The monks endeavoured to appease them, and, seeking out the thirty Spaniards, represented to them the great evil they were doing, and required them to leave the country; but the Spaniards refused, and consummated their wickedness by telling the Indians that the priests themselves had induced them to come into the country. The Indians were now roused beyond all forbearance, and determined to murder the priests, who, having notice of this intention, escaped at night. Very soon, however, the Indians repented, and, remembering the purity of their lives, and satisfied of their innocence, they sent after the monks fifty leagues, and begged them to return. The monks, zealous only for their souls, forgave them and returned; but, finding that the Spaniards would not leave the country, and that they were constantly aggrieving the Indians, and especially that they could not preach in peace, nor without continual dread, they determined to leave the country and return to Mexico. Thus Yucatan remained without the light and help of the doctrine, and the miserable Indians in the darkness of ignorance.

Such is the account of the mission of these monks given by the old Spanish historians, but the cautious reader of the present day will hardly credit that these good priests, "ignorant of the language, and without interpreters who understood the idiom," could in forty days bring the Indians to throw their idols at their feet; and still less, that this warlike people, who had made such fierce resistance to Cordova, Grijalva, Cortez, and the adelantado, would all at once turn cravens before thirty vagabond Spaniards; but says the historian, these are secrets of Divine justice; perhaps for their many sins they did not deserve that at that time the word should be preached to them.

We return now to the adelantado, whom we left at Tobasco. Severe wars with the Indians, want of arms and provisions, and, above all, desertions instigated by the fame of Peruvian riches, had left him at a low ebb. In this situation he was joined by Captain Gonzalo Nieto and the small band which had been compelled to evacuate Yucatan, and by the presence of these old companions his spirits were again roused.

But the pacification of Tobasco was much more difficult than was supposed. By communication with the Spaniards, the Indians had lost their fears of them. The country was bad for carrying on war, particularly with cavalry, on account of the marshes and pools; their provisions were again cut off; many of the soldiers went away disgusted, and others, from the great humidity and heat, sickened and died.

While they were in this extremity, the Captain Diego de Contreras, with no fixed destination, and ready to embark in any of the great enterprises which at that time attracted the adventurous soldier, arrived at the port. He had with him a vessel of his own, with provisions and other necessaries, his son, and twenty Spaniards. The adelantado represented to him the great service he might render the king, and by promises of reward induced him to remain. With this assistance he was enabled to sustain himself in Tobasco until, having received additional reenforcements, he effected the pacification of the whole of that country.

The adelantado now made preparations to return to Yucatan. Champoton was selected as the place of disembarcation. According to some of the historians, he did not himself embark on this expedition, but sent his son. It seems more certain, however, that he went in person as commander-in-chief of the armada, and leaving his son, Don Francisco de Montejo, in command of the soldiers, returned to Tobasco, as being nearer to Mexico, from which country he expected to receive and send on more recruits and necessaries. The Spaniards landed some time in the year 1537, and again planted the royal standard in Yucatan. The Indians allowed them to land without noise or opposition, but they were only lying in wait for an opportunity to destroy them. In a few days a great multitude assembled, and at midnight they crept silently up the paths and roads which led to the camp of the Spaniards, seized one of the sentinels, and killed him; but the noise awoke the Spaniards, who, wondering less at the attack than at its being made by night, rushed to their arms. Ignorant as they were of the ground, in the darkness all was confusion. On the east, west, and south they heard the clamour and outcries of the Indians. Nevertheless, they made great efforts, and the Indians, finding their men falling, and hearing the groans of the wounded and dying, relaxed in the fury of their attack, and at length retreated. The Spaniards did not pursue them, but remained in the camp, keeping watch till daylight, when they collected and buried the bodies of their own dead.

For some days the Indians did not make any hostile demonstrations, but they kept away or concealed as much as possible all supplies of provisions. The Spaniards were much straitened, and obliged to sustain themselves by catching fish along the shores. On one occasion two Spaniards, who had straggled to some distance from the camp, fell into the hands of the Indians, who carried them away alive, sacrificed them to their idols, and feasted upon their bodies.

During this time the Indians were forming a great league of all the caciques in the country, and gathered in immense numbers at Champoton. As soon as all the confederates were assembled, they attacked with a horrible noise the camp of the Spaniards, who could not successfully contend against such a multitude. Many Indians fell, but they counted as well lost a thousand of their own number for the life of one Spaniard. There was no hope but in flight, and the Spaniards retreated to the shore. The Indians pursued them, heaping insults upon them, entered their camp, loaded themselves with the clothing and other things, which in the hurry of retreat they had been obliged to leave behind, put on their dresses, and from the shore mocked and scoffed at them, pointing with their fingers, taunting them with cowardice, and crying out, "Where is the courage of the Spaniards?" The latter, hearing from their boats these insults, resolved that death and fame were better than life and ignominy, and, wounded and worn out as they were, took up their arms and returned to the shore. Another fierce battle ensued; and the Indians, dismayed by the resolution with which these vanquished men again made front against them, retired slowly, leaving the Spaniards masters of the field. The Spaniards cared for no more, content to recover the ground they had lost.

From this time the Indians determined not to give battle again, and the great multitude, brought together from different places, dispersed, and returned to their homes. The Spaniards remained more at their ease. The Indians, seeing that they could not be driven out of the country, and did not intend to leave it, contracted a sort of friendship with them, but they were not able to make any advances into the interior. On every attempt they were so badly received that they were compelled to return to their camp in Champoton, which was, in fact, their only refuge.

As Champoton was on the coast, which now began to be somewhat known, vessels occasionally touched there, from which the poor Spaniards relieved some of their necessities. Occasionally a new companion remained, but their numbers still diminished, many, seeing the delay and the little fruit derived from their labours, abandoning the expedition. The time came when there were only nineteen Spaniards in Champoton, the names of some of whom are still preserved, and they affirm in their judicial declaration, that in this critical situation they owed their preservation to the prudence and good management of Don Francisco Montejo, the son of the adelantado.

Again they were relieved, and again their force dwindled away. The fame of the riches of Peru was in every mouth. The poverty of Yucatan was notorious. There were no mines; there was but little encouragement for others to join the expedition, and those in Champoton were discouraged. Struggling with continual hardships and dangers, they made no advance toward the conquest of the country; all who could, endeavoured to get away, some going in canoes, others by land, as occasion offered. In order to confer upon some means of bettering the condition of things, it was necessary for the son of the adelantado to visit his father at Tobasco, and he set out, leaving the soldiers at Champoton under the command of his cousin, a third Don Francisco.

During his absence matters became worse. The people continued going away, and Don Francisco knew that if they lost Champoton, which had cost them so much, all was lost. Consulting with a few who were most desirous of persevering in the enterprise, he brought together those who were suspected of meditating desertion, and told them to go at once, and leave the rest to their fate. The poor soldiers, embarrassed, and ashamed at being confronted with companions whom they intended to desert, determined to remain.

But the succour so earnestly hoped for was delayed. All the expedition which the son of the adelantado could make was not sufficient for those who remained in Champoton. They had been nearly three years without making any advances or any impression upon the country. Despairing of its conquest, and unable to exist in the straits in which they found themselves, they talked openly of disbanding, and going where fortune might lead them. The captain did all that he could to encourage them, but in vain. All had their luggage and ship-stores ready to embark, and nothing was talked of but leaving the country.

The exertions of the captain induced them to take better counsel, and they agreed not to execute their resolution hastily, but, to save themselves from injurious imputations, first to send notice of their intention to the adelantado. Juan de Contreras was sent with the despatches, who gave the adelantado, besides, a full account of the desperate condition in which they remained at Champoton.

His intelligence gave the adelantado much anxiety. All his resources were exhausted; he had been unable to procure the succour necessary, and he knew that if the Spaniards abandoned Champoton, it would be impossible to prosecute the conquest of Yucatan. Aware of their necessities, when the news arrived, he had some Spaniards collected to go to their assistance, and now, by gifts and promises, he made some additions; and while waiting until these could be got ready, despatched Alonzo Rosado, one of the new recruits, to give notice of the succour at hand.

It does not appear whether the adelantado went to Champoton in person, but vessels arrived carrying soldiers, provisions, clothing, and arms, and toward the end of the year 1539 his son returned, with twenty horsemen, from New Spain. The drooping spirits of the Spaniards were revived, and again they conceived hopes of achieving the conquest of the country.

About this time, too, the adelantado, grieving over the common misfortune of himself and those who had been constant and enduring, but doubting his own fortune, and confiding in the valour of his son Don Francisco, determined to put into the hands of the latter the pacification of Yucatan. He was at that time settled in the government of Chiapas, to which place he summoned his son, and by a formal act substituted him in all the powers given to himself by the king. The act of substitution is creditable alike to the head and heart of the adelantado. It begins with an injunction "that he should strive that the people under his charge should live and be as true Christians, separating themselves from vices and public sins, not permitting them to speak ill of God, nor his blessed mother, nor the saints;" and it concludes with the words, "because I know that you are a person who will know how to do it well, putting first God our Lord, and the service of his majesty, and the good of the country, and the execution of justice."

Within a month from the time when he was called away by his father, Don Francisco returned to Champoton with all the provisions necessary for prosecuting, on his own accout, the conquest of Yucatan. From this time the door of better fortune seemed opened to the Spaniards.

Don Francisco determined forthwith to undertake the march to Campeachy. At a short distance from Champoton they encountered a large body of Indians, routed them, and, determined not to make any retrograde movement, encamped upon the spot.

From this place the Indians, mortified and incensed at their defeat, erected fortifications along the whole line of march. The Spaniards could not advance without encountering walls, trenches, and embankments, vigorously defended. All these they gained in succession; and so great was the slaughter of the Indians, that at times their dead bodies obstructed the battle, and the Spaniards were obliged to pass over the dead to fight with the living. In one day they had three battles, in which the Spaniards were almost worn out with fighting.

Here, again, the history fails, and it does not appear how they were received in Campeachy; but it is manifest from other authorities that in the year 1540 they founded a city under the name of San Francisco de Campeche.

Remaining in this place till things were settled, Don Francisco, in pursuance of his father's instructions, determined on descending to the province of Quepech, and founding a city in the Indian town of Tihoo. Knowing that delay was dangerous, he sent forward the Captain Francisco de Montejo, his cousin, with fifty-seven men. He himself remained in Campeachy to receive and organize the soldiers, who, stimulated by the tidings of his improving fortunes, were every day coming in from his father.

Don Francisco set out for Tihoo, and in all the accounts there is a uniform correspondence in regard to the many dangers they encountered on that journey from the smallness of their numbers, the great multitudes of warlike Indians, and the strong walls and other defences which they found at every step to obstruct their progress. The Indians concealed the wells and ponds, and as there were no streams or fountains, they were perishing with thirst. Provisions were cut off, and they had war, thirst, and hunger on their path. The roads were mere narrow passes, with thick woods on both sides, encumbered with the dead bodies of men and animals, and their sufferings from want of water and provisions were almost beyond endurance.

Arriving at a town called Pokboc, they pitched and fortified their camp, with the intention of making a halt, but at night they were roused by finding the camp on fire. All ran to arms, thinking less of the fire than of the Indians, and in darkness and silence waited to discover the quarter whence the attack would come; but hearing no noise, and relieved from the apprehension of enemies, they attempted to extinguish the flames. By this time, however, the whole camp, and almost everything that they had, were burned up. But they were not dismayed. The captain gave notice of this misfortune to his cousin in Campeachy, and resumed his march. In the year 1540 he arrived at Tihoo.

In a few days he was joined by forty other Spaniards, who were sent on by Don Francisco Montejo, and at this time some Indians came to them and said, "What are you doing here, Spaniards? more Indians are coming against you, more than there are hairs on the skin of a deer." The Spaniards answered that they would go out to seek them; and, leaving the guard in the camp, the Captain Don Francisco Montejo immediately set out, came upon them at a place five leagues distant, and attacked them with such vigour, that, though they at first defended themselves bravely, the Spaniards gained upon them, and killing many, the rest became disheartened and took to flight.

In the mean time the son of the adelantado arrived from Campeachy; and being now all united, and the Indians at first withholding all supplies, they very soon began to suffer from want of provisions. While in this condition, unexpectedly a great cacique from the interior came to them voluntarily (the circumstances will appear hereafter) and made submission. Some neighbouring caciques of Tihoo, either moved by this example, or finding that, after so many years of war, they could not prevail against the Spaniards, also submitted. Encouraged by the friendship of these caciques, and believing that they might count upon their succour until they had finished the subjection of the country, the Spaniards determined to found a city on the site occupied by Tihoo; but in the mean time a terrific storm was gathering over their heads. All the Indians from the east of Tihoo were drawing together; and in the month of June, toward the evening of the feast of Barnaby the apostle, an immense body, varying, according to manuscript accounts, from forty to seventy thousand, came down upon the small band of a little more than two hundred then in Tihoo. The following day they attacked the

Spanish camp on all sides. The most terrible battle the Spaniards had ever encountered ensued. "Divine power," says the pious historian, "works more than human valour. What were so few Catholics against so many infidels?" The battle lasted the greater part of the day. Many Indians were killed, but immediately others took their places, for they were so many that they were like the leaves on the trees. The arquebuses and crossbows made great havoc, and the horsemen carried destruction wherever they moved, cutting down the fugitives, trampling under foot the wounded and dying. Piles of dead bodies stopped the Spaniards in their pursuit. The Indians were completely routed, and for a great distance the ground was covered with their dead.

The fame of the Spaniards rose higher than before, and the Indians never rallied again for a general battle. All this year the invaders were occupied in drawing to them and conciliating the neighbouring caciques, and on the sixth of January, 1542, they founded, with all legal formalities, on the site of the Indian town of Tihoo, the "very loyal and noble" city of Merida.

Here I shall leave them; and I make no apology for presenting this history. It was forty years since a straggling canoe at the island of Guanaja first gave intelligence of the existence of such a country as Yucatan, and sixteen since Don Francisco Montejo received the royal authority to conquer and people it. During that time Cortez had driven Montezuma from the throne of Mexico, and Pizarro had seized the sceptre of the Peruvian Incas. In the glory of these conquests Yucatan was unnoticed, and has been to this day. The ancient historians refer to it briefly and but seldom. The only separate account of it is that of Cogolludo, a native historian.

The work of this author was published in the year 1658. It is voluminous, confused, and ill-digested, and might almost be called a history of the Franciscan Friars, to which order he belonged. It is from this work principally that, with no small labour, I have gathered the events subsequent to the grant made by the king to Don Francisco Montejo; it is the only work that purports to give an account of those events, and as it has never been translated, and is scarcely known out of Yucatan, and even in that country is almost out of print, it must at least be new to the reader.

CHAPTER IV

From the time of the conquest, Yucatan existed as a distinct captain-generalcy, not connected with Guatimala, nor subject to the viceroy of Mexico. So it continued down to the Mexican revolution. The independence of Yucatan followed that of Mexico without any struggle, and actually by default of the mother-country in not attempting to keep it in subjection.

Separated from Spain, in an evil hour Yucatan sent commissioners to Mexico to deliberate upon forming a government; and on the return of these commissioners, and on their report, she gave up her independent position, and entered into the Mexican confederation as one of the states of that republic. Ever since she had been suffering from this unhappy connexion, and, a short time before our former visit, a revolution broke out all over the country; in the successful progress of which, during that visit, the last Mexican garrison was driven out of Yucatan. The state assumed the rights of sovereignty, asserting its independent powers, at the same time not disconnecting itself entirely from Mexico, but declaring itself still a component part of that republic upon certain conditions. The declaration of its independence was still a moot question. The assembly had passed a bill to that effect, but the senate had not yet acted upon it, and its fate in that body was considered doubtful. In the mean time, a commissioner had been sent to Texas, and two days after our arrival at Merida the Texan schooner of war San Antonio arrived at Sisal, bringing a proposition for Yucatan to pay $8000 per month toward the support of the Texan navy, and for the Texan vessels to remain upon the coast of Yucatan and protect it against invasion by Mexico. This proposition was accepted immediately, and negotiations were pending for farther co-operation in procuring a recognition of their mutual independence. Thus, while shrinking from an open declaration of independence, Yucatan was widening the breach, and committing an offence which Mexico could never forgive, by an alliance with a people whom that government, or rather Santa Ana, regarded as the worst of rebels, and whom he was bent upon exerting the whole power of the country in an effort to reconquer. Such was the disjointed and false position in which Yucatan stood at the time of our presentation to the governor.

Our visit to him was made at his private residence, which was one befitting his station as a private gentleman, and not unworthy of his public character. His reception-room was in the sala or parlour of his house, in the centre of which, after the fashion of Merida, three or four large chairs covered with morocco were placed facing each other.

Don Santiago Mendez was about fifty years of age, tall and thin, with a fine intellectual face, and of very gentlemanly appearance and deportment. Free from internal wars, and saved by her geographical position from the sanguinary conflicts common in the other Mexican states, Yucatan has had no school for soldiers; there are no military chieftains and no prepossessions for military glory. Don Santiago Mendez was a merchant, until within a few years, at the head of a respectable commercial house in Campeachy. He was so respected for uprightness and integrity, that in the unsettled state of affairs he was agreed upon by the two opposite parties as the best person in the state to place at the head of the government. His popularity, however, was now somewhat on the wane, and his position was neither easy nor enviable. From a quiet life and occupations, he found himself all at once in the front rank of a wide-spread rebellion. An invasion from Mexico was constantly apprehended, and should it prove successful, while others would escape by reason of their insignificance, his head would be sure to fall. The two great parties, one in favour of keeping open the door of reconciliation with Mexico, and the other for immediate and absolute separation, were both urging him to carry out their views. The governor shrank from the hazard of extremes, was vacillating, undecided, and unequal to the emergency. In the mean time, the enthusiasm which led to the revolution, and which might have achieved independence, was wearing away. Dissatisfaction and discontent prevailed. Both parties blamed the governor, and he did not know himself to which he belonged.

There was nothing equivocal, however, in his reception of us. He knew the object of our return to the country, and offered us all the facilities the government could bestow. Whatever was to be the fate of Yucatan, it was fortunate for us that it was then free from the dominion of Mexico, and repudiated entirely the jealous policy which threw impediments in the way of strangers seeking to explore the antiquities of the country; and it was also fortunate, that on my former visit Yucatan had impressed me favourably; for, had it been otherwise, my situation might have been made uncomfortable, and the two journals of Merida, the "Commercial Bulletin" and the "Nineteenth Century," instead of giving us a cordial welcome, and bespeaking favour for us, might have advised us to return home by the same vessel that brought us out.

Our only business in Merida was to make inquiries about ruins and arrangements for our journey into the interior, but in the mean time we had no lack of other occupation.

The house of the Doña Micaela was the rendezvous of all strangers in Merida, and a few days after our arrival there was an unprecedented gathering. There were Mr. Auchincloss and his son, Mr. Tredwell, Mr. Northrop, Mr. Gleason, and Mr. Robinson, formerly United States consul at Tampico, who had come out passengers by the Lucinda, all citizens of the United States; and, besides these, the arrival of the schooner of war San Antonio, from Texas, brought among us a citizen of the world, or, at least, of a great part of it. Mr. George Fisher, as appeared by his various papers of naturalization, was "natural de la ciudad y fortaleza de Belgrada en la provincia de Servia del Imperio Ottomano," or a "native of the city and fortress of Belgrade, in the province of Servia, in the Ottoman Empire." His Sclavonic name was Ribar, which in the German language means a Fischer, and at school in Austria it was so translated, from which in the United States it became modified to Fisher. At seventeen he embarked in a revolution to throw off the yoke of the sultan, but the attempt was crushed, and forty thousand Sclavonians, men, women, and children, were driven across the Danube, and took refuge in the Austrian territory. The Austrian government, not liking the presence of so many revolutionists within its borders, authorized the organizing of a Sclavonic legion. Mr. Fisher entered it, made a campaign in Italy, and, at the end of the year, in the interior of the country, where there was no danger of their disseminating revolutionary notions, the legion was disbanded. After expeditions of various kinds along the Danube, in Turkey, to Adrianople, and along the Adriatic, he traded back, most of the way on foot, until he reached Hamburgh, where, in 1815, he embarked for Philadelphia. Hence he crossed over to the Ohio River, and in the State of Mississippi, by five years' residence, and abjuring all other allegiance, became a citizen of the United States. Mexico obtained her independence, and he moved on to that country, becoming, by due process of law, a Mexican citizen. Here he established a newspaper, which, during the presidency of Santa Ana, became so conspicuous for its liberal opinions, that one fine morning an officer waited upon him with a paper containing permission for him to leave the country "por el tiempo necessario," which being translated, meant, not to return very soon. With this he "sloped" for Texas, and became a citizen of that young republic. It was strange in that remote and secluded place to meet one from a region still more distant and even less known, speaking every language in Europe, familiar with every part of it, with the history of every reigning family, the territorial limits of every prince, and at the same time a citizen of so many republics.

His last allegiance was uppermost; his feelings were all Texan, and he gave us many interesting particulars touching the condition and prospects of that country. He was, of course, soon at home in the politics of Yucatan, and he had some little personal interest in watching them closely; for, should Santa Ana regain the ascendancy, the climate would be altogether too warm for him. He had saddle and bridle, sword and pistols—all that he needed except a horse—hanging up in his room, and at a moment's notice he was ready to mount and ride.

Our meeting with this gentleman added much to the interest of our time in Merida. In the evening, when we had settled the affairs of Yucatan, we made an excursion into Illyria or the interior of Turkey. He was as familiar with the little towns in those countries as with those in Mexico. His knowledge of persons and places, derived from actual observation, was most extensive; in short, his whole life had been a chapter of incidents and adventures; and these were not yet ended. He had a new field opened to him in Yucatan. We parted with him in Merida, and the next that we heard of him was of his being in a situation quite as strange as any he had ever been in before. Yet there was nothing reckless, restless, or unsettled about him; he was perfectly fixed and methodical in all his notions and modes of ac-tion; in Wall-street he would be considered a staid, regular, quiet, middle-aged man, and he was systematic enough in his habits to be head director of the Bank of England.

I must not omit to mention, among those whom we were in the habit of seeing every day, another old acquaintance, of the Spanish Hotel in Fulton-street, Don Vicente Calera, who, at the time of our former visit, was still travelling in the United States. In the mean time he had returned, married, and was again domesticated in his native city.

Under his escort we traversed Merida in every direction, and visited all the public buildings and institutions.

The population of Merida is probably about twenty-three thousand. Two tables are published in the Appendix; but both purport to give the population of the district, and neither that of the city alone. The city stands on a great plain, on a surface of limestone rock, and the temperature and climate are very uniform. During the thirteen days that we were in Merida the thermometer varied but nine degrees; and, according to a table of observations kept for many years by the much-esteemed Cura Villamil, it appears that during the year beginning on the first of September, 1841, which included the whole time that we were in the country, the greatest variation was but twenty-three degrees. By the kindness of the cura, I have been furnished with a copy of this table, from which I extract the observations for the days that we passed in Merida. The entire table is published in the Appendix. The observations were made by a Fahrenheit thermometer kept in the open air and in the shade, and noted at six in the morning, midday, and six in the afternoon.

	6 A.M.	12 M.	6 P.M.
Oct. 30	78	81	81
" 31	81	82	82
Nov. 1	82	83	82
" 2	80	82	81
" 3	78	80	80
" 4	80	77	77
" 5	77	78	78
" 6	74	77	76
" 7	74	76	76
" 8	75	78	78
" 9	75	78	78
" 10	74	79	79
" 11	76	79	79

I may remark, however, that in the interior of the country we found a much greater variation than any noted in the table published in the Appendix.

The general aspect of the city is Moorish, as it was built at a time when the Moorish style prevailed in Spanish architecture. The houses are large, generally of stone, and one story in height, with balconies to the windows and large courtyards. In the centre of the city stands the plaza major, a square of about six hundred feet. The whole of the east side is occupied by the cathedral and the bishop's palace. On the west stand the house of the municipality and that of the Doña Joaquina Peon. On the north is the palace of the government, and on the south a building which on our first visit arrested our attention the moment we entered the plaza. It is distinguished by a rich sculptured façade of curious design and workmanship. In it is a stone with this inscription:

Esta obra mando hacerla el
Adelantado D. Francisco de Montejo
Año de MDXLIX.

The Adelantado Don Francisco Montejo caused this to be made
in the year 1549.

The subject represents two knights in armour, with visors, breastplates, and helmets, standing upon the shoulders of crushed naked figures, probably intended to represent the conquering Spaniard trampling upon the Indian. Mr. Catherwood attempted to make a drawing of it, and, to avoid the heat of the sun, went into the plaza at daylight for that purpose; but he was so annoyed by the crowd that he was obliged to give it up. There is reason to believe that it is a combination of Spanish and Indian art. The design is certainly Spanish, but as, at that early period of the conquest, but five years after the foundation of Merida, Spaniards were but few, and each man considered himself a conqueror, probably there were none who practised the mechanic arts. The execution was no doubt the work of Indians; and perhaps the carving was done with their own instruments, and not those furnished them by the Spaniards.

The history of the erection of this building would be interesting and instructive; and, with the hope of learning something about it, I proposed to examine thoroughly the archives of the cabildo; but I was advised that all the early archives were lost, or in such confusion that it would be a Herculean labour to ex-

61

plore them, and I saw that it would consume more time than I should be able to devote to it.

Besides the inscription on the stone, the only information that exists in regard to this building is a statement in Cogolludo, that the façade cost fourteen tl ousand dollars. It is now the property of Don Simon Peon, and is occupied by his family. It has been lately repaired, and some of the beams are no doubt the same which held up the roof over the adelantado.

Eight streets lead from the plaza, two in the direction of each cardinal point. In every street, at the distance of a few squares, is a gate, now dismantled, and beyond are the barrios, or suburbs.

The streets are distinguished in a manner peculiar to Yucatan. In the angle of the corner house, and on the top, stands a painted wooden figure of an elephant, a bull, a flamingo, or some other visible object, and the street is called by the name of this object. On one corner there is the figure of an old woman with large spectacles on her nose, and the street is called la Calle de la Vieja, or the Street of the Old Woman. That in which we lived had on the corner house a flamingo, and was called the Street of the Flamingo; and the reason of the streets being named in this way gives some idea of the character of the people. The great mass of the inhabitants, universally the Indians, cannot read. Printed signs would be of no use, but every Indian knows the sign of an elephant, a bull, or a flamingo.

In the front wall of a house in a street running north from the plaza, and also in a corner house near the square of the Alameda, are sculptured figures from the ruins of ancient buildings, of which Mr. Catherwood made drawings, but, in the multiplicity of other subjects, we do not think it worth while to present them to the reader.

The great distinguishing feature of Merida, as of all the cities of Spanish America, is in its churches. The great Cathedral; the parish church and convent of San Cristoval; the church of the Jesuits; the church and convent of the Mejorada; the chapels of San Juan Bautista; of Our Lady of Candelaria; of the Santa Lucia and the Virgin, and the convent de las monjas, or the nunnery, with its church and enclosures occupying two whole squares, are all interesting in their history. Some are of good style in architecture, and rich in ornaments; but there is one other, not yet mentioned, which I regard as the most interesting and remarkable edifice in Merida. It is the old Franciscan convent. It stands on an eminence in the eastern part of the city, and is enclosed by a high wall, with turrets, forming what is now called the Castillo. These walls and turrets are still erect, but within is ruin irretrievable.

In 1820 the new constitution obtained by the patriots in Spain reached the colonies, and on the 30th of May Don Juan Rivas Vertiz, then Gefe Politico, and now living in Merida, a fine memorial of the olden time, published it in the plaza. The church sustained the old order of things, and the Franciscan friars, confident in their hold upon the feelings of the populace, endeavoured to put down this demonstration of liberal feeling. A mob gathered in the plaza; friars appeared among them, urging them on; field-pieces were brought out, the mob dispersed, and Don Juan Rivas marched to the Franciscan convent, opened the doors, drove out the monks, above 300 in number, at the point of the bayonet, and gave up the building to destruction. The superior and some of the brothers became seculars or regular priests; others turned to worldly pursuits; and of this once powerful order, but eleven are now left who wear the garb of the Franciscan monks.

It was in company with one of these that I paid my last visit to this convent. We entered by the great portal of the castle wall into an overgrown courtyard. In front was the convent, with its large corridors and two great churches, the walls of all three standing, but without doors or windows. The roof of one of the churches had fallen, and the broad glare of day was streaming into the interior. We entered the other—the oldest, and identified with the times of the conquerors. Near the door was a blacksmith's forge. A Mestizo was blowing at the bellows, hauling out a red-hot bar of iron, and hammering it into spikes. All along the floor were half-naked Indians and brawny Mestizoes, hewing timber, driving nails, and carrying on the business of making gun-carriages for artillery. The altars were thrown down and the walls defaced; half way up were painted on them, in coarse and staring red characters (in Spanish,) "First squadron," "Second squadron;" and at the head of the church, under a golden gloria, were the words "Comp'y Light Infantry." The church had been occupied as barracks, and these were the places where they stacked their arms. As we passed through, the workmen stared at my companion, or rather at the long blue gown, the cord around his waist, and the cross dangling from it—the garb of his scattered order. It was the first time he had visited the place since the expulsion of the monks. To me it was mournful to behold the destruction and desecration of this noble building; what, then, must it have been to him? In the floor of the church near the altar and in the sacristia were open vaults, but the bones of the monks had been thrown out and scattered on the floor. Some of these were the bones of his earliest friends. We passed into the refectory, and he pointed out the position of the long table at which the brotherhood took their meals, and the stone fountain at which they performed their ablutions. His old companions in their long blue gowns rose up before him, now scattered forever, and their home a desolation and ruin.

But this convent contains one memorial far more interesting than any connected with its own ruin; one that carries the beholder back through centuries of time, and tells the story of a greater and a sadder fall.

In one of the lower cloisters going out from the north, and under the principal dormitory, are two parallel corridors. The outer one faces the principal patio, and this corridor has that peculiar arch so often referred to in my previous volumes, two sides rising to meet each other, and covered, when within about a foot of forming an apex, by a flat layer of stones. There can be no mistake about the character of this arch; it cannot for a moment be supposed that the Spaniards constructed anything so different from their known rules of architecture; and beyond doubt it formed part of one of those mysterious buildings which have given rise to so much speculation; the construction of which has been ascribed to the most ancient people in the Old World, and to races lost, perished, and unknown.

I am happy thus early in these pages to have an opportunity of recurring to the opinion expressed in my former volumes, in regard to the builders of the ancient American cities.

The conclusion to which I came was, that "there are not sufficient grounds for belief in the great antiquity that has been ascribed to these ruins;" "that we are not warranted in going back to any ancient nation of the Old World for the builders of these cities; that they are not the works of people who have passed away, and whose history is lost; but that there are strong reasons to believe them the creation of the same races who inhabited the country at the time of the Spanish conquest, or of some not very distant progenitors."

This opinion was not given lightly, nor without due consideration. It was adverse to my feelings, which would fain have thrown around the ruins the interest of mystery and hoary age; and even now, though gratified at knowing that my opinion has been fully sustained, I would be willing to abandon it, and

64

involve the reader and myself in doubt, did circumstances warrant me in so doing; but I am obliged to say that subsequent investigations have fortified and confirmed my previous conclusions, and, in fact, have made conviction what before was mere matter of opinion.

When I wrote the account of my former journey, the greatest difficulty attending the consideration of this subject was the absence of all historical record concerning the places visited. Copan had some history, but it was obscure, uncertain, and unsatisfactory. Quirigua, Palenque, and Uxmal had none whatever; but a ray of historic light beams upon the solitary arch in the ruined convent of Merida.

In the account of the conquest of Yucatan by Cogolludo it is stated, that on the arrival of the Spaniards at the Indian town of Tihoo, on the site of which, it will be remembered, Merida now stands, they found many cerros hechos a mano, *i. e.*, hills made by hand, or artificial mounds, and that on one of these mounds the Spaniards encamped.

This mound, it is stated, stood on the ground now occupied by the plaza major. East of it was another large mound, and the Spaniards laid the foundation of the city between these two, because, as it is assigned, the stones in them were a great convenience in building, and economized the labour of the Indians. These mounds were so large, it is added, that with the stones the Spaniards built all the edifices in the city, so that the ground which forms the plaza major remained nearly or quite level. The buildings erected are specified, and it is added that there was abundance of material for other edifices which the Spaniards wished to erect.

Other mounds are mentioned as obstructing the laying out of streets according to the plan proposed, and there is one circumstance which bears directly upon this point, and, in my opinion, is conclusive.

In the history of the construction of the Franciscan convent, which was founded in the year 1547, five years after the arrival of the Spaniards in Tihoo, it is expressly stated that it was built upon a small artifical mound, one of the many that were then in the place, on which mound, it is added, were *some ancient buildings*. Now we must either suppose that the Spaniards razed these buildings to the ground, and then constructed this strange arch themselves, which supposition is, I think, utterly untenable, or that this corridor formed part of the ancient buildings which, according to the historical account, stood on this artificial mound, and that for some purpose or other the monks incorporated it with their convent.

There is but one way to overthrow this latter conclusion, and that is by contending that these mounds were all ruined, and this building too, at the time when it was made to form part of the convent; but then we are reduced to the necessity of supposing that a great town, the fame of which reached the Spaniards at Campeachy, and which made a desperate and bloody resistance to their occupation of it, was a mere gathering of hordes around the ruined buildings of another race; and, besides, it is a matter of primary importance to note that these artificial mounds are mentioned, not in the course of describing the Indian town, for no description whatever is attempted, but merely incidentally, as affording conveniences to the Spaniards in furnishing materials for building the city, or as causing obstructions in the laying out of streets regularly and according to the plan proposed. The mound on which the convent stands would perhaps not have been mentioned at all but for the circumstance that the Padre Cogolludo was a Franciscan friar, and the mention of it enabled him to pay a tribute to the memory of the blessed father Luis de Villpando, then superior of the convent, and to show the great estimation in which he was held, for he says that the adelantado had fixed upon this mound for the site of one of his fortresses, but on the application of the superior he yielded it to him readily for the site of the convent; and, more than all this, even in the incidental way in which these mounds are referred to, there is one circumstance which shows clearly that they were not at that time disused and in ruins, but, on the contrary, were then in the actual use and occupation of the Indians; for Cogolludo mentions particularly and with much detail one that completely obstructed the running of a particular street, which, he says, was called El grande de los Kues, adoratorio que era de los idolos. Now the word "Kues," in the Maya language, as spoken by the Indians of Yucatan at the present day, means their ancient places of worship, and the word "adoratorio," as defined in the Spanish dictionary, is the name given by the Spaniards to the temples of idols in America. So that when the historian describes this mound as El grande de los Kues el adoratorio de los idolos, he means to say that it was the great one, or the greatest among the places of worship of the Indians, or the temples of their idols.

It is called the "great one" of their places of worship, in contradistinction to the smaller ones around, among which was that now occupied by the Franciscan convent. In my opinion, the solitary arch found in this convent is very strong, if not conclusive, evidence that all the ruined buildings scattered over Yucatan were erected by the very Indians who occupied the country at the time of the Spanish conquest, or, to fall back upon my old ground, that they were the work "of the same race of people," or "their not very distant progenitors."

Who these races were, whence they came, or who were their progenitors, I did not undertake to say, nor do I now.

CHAPTER V

But the reader must not suppose that our only business in Merida was the investigation of antiquities; we had other operations in hand which gave us plenty of employment. We had taken with us a Daguerreotype apparatus, of which but one specimen had ever before appeared in Yucatan. Great improvements had been since made in the instrument, and we had reason to believe that ours was one of the best; and having received assurances that we might do a large business in that line, we were induced to set up as ladies' Daguerreotype portrait takers. It was a new line for us, and rather venturesome, but not worse than for the editor of a newspaper to turn captain of a steamboat; and, besides, it was not like banking—we could not injure any one by a failure.

Having made trials upon ourselves until we were tired of the subjects, and with satisfactory results, we considered ourselves sufficiently advanced to begin; and as we intended to practice for the love of the art, and not for lucre, we held that we had a right to select our subjects. Accordingly, we had but to signify our wishes, and the next morning put our house in order for the reception of our fair visiters. We cleared everything out of the hammock, took the washhand basin off the chair, and threw odds and ends into one corner; and as the sun was pouring its rays warmly and brightly into our door, it was farther lighted up by the entry of three young ladies, with their respective papas and mammas. We had great difficulty in finding them all seats, and were obliged to put the two mammas into the hammock together. The young ladies were dressed in their prettiest costume, with earrings and chains, and their hair adorned with flowers. All were pretty, and one was much more than pretty; not in the style of Spanish beauty, with dark eyes and hair, but a delicate and dangerous blonde, simple, natural, and unaffected, beautiful without knowing it, and really because she could not help it. Her name, too, was poetry itself. I am bound to single her out, for, late on the evening of our departure from Merida, she sent us a large cake, measuring about three feet in circumference by six inches deep, which, by-the-way, everything being packed up, I smothered into a pair of saddle-bags, and spoiled some of my scanty stock of wearing apparel.

The ceremonies of the reception over, we made immediate preparations to begin. Much form and circumstance were necessary in settling preliminaries; and as we were in no hurry to get rid of our subjects, we had more formalities than usual to go through with.

Our first subject was the lady of the poetical name. It was necessary to hold a consultation upon her costume, whether the colours were pretty and such as would be brought out well or not; whether a scarf around the neck was advisable; whether the hair was well arranged, the rose becoming, and in the best position; then to change it, and consider the effect of the change, and to say and do many other things which may suggest themselves to the reader's imagination, and all which gave rise to many profound remarks in regard to artistical effect, and occupied much time.

The lady being arrayed to the best advantage, it was necessary to seat her with reference to a right adjustment of light and shade; to examine carefully the falling of the light upon her face; then to consult whether it was better to take a front or a side view; to look at the face carefully in both positions; and, finally, it was necessary to secure the head in the right position; that it should be neither too high nor too low; too much on one side nor on the other; and as this required great nicety, it was sometimes actually indispensable to turn the beautiful little head with our own hands, which, however, was a very innocent way of turning a young lady's head.

Next it was necessary to get the young lady into focus—that is, to get her into the box, which, in short, means, to get a reflec-

69

tion of her face on the glass in the camera obscura at that one particular point of view which presented it better than any other; and when this was obtained, the miniature likeness of the object was so faithfully reflected, that, as artists carried away by enthusiasm, we were obliged to call in the papas and mammas, who pronounced it beautiful—to which dictum we were in courtesy obliged to respond.

The plate was now cleaned, put into the box, and the light shut off. Now came a trying time for the young lady. She must neither open her lips nor roll her eyes for one minute and thirty seconds by the watch. This eternity at length ended, and the plate was taken out.

So far our course had been before the wind. Every new formality had but increased our importance in the eyes of our fair visiters and their respectable companions. Mr. Catherwood retired to the adjoining room to put the plate in the mercury bath, while we, not knowing what the result might be, a little fearful, and neither wishing to rob another of the honour he might be justly entitled to, nor to be dragged down by another's failure, thought best to have it distinctly understood that Mr. Catherwood was the maestro, and that we were merely amateurs. At the same time, on Mr. Catherwood's account, I took occasion to suggest that the process was so complicated, and its success depended upon such a variety of minute circumstances, it seemed really wonderful that it ever turned out well. The plate might not be good, or not well cleaned; or the chemicals might not be of the best; or the plate might be left too long in the iodine box, or taken out too soon; or left too long in the bromine box, or taken out too soon; or a ray of light might strike it on putting it into the camera or in taking it out; or it might be left too long in the camera or taken out too soon; or too long in the mercury bath or taken out too soon; and even though all these processes were right and regular, there might be some other fault of omission or commission which we were not aware of; besides which, climate and atmosphere had great influence, and might render all of no avail. These little suggestions we considered necessary to prevent too great a disappointment in case of failure; and perhaps our fair visiters were somewhat surprised at our audacity in undertaking at all such a doubtful experiment, and using them as instruments. The result, however, was enough to induce us never again to adopt prudential measures, for the young lady's image was stamped upon the plate, and made a picture which enchanted her and satisfied the critical judgment of her friends and admirers.

Our experiments upon the other ladies were equally successful, and the morning glided away in this pleasant occupation.

We continued practising a few days longer; and as all our good results were extensively shown, and the poor ones we took care to keep out of sight, our reputation increased, and we had abundance of applications.

In this state of things we requested some friends to whom we were under many obligations, to be permitted to wait upon them at their houses. On receiving their assent, the next morning at nine o'clock Mr. C. in a caleza, with all the complicated apparatus packed around him, drove up to their door. I followed on foot. It was our intention to go through the whole family, uncles, aunts, grandchildren, down to Indian servants, as many as would sit; but man is born to disappointment. I spare the reader the recital of our misfortunes that day. It would be too distressing. Suffice it to say that we tried plate after plate, sitting after sitting, varying light, time, and other points of the process; but it was all in vain. The stubborn instrument seemed bent upon confounding us; and, covering our confusion as well as we could, we gathered up our Daguerreotype and carried ourselves off. What was the cause of our complete discomfiture we never ascertained, but we resolved to give up business as ladies' Daguerreotype portrait takers.

There was one interesting incident connected with our short career of practice. Among the portraits put forth was one of a lady, which came to the knowledge of a gentleman particularly interested in the fair original. This gentleman had never taken any especial notice of us before, but now he called upon us, and very naturally the conversation turned upon that art of which we were then professors. The portrait of this lady was mentioned, and by the time he had finished his third straw cigar, he unburdened himself of the special object of his visit, which was to procure a portrait of her for himself. This seemed natural enough, and we assented, provided he would get her to sit; but he did not wish either her or her friends to know anything about it. This *was* a difficulty. It was not very easy to take it by stealth. However strong an impression a young lady may make by a glance upon some substances, she can do nothing upon a silver plate. Here she requires the aid of iodine, bromine, and mercury. But the young man was fertile in expedients. He said that we could easily make some excuse, promising her something more perfect, and in making two or three impressions, could slip one away for him. This was by no means a bad suggestion, at least so far as he was concerned, but we had some qualms of conscience. While we were deliberating, a matter was introduced which perhaps lay as near Doctor Cabot's heart as the young lady did that of our friend. That was a pointer or setter dog for hunting, of which the doctor was in great want. The gentlemen said he had one—the only one in Merida—and he would give it for the portrait. It was rather an odd proposition, but to offer a dog for his mistress's portrait was very different from offering his mistress's portrait for a dog. It was clear that the young man was in a bad way; he would lay down his life, give up smoking, part with his dog or commit any other extravagance. The case was touching. The doctor was really interested; and, after all, what harm could it do? The doctor and I went to look at the dog, but it turned out to be a mere pup, entirely unbroken, and what the result might have been I do not know, but all farther negotiations were broken off by the result of our out-of-door practice and disgust for the business.

There is no immediate connexion between taking Daguerreotype portraits and the practice of surgery, but circumstances bring close together things entirely dissimilar in themselves, and we went from one to the other. Secluded as Merida is, and seldom visited by strangers, the fame of new discoveries in science is slow in reaching it, and the new operation of Mons. Guerin for the cure of strabismus had not been heard of. In private intercourse we had spoken of this operation, and, in order to make it known, and extend its benefits, Doctor Cabot had offered to perform it in Merida. The Merida people have generally fine eyes, but, either because our attention was particularly directed to it, or that it is really the case, there seemed to be more squinting eyes, or biscos, as they are called, than are usually seen in any one town, and in Merida, as in some other places, this is not esteemed a beauty; but, either from want of confidence in a stranger, or a cheap estimation of the qualifications of a medico who asked no pay for his services, the doctor's philanthropic purposes were not appreciated. At least, no one cared to be the first; and as the doctor had no sample of his skill with him, no subject offered.

We had fixed the day for our departure; and the evening but one before, a direct overture was made to the doctor to perform the operation. The subject was a boy, and the application in his behalf was made by a gentleman who formed one of a circle in which we were in the habit of visiting, and whom we were all happy to have it in our power to serve.

The time was fixed at ten o'clock the next day. After breakfast our sala was put in order for the reception of company, and the doctor for the first time looked to his instruments. He had some misgivings. They were of very fine workmanship, made in Paris, most sensitive to the influence of the atmosphere, and in that climate it was almost impossible to preserve anything metallic from rust. The doctor had packed the case among his clothing in the middle of his trunk, and had taken every possible precaution, but, as usual upon such occasions, the most important instrument had rusted at the point, and in that state was utterly useless. There was no cutler in the place, nor any other person competent to touch it. Mr. Catherwood, however, brought out an old razor hone, and between them they worked off the rust.

At ten o'clock the doctor's subject made his appearance. He was the son of a widow lady of very respectable family, about fourteen years old, but small of stature, and presenting even to the most casual glance the stamp of a little gentleman. He had large black eyes, but, unluckily, their expression was very much injured by an inward squint. With the light heart of boyhood, however, he seemed indifferent to his personal appearance, and came, as he said, because his mother told him to do so. His handsome person, and modest and engaging manners, gave us immediately a strong interest in his favour. He was accompanied by the gentleman who had spoken of bringing him, Dr. Bado, a Guatimalian educated in Paris, the oldest and principal physician of Merida, and by several friends of the family, whom we did not know.

Preparations were commenced immediately. The first movement was to bring out a long table near the window; then to spread upon it a mattress and pillow, and upon these to spread the boy. Until the actual moment of operating, the precise character of this new business had not presented itself to my mind, and altogether it opened by no means so favourably as Daguerreotype practice.

Not aiming to be technical, but desiring to give the reader the benefit of such scraps of learning as I pick up in my travels, modern science has discovered that the eye is retained in its orbit by six muscles, which pull it up and down, inward and outward, and that the undue contraction of either of these muscles produces that obliquity called squinting, which was once supposed to proceed from convulsions in childhood, or other un-

known causes. The cure discovered is the cutting of the contracted muscle, by means of which the eye falls immediately into
its proper place. This muscle lies under the surface; and, as it is
necessary to pass through a membrane of the eye, the cutting
cannot be done with a broadaxe or a handsaw. In fact, it requires a knowledge of the anatomy of the eye, manual dexterity,
fine instruments, and Mr. Catherwood, and myself for assistants.

Our patient remained perfectly quiet, with his little hands
folded across his breast; but while the knife was cutting through
the muscle he gave one groan, so piteous and heart-rending, that
it sent into the next room all who were not immediately engaged.
But before the sound of the groan had died away the operation
was over, and the boy rose with his eye bleeding, but perfectly
straight. A bandage was tied over it, and, with a few directions
for its treatment, amid the congratulations and praises of all
present, and wearing the same smile with which he had entered,
the little fellow walked off to his mother.

The news of this wonder spread rapidly, and before night
Dr. Cabot had numerous and pressing applications, among which
was one from a gentleman whom we were all desirous to oblige,
and who had this defect in both eyes.

On his account we determined to postpone our departure
another day; and, in furtherance of his original purpose, Dr.
Cabot mentioned that he would perform the operation upon all
who chose to offer. We certainly took no trouble to spread this
notice, but the next morning, when we returned from breakfast,
there was a gathering of squint-eyed boys around the door, who,
with their friends and backers, made a formidable appearance,
and almost obstructed our entrance. As soon as the door opened
there was a rush inside; and as some of these slanting eyes might
not be able to distinguish between meum and tuum, we were
obliged to help their proprietors out into the street again.

At ten o'clock the big table was drawn up to the window,
and the mattress and pillow were spread upon it, but there was
such a gathering around the window that we had to hang up a
sheet before it. Invitations had been given to Dr. Bado and Dr.
Munoz, and all physicians who chose to come, and having met
the governor in the evening, I had asked him to be present.
These all honoured us with their company, together with a
number of self-invited persons, who had introduced themselves,
and could not well be turned out, making quite a crowded room.

The first who presented himself was a stout lad about nineteen or twenty, whom we had never seen or heard of before. Who

he was or where he came from we did not know, but he was a
bisco of the worst kind, and seemed able-bodied enough to undergo anything in the way of surgery. As soon as the doctor began
to cut the muscle, however, our strapping patient gave signs of
restlessness; and all at once, with an actual bellow, he jerked his
head on one side, carried away the doctor's hook, and shut his
eye upon it with a sort of lockjaw grip, as if determined it should
never be drawn out. How my hook got out I have no idea; fortunately, the doctor let his go, or the lad's eye would have been
scratched out. As it was, there he sat with the bandage slipped
above one eye, and the other closed upon the hook, the handle
of which stood out straight. Probably at that moment he would
have been willing to sacrifice pride of personal appearance, keep
his squint, and go through life with his eye shut, the hook in it,
and the handle sticking out; but the instrument was too valuable
to be lost. And it was interesting and instructive to notice the
difference between the equanimity of one who had a hook in his
eye, and that of lookers-on who had not. All the spectators up-
braided him with his cowardice and want of heart, and after a
round of reproof to which he could make no answer, he opened
his eye and let out the hook. But he had made a bad business of
it. A few seconds longer, and the operation would have been
completed. As it was, the whole work had to be repeated. As the
muscle was again lifted under the knife, I thought I saw a glare
in the eyeball that gave token of another fling of the head, but
the lad was fairly browbeaten into quiet; and, to the great satisfaction of all, with a double share of blackness and blood, and
with very little sympathy from any one, but with his eye straight,
he descended from the table. Outside he was received with a loud
shout by the boys, and we never heard of him again.

The room was now full of people, and, being already disgusted with the practice of surgery, I sincerely hoped that this
exhibition would cure all others of a wish to undergo the operation, but a little Mestizo boy, about ten years old, who had been
present all the time, crept through the crowd, and, reaching the
table, squinted up at us without speaking, his crisscross expression telling us very plainly what he wanted. He had on the usual
Mestizo dress of cotton shirt and drawers and straw hat, and
seemed so young, simple, and innocent, that we did not consider
him capable of judging for himself. We told him he must not be
operated on, but he answered, in a decided though modest tone,
"Yo quiero, yo quiero," "I wish it, I wish it." We inquired if
there was any one present who had any authority over him, and

a man whom we had not noticed before, dressed, like him, in shirt and drawers, stepped forward and said he was the boy's father; he had brought him there himself on purpose, and begged Doctor Cabot to proceed. By his father's directions, the little fellow attempted to climb up on the table, but his legs were too short, and he had to be lifted up. His eye was bandaged, and his head placed upon the pillow. He folded his hands across his breast, turned his eye, did in all things exactly as he was directed, and in half a minute the operation was finished. I do not believe that he changed his position a hair's breadth or moved a muscle. It was an extraordinary instance of fortitude. The spectators were all admiration, and, amid universal congratulation, he was lifted from the table, his eye bound up, and, without a word, but with the spirit of a little hero, he took his father's hand and went away.

At this time, amid a press of applicants, a gentleman came to inform us that a young lady was waiting her turn. This gave us an excuse for clearing the room, and we requested all except the medical gentlemen and the immediate friends to favour us with their absence. Such was the strange curiosity these people had for seeing a most disagreeable spectacle, that they were very slow in going away, and some slipped into the other rooms and the yard, but we ferreted them out, and got the room somewhat to ourselves.

The young lady was accompanied by her mother. She was full of hesitation and fears, anxious to be relieved, but doubting her ability to endure the pain, and the moment she saw the instruments, her courage entirely forsook her. Doctor Cabot discouraged all who had any distrust of their own fortitude, and, to my mingled joy and regret, she went away.

The next in order was the gentleman on whose account we had postponed our departure. He was the oldest general in the Mexican service, but for two years an exile in Merida. By the late revolution, which placed Santa Ana in power, his party was uppermost; and he had strong claims upon our good feelings, for, in a former expatriation from Mexico, he had served as volunteer aid to General Jackson at the battle of New-Orleans. This gentleman had an inward squint in both eyes, which, however, instead of being a defect, gave character to his face; but his sight was injured by it, and this Doctor Cabot thought might be improved. The first eye was cut quickly and successfully, and while the bloody orb was rolling in its socket, the same operation was performed on the other. In this, however, fearing that the eye might be drawn too far in the opposite direction, the doctor had not thought it advisable to cut the muscle entirely through, and, on examining it, he was not satisfied with the appearance. The general again laid his head upon the pillow, and the operation was repeated, making three times in rapid succession. Altogether, it was a trying thing, and I felt immensely happy when it was over. With his eyes all right and both bandaged, we carried him to a caleza in waiting, where, to the great amusement of the vagabond boys, he took his seat on the footboard, with his back to the horse, and it was some time before we could get him right.

In the mean time the young lady had returned with her mother. She could not bear to lose the opportunity, and though unable to make up her mind to undergo the operation, she could not keep away. She was about eighteen, of lively imagination, picturing pleasure or pain in the strongest colours, and with a smile ever ready to chase away the tear. At one moment she roused herself to the effort, and the next, calling herself coward, fell into her mother's arms, while her mother cheered and encouraged her, representing to her, with that confidence allowed before medical men, the advantage it would give her in the eyes of our sex. Her eyes were large, full, and round, and with the tear glistening in them, the defect was hardly visible; in fact, all that they wanted was to be made to roll in the right direction.

I have given the reader a faint picture of Daguerreotype practice with young ladies, but this was altogether another thing, and it was very different from having to deal with boys or men. It is easy enough to spread out a boy upon a table, but not so with a young lady; so, too, it is easy enough to tie a bandage around a boy's head, but vastly different among combs and curls, and long hair done up behind. As the principal assistant of Doctor Cabot, this complicated business devolved upon me; and having, with the help of her mother, accomplished it, I laid her head upon the pillow as carefully as if it had been my own property. In all the previous cases I had found it necessary, in order to steady my hand, to lean my elbow on the table, and my wrist on the forehead of the patient. I did the same with her, and, if I know myself, I never gazed into any eyes as I did into that young lady's one eye in particular. When the doctor drew out the instrument, I certainly could have taken her in my arms, but her imagination had been too powerful; her eyes closed, a slight shudder seized her, and she fainted. That passed off, and she rose with her eyes all right. A young gentleman was in attendance to escort her to her home, and the smile had again returned to her cheek as he told her that now her lover would not know her.

This case had occupied a great deal of time; the doctor's labours were doubled by the want of regular surgical aid, he was fatigued with the excitement, and I was worn out; my head was actually swimming with visions of bleeding and mutilated eyes, and I almost felt doubtful about my own. The repetition of the operations had not accustomed me to them; indeed, the last was more painful to me than the first, and I felt willing to abandon forever the practice of surgery. Doctor Cabot had explained the modus operandi fully to the medical gentlemen, had offered to procure them instruments, and considering the thing fairly introduced into the country, we determined to stop. But this was not so easy; the crowd out of doors had their opinion on the subject; the biscos considered that we were treating them outrageously, and became as clamorous as a mob in a western city about to administer Lynch law. One would not be kept back. He was a strapping youth, with cast enough in his eye to carry everything before him, and had probably been taunted all his life by merciless schoolboys. Forcing himself inside, with his hands in his pockets, he said that he had the money to pay for it, and would not be put off. We were obliged to apologize, and, with a little wish to bring him down, gave him some hope that he should be attended to on our return to Merida.

The news of these successes flew like wild-fire, and a great sensation was created throughout the city. All the evening Doctor Cabot was besieged with applications, and I could but think how fleeting is this world's fame! At first my arrival in the country had been fairly trumpeted in the newspapers; for a little while Mr. Catherwood had thrown me in the shade with the Daguerreotype, and now all our glories were swallowed up by Doctor Cabot's cure of strabismus. Nevertheless, his fame was reflected upon us. All the afternoon squint-eyed boys were passing up and down the street, throwing slanting glances in at the door, and toward evening, as Mr. Catherwood and I were walking to the plaza, we were hailed by some vagabond urchins with the obstreperous shout, "There go the men who cure the biscos."

CHAPTER VI

On Thursday, the twelfth day of November, we rose for our departure from Merida. The plan of our route, and all the arrangements for our journey, were made by our friend Don Simon Peon. Early in the morning our luggage was sent forward on the backs of mules and Indians, and we had only to take leave of our friends. Our landlord refused to receive the four dollars due to him for rent. The pleasure of our society, he said, was compensation enough, and between friends house-rent was not to be thought of. We bade him an affectionate farewell, and in all probability "we ne'er shall see his like again," at least in this matter of house-rent. We breakfasted for the last time with our countrymen, including Mr. Fisher and Captain M'Kinley, who had arrived that morning direct from New-York, at the house of the Doña Micaela, and, attended by the good wishes of all for our safety and success, mounted for our journey into the interior.

It was our intention to resume our explorations at Uxmal, the point where we were interrupted by the illness of Mr. Catherwood. We had received intelligence, however, of the ruins of Mayapan, an ancient city which had never been visited, about eight leagues distant from Merida, and but a few leagues aside from the road, by the haciendas, to Uxmal. The accounts which we could obtain were meager, and it was represented as completely in ruins; but, in fulfillment of the purpose we at that time entertained of going to every place of which we heard any account whatever, we determined to visit this on our way to Uxmal. It was for Mayapan, therefore, that we were now setting out.

Our saddles, bridles, holsters, and pistols, being entirely different from the mountings of horsemen in that country, attracted all eyes as we rode through the streets. A friend accompanied us beyond the suburbs, and put us into a straight road, which led, without turning, to the end of our day's journey. Instead of the ominous warnings we were accustomed to receive in Central America, his parting words were, that there was no danger of robbers, or of any other interruptions.

Under these favourable circumstances, in good health and spirits, with recommendations from the government to its officers in different sections of the country, and through the newspapers to the hospitality of citizens in the interior, we set out on our journey. We had before us a new and unexplored region, in which we might expect to find new scenes every day. There was but one drawback. We had no servant or attendant of any kind, our friends having been disappointed in procuring those which were expected. This, however, did not give us much uneasiness.

The day was overcast, which saved us from the scorching sun, that otherwise, at this hour, would have molested us. The road was straight, level, stony, and uninteresting. On both sides were low, thick woods, so that there was no view except that of the road before us; and already, in the beginning of our journey, we felt that, if we were safe from the confusion and danger which had attended us in Central America, we had lost, too, the mountains, valleys, volcanoes, rivers, and all the wild and magnificent scenery that gave a charm to the country in spite of the difficulties and dangers by which travelling was there attended.

I would remark that no map of Yucatan at all to be depended on has ever been published. The Doña Joaquina Peon had one in manuscript, which she was so kind as to place at our disposal, but with notice that it was not correct; and, in order to keep a record of our own track from the time we left Merida until we returned to it, we took the bearings of the roads, noted the number of hours on each day's journey, and the pace of our horses, and at some places Mr. Catherwood took an observation for latitude. From these memoranda our map is prepared. It is correct so far as regards our route, but does not fix accurately the location of places which we did not visit.

At the distance of a league we passed a fine cattle hacienda, and at twenty minutes past one reached Timucui, a small village five leagues from Merida. This village consisted of a few Indian huts, built around a large open square, and on one side was a sort of shed for a casa real. It had no church or cura, and already we experienced a difficulty which we did not expect to encounter so soon. The population consisted entirely of Indians, who in general throughout the country speak nothing but the Maya; there was not a white man in the place, nor any one who could speak in any tongue that we could comprehend. Fortunately, a muleteer from the interior, on his way to Merida, had stopped to bait his mules under the shade of a large tree, and was swinging in a hammock in the casa real. He was surprised at our undertaking alone a journey into the interior, seeing that we were brought to a stand at the first village from the capital; but, finding us somewhat rational in other respects, he assisted us in procuring ramon leaves and water for the horses. His life had been passed in driving mules from a region of country called the Sierra, to the capital; but he had heard strange stories about foreign countries, and, among others, that in El Norte a man could earn a dollar a day by his labour; but he was comforted when he learned that a real in his country was worth more to him than a dollar would be in ours; and as he interpreted to his nearly naked companions, crouching in the shade, nothing touched them so nearly as the idea of cold and frost, and spending a great portion of the day's earnings for fuel to keep from freezing.

At three o'clock we left the hamlet, and at a little after four we saw the towers of the church of Tekoh. In the suburbs of this village we passed the campo santo, a large enclosure with high stone walls; over the gateway of which, and in niches along the top of the wall, was a row of human skulls. Inside the enclosure, at the farthest extremity, was a pile of skulls and bones, which, according to a custom of the Indians observed from time immemorial, had been dug up from the graves and thrown into this shallow pit, a grim and ghastly charnel-house.

The village consisted of a long, straight street, with houses or huts almost hidden by foliage, and inhabited exclusively by Indians. We rode up to the plaza without meeting a single person. At one side of the plaza, on a high stone platform, stood a gigantic church, with two lofty towers, and in front and on each side was a broad flight of stone steps. Crossing the plaza we saw an Indian woman, to whom we uttered the word *convento*, and, following the direction of her hand, rode up to the house of the cura. It was in the rear of the church, and enclosed by a large wall. The gate was closed, but we opened it without knocking. The convent stood on the same platform with the church, and had a high flight of stone steps. A number of Indian servants ran out to the corridor, to stare at such strange-looking persons, and we understood that the padre was not at home; but we were too well pleased with the appearance of things to think of going elsewhere. We tied our horses in the yard, ascended the steps, and strolled through the corridor of the convent and along the platform of the church, overlooking the village.

Before the door of the church lay the body of a child on a bier. There was no coffin, but the body was wrapped in a tinsel dress of paper of different colours, in which red and gold were predominant; and amid this finery worms several inches long were issuing from its nostrils, curling and twisting over its face: a piteous and revolting spectacle, showing the miserable lot of the children of the poor in these Indian villages.

In a few minutes the ministro, or assistant of the cura, joined us, from whom we learned that the cura was preparing to bury this child, and as soon as it was over, would come to receive us. In the mean time, under his escort, we ascended to the top of the church.

The ascent was by a large stone staircase within one of the towers. The top commanded a view of a great plain, covered by an almost boundless forest, extending on one side to the sea, and on the other to the sierra which crosses the peninsula of Yucatan, and runs back to the great traversing range in Guatimala, broken only by a high mound, which at three leagues' distance towered above the plain, a mourning monument of the ruins of Mayapan, the capital of the fallen kingdom of Maya.

On our return we found the cura, Don José Canuta Vela, waiting to receive us; he had been notified of our coming, and had expected us the day before. His curacy consisted of nearly two thousand souls, and, except his ministro, we did not see a white man among this population. He was under thirty, born and bred in Merida, and in manners and attainments apparently out of place in such a position; but his feelings and sympathies were identified with the people under his charge. The convent was a great stone building, with walls several feet thick, and in size corresponded with the church. Being so near Merida, it was more than ordinarily well supplied with comforts; and, among other things, the cura had a small collection of books, which, for that country, constituted quite a library.

He relieved us of all difficulty arising from the want of an interpreter, and, sending for the Indian alcaldes, made immediate arrangements to forward our luggage, and to accompany us himself the next day to the ruins of Mayapan. We had again made a beginning with the padres, and this beginning, in heartiness of welcome and goodness of cheer, corresponded with all that we had before received at their hands. We had the choice of cot or hammock for the night, and at breakfast a group of Indian musicians were seated under the corridor, who continued making a noise, which they called la musica, till we mounted to depart.

The cura accompanied us, mounted on one of the best horses we had seen in the country; and as it was a rare thing for him to absent himself a day from his parochial duties, he set out as for a holy-day excursion, worrying our poor nags, as well as ourselves, to keep up with him.

The road upon which we entered turned off abruptly from the camino real. This royal road itself, like most of the others which bore that name, would not be considered, in other countries, as indicating a very advanced state of internal improvement, but the one into which we now struck was much rougher and more stony, entirely new, and in some places still unfinished. It had been but lately opened, and the reason of its being opened at all illustrates one striking feature in the character of the Indians. The village to which it leads was under the pastoral charge of our friendly companion, and was formerly reached by a road, or rather path, so circuitous and difficult that, on account of his other duties, he was obliged to give notice that he would be compelled to give it up. To prevent this calamity, all the Indians, in a body, turned out and made this new road, being a straight cut through the woods, two leagues in length.

The padre took a lively interest in the zeal lately awakened for exploring the antiquities of the country, and told us that this particular region abounded with traces of the ancient inhabitants. At a short distance from the camino real we came to a line of fallen stones, forming what appeared to be the remains of a wall which crossed the road, and ran off into the forest on both sides, traversing, he said, the country for a great distance in both directions.

A short distance beyond, we turned off to a large hollow basin perfectly dry, which he called an aguada, and said it was an artificial formation, excavated and walled around, and had been used by the ancients as a reservoir for water. At the time, we did not agree with him, but considered the basin a natural formation, though, from what we saw afterward, we are induced to believe that his account may have been correct.

At ten o'clock we reached the small village of Telchaquillo, containing a population of six hundred souls, and these, again, were all Indians. It was they who had made the road we had travelled over, and the church was under our friend's pastoral charge. We rode to the convent, and dismounted. Immediately the bell of the church tolled, to give notice of his arrival, that all who wished to confess or get married, who had sick to be visited, children to be baptized, or dead to be buried, might apply to him, and have their wants attended to.

The village consisted entirely of huts, or casas de paja. The church had been commenced on a large scale, under the direction of a former cura, who afterward became dissatisfied with the people, and discontinued the building. One end was covered over, and fitted up rudely as a chapel; beyond were two high walls, but roofless.

In the square of this little village was a great senote, or subterraneous well, which supplied all the inhabitants with water. At a distance the square seemed level and unbroken; but women walking across it with cantaros or water-jars suddenly disappeared, and others seemed to rise out of the earth. On a nearer approach, we found a great orifice or opening in the rocky surface, like the mouth of a cave. The descent was by irregular steps cut and worn in the rocks. Over head was an immense rocky roof, and at a distance of perhaps five hundred feet from the mouth was a large basin or reservoir of water. Directly over the water the roof was perhaps sixty feet high; and there was an opening above which threw down a strong body of light. The water had no current, and its source was a mystery. During the rainy season it rises a little, but never falls below a certain point, and at all times it is the only source of supply to the inhabitants. Women, with their water-jars, were constantly ascending and descending; swallows were darting through the cave in every direction, and the whole formed a wild, picturesque, and romantic scene.

At this village we found waiting for us the major domo of the hacienda of San Joaquin, on which stand the ruins of Mayapan. Leaving the senote, we mounted and followed him.

At the distance of half a mile he stopped near a great cave that had lately been discovered, and which, he said, had no end.

Tying our horses to the bushes, we turned off to visit it. The major domo cut a path a short distance into the woods, following which we came to a large hollow, overgrown with trees, and, descending, entered a great cavern with a lofty roof, and gigantic passages branching off in different directions, and running no one knew whither. The cave had been discovered by the major domo and some vaqueros while in pursuit of robbers who had stolen a bull; and no robber's cave in romantic story could equal it in wildness. The major domo said he had entered it with ten men, and had passed four hours in exploration without finding any end. The cave, its roof, base, and passages, were an immense fossil formation. Marine shells were conglomerated together in solid masses, many of them perfect, showing a geological structure which indicated that the whole country, or, at least, that portion of it, had been once, and probably at no very remote period, overflowed by the sea.

We could have passed a day with much satisfaction in rambling through this cave, but, remaining only a few minutes, and taking away some curious and interesting specimens, we remounted, and very soon reached mounds of earth, fragments of sculptured stones, broken walls, and fallen buildings, indicating that we were once more treading upon the sepulchre of an aboriginal city.

At eleven o'clock we came to a clearing, in which was situated the hacienda of San Joaquin. The building was a mere rancho, erected only for the residence of a mayoral, a person inferior to a major domo; but there was a fine clearing around it, and the situation was wild and beautiful. In the cattle-yard were noble trees. In the platform of the well were sculptured stones taken from the ancient buildings; it was shaded by the spreading branches of a fine ramon or tropical oak, with a foliage of vivid green; and crowning the top, and apparently growing out of it, were the long pale leaves of the cocoanut.

The hacienda, or rather rancho, of San Joaquin, on which the ruins of Mayapan lie scattered, is ten leagues south from Merida. It forms part of the great hacienda of Xcanchakan, the property of Don José Maria Meneses, the venerable cura of San Cristoval, formerly provesor of the Church of Yucatan. We had made the acquaintance of this gentleman at the house of his friend Señor Rejon, secretary of state, and he had sent instructions to his major domo, the same who had met us at the last village, to place at our command all the disposable force of the hacienda.

85

The ruins of Mayapan cover a great plain, which was at that time so overgrown that hardly any object was visible until we were close upon it, and the undergrowth was so thick that it was difficult to work our way through it. Our's was the first visit to examine these ruins. For ages they had been unnoticed, almost unknown, and left to struggle with rank tropical vegetation; and the major domo, who lived on the principal hacienda, and had not seen them in twenty-three years, was more familiar with them than any other person we could find. He told us that within a circumference of three miles, ruins were found, and that a strong wall once encompassed the city, the remains of which might still be traced through the woods.

Fig. 1

At a short distance from the hacienda, but invisible on account of the trees, rises the high mound which we had seen at three leagues' distance, from the top of the church at Tekoh, and which is represented in Figure 1. It is sixty feet high, and one hundred feet square at the base; and, like the mounds at Palenque and Uxmal, it is an artificial structure, built up solid from the plain. Though seen from a great distance above the tops of the trees, the whole field was so overgrown that it was scarcely visible until we reached its foot; and the mound itself, though retaining the symmetry of its original proportions, was also so overgrown that it appeared a mere wooded hill, but peculiar in its regularity of shape. Four grand staircases, each twenty-five feet wide, ascended to an esplanade within six feet of the top. This esplanade was six feet in width, and on each side was a smaller staircase leading to the top. These staircases are in a ruinous condition; the steps are almost entirely gone, and we climbed up by means of fallen stones and trees growing out of its sides. As we ascended, we scared away a cow, for the wild cattle roaming on these wooded wastes pasture on its sides, and ascend to the top.

The summit was a plain stone platform, fifteen feet square. It had no structure upon it, nor were there vestiges of any. Probably it was the great mound of sacrifice, on which the priests, in the sight of the assembled people, cut out the hearts of human victims. The view commanded from the top was a great desolate plain, with here and there another ruined mound rising above the trees, and far in the distance could be discerned the towers of the church at Tekoh.

Around the base of this mound, and throughout the woods, wherever we moved, were strewed sculptured stones. Most of them were square, carved on the face, and having a long stone tenon or stem at the back; doubtless they had been fixed in the wall, so as to form part of some ornament, or combination of ornaments, in the façade, in all respects the same as at Uxmal.

Besides these, there were other and more curious remains. These were representations of human figures, or of animals, with hideous features and expressions, in producing which the skill of the artist seems to have been expended. The sculpture of these figures was rude, the stones were timeworn, and many were half buried in the earth. Figure 2 represents two of them. One is four, and the other three feet high. The full length seems intended to represent a warrior with a shield. The arms are broken off, and to my mind they conveyed a lively idea of the figures or idols which Bernal Dias met with on the coast, containing hideous faces of demons. Probably, broken and half buried as they lie, they were once objects of adoration and worship, and now exist as mute and melancholy memorials of ancient paganism.

At a short distance from the base of the mound was an open-

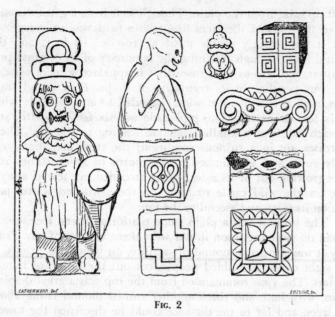

CATHERWOOD Del.   LOSSING Sc.

FIG. 2

ing in the earth, forming another of those extraordinary caves
before presented to the reader. The cura, the major domo, and
the Indians called it a senote, and said that it had supplied the
inhabitants of the old city with water. The entrance was by a
broken, yawning mouth, steep, and requiring some care in the
descent. At the first resting-place, the mouth opened into an extensive subterraneous chamber, with a high roof, and passages
branching off in every direction. In different places were remains
of fires and the bones of animals, showing that it had at times
been the place of refuge or residence of men. In the entrance of
one of the passages we found a sculptured idol, which excited us
with the hope of discovering some altar or sepulchre, or perhaps
mummied figures. With this hope, we sent the Indians to procure torches; and while Mr. Catherwood was making some
sketches, Doctor Cabot and myself passed an hour in exploring
the recesses of the cave. In many places the roof had fallen, and
the passages were choked up. We followed several of them with
much toil and disappointment, and at length fell into one, low
and narrow, along which it was necessary to crawl on the hands
and feet, and where, from the flame and smoke of the torches, it
was desperately hot. We at length came to a body of water, which,
on thrusting the hand into it, we found to be incrusted with a

88

thin coat of sulphate of lime, that had formed on the top of the water, but decomposed on being brought into the air.

Leaving the cave or senote, we continued rambling among the ruins. The mounds were all of the same general character, and the buildings had entirely disappeared on all except one; but this was different from any we had at that time seen, though we afterward found others like it.

FIG. 3

It stood on a ruined mound about thirty feet high. What the shape of the mound had been it was difficult to make

89

out, but the building was circular. Figure 3 represents this edifice, with the mound on which it stands. The exterior is of plain stone, ten feet high to the top of the lower cornice, and fourteen more to that of the upper one. The door faces the west, and over it is a lintel of stone. The outer wall is five feet thick; the door opens into a circular passage three feet wide, and in the centre is a cylindrical solid mass of stone, without any doorway or opening of any kind. The whole diameter of the building is twenty-five feet, so that, deducting the double width of the wall and passage, this centre mass must be nine feet in thickness. The walls had four or five coats of stucco, and there were remains of painting, in which red, yellow, blue, and white were distinctly visible.

On the southwest side of the building, and on a terrace projecting from the side of the mound, was a double row of columns eight feet apart, of which only eight remained, though probably, from the fragments around, there had been more, and, by clearing away the trees, more might have been found still standing. In our hurried visit to Uxmal, we had seen objects which we supposed might have been intended for columns, but were not sure; and though we afterward saw many, we considered these the first decided columns we had seen. They were two feet and a half in diameter, and consisted of five round stones, eight or ten inches thick, laid one upon another. They had no capitals, and what particular connexion they had with the building did not appear.

So far, although the fragments of sculpture were of the same general character as at Uxmal, we had not found any edifice sufficiently entire to enable us to identify that peculiar arch which we had found in all the ruined buildings of this country; but it was not wanting. At some distance from this place, and on the other side of the hacienda, were long ranges of mounds. These had once been buildings, the tops of which had fallen, and almost buried the structures. At the end was a doorway, encumbered and half filled with rubbish, crawling through which, we stood upright in apartments exactly similar to those at Uxmal, with the arch formed of stones overlapping, and a flat stone covering the top. The apartments were ruder and narrower, but they were of precisely the same character with all the others we had seen.

The day was now nearly spent; with the heat and labour we were exceedingly fatigued, and the Indians insisted that we had seen all the principal remains. The place was so overgrown with trees that it would have taken a long time to clear them away, and for the present at least it was out of the question. Besides, the only result we could promise ourselves was the bringing to light of fragments and single pieces of buried sculpture. Of one thing, however, we had no doubt: the ruins of this city were of the same general character with those at Uxmal, erected by the same builders, probably of older date, and suffering more from the corrosion of the elements, or they had been visited more harshly by the destroying hand of man.

Fortunately, at this place again we have a ray of historic light. According to the best accounts, the region of country now called Yucatan was known to the natives, at the time of the Spanish invasion, by the name of Maya, and before that time it had never been known by any other. The name of Yucatan was given to it by the Spaniards. It is entirely arbitrary and accidental, and its origin is not known with certainty. It is supposed by some to be derived from the plant known in the islands by the name of *Yuca,* and *tal* or *thale,* the heap of earth in which this plant grows; but more generally it is derived from certain words supposed to have been spoken by the natives in answer to a question asked by the Spaniards on their first arrival. The supposed question is, "What is the name of this country?" or, "How is this country called?" and the conjectured answer, "I do not understand those words," or, "I do not understand your words," either of which expressions, in the language of the natives, has some resemblance in pronunciation to the word Yucatan. But whatever was its origin, the natives have never recognised the name, and to this day, among themselves, they speak of their country only under its ancient name of Maya. No native ever calls himself a Yucateco, but always a Macegual, or native of the land of Maya.

One language, called the Maya, extended throughout the whole peninsula; and though the Spaniards found the country parcelled into different governments, under various names and having different caciques, hostile to each other, at an earlier period of its history the whole land of Maya was united under one head or supreme lord. This great chief or king had for the seat of his monarchy a very populous city called Mayapan, and had under him many other lords and caciques, who were bound to pay him tribute of cotton clothes, fowls, cacao, and gum or resin for incense; to serve him in wars, and day and night in the temples of the idols, at festivals and ceremonies. These lords, too, had under them cities and many vassals. Becoming proud and ambitious, and unwilling to brook a superior, they rebelled against the power of the supreme lord, united all their forces, and besieged and destroyed the city of Mayapan. This destruction took place in the year of our Lord 1420, about one hundred years, or, according to Herrera, about seventy years, before the arrival of the Spaniards in Yucatan; and, according to the computation of the ages of the Indians, two hundred and seventy years from the foundation of the city. The account of all the details is confused and indistinct; but the existence of a principal city called Mayapan, and its destruction by war at about the time indicated, are mentioned by every historian. This city was occupied by the same race of people who inhabited the country at the time of the conquest, and its site is identified as that which has just been presented to the reader, retaining, through all changes and in its ruins, its ancient name of Mayapan.

CHAPTER VII

The interest of our day at Mayapan came near being marred by an unlucky accident. Just as we were leaving the ruins a messenger came to inform us that one of our pistols had shot an Indian. These pistols had never shown any particular antipathy to Indians, and had never shot one before; but, hurrying back to the hacienda, we found the poor fellow with two of his fingers nearly shot off. The ball had passed through his shirt, making two holes in it, fortunately without hitting his body. The Indians said that the pistol had gone off itself while they were only looking at it. We felt sure that this was not exactly the case, knowing that pistols are not free agents, and laid the blame upon them; but it was a great satisfaction that the accident was no worse, and also that Doctor Cabot was at hand to dress the wound. The Indian seemed to think less of it than we did.

It was late when we left the hacienda. Our road was a mere bridle-path through a wilderness. At some distance we crossed a broken range of stones, rising on each side to a wall, which the major domo said was the line of wall that encompassed the ancient city.

It was nearly dark when we reached the stately hacienda of Xcanchakan, one of the three finest in Yucatan, and containing nearly seven hundred souls. Plate I represents the front of this hacienda. The house is perhaps one of the best in the country, and being within one day's ride of the capital, and accessible by calesa, it is a favourite residence of its venerable proprietor. The

Plate I

HACIENDA OF XCANCHAKAN.

Catherwood

Rolph

whole condition of the hacienda showed that it was often subject to the master's eye, and the character of that master may be judged of from the fact that his major domo, the same who was attendant upon us, had been with him twenty-six years.

I have given the reader some idea of a hacienda in Yucatan, with its cattle-yard, its great tanks of water and other accessories. All these were upon a large and substantial scale, equal to any we had seen; and there was one little refinement in their arrangement, which, though not, perhaps, intended for that purpose, could not fail to strike the eye of a stranger. The passage to the well was across the corridor, and, sitting quietly in the shade, the proprietor could see every day, passing and repassing, all the women and girls belonging to the estate.

Our friend the cura of Tekoh was still with us, and the Indians of the hacienda were within his curacy. Again immediately upon our arrival the bell of the church was tolled to announce his arrival to the sick, those who wished to confess, marry, or be baptized. This over, it struck the solemn note of the *oracion,* or vesper prayers. All rose, and, with uncovered heads stood silent till the last note died away, all, according to the beautiful injunction of the Catholic Church, breathing an inward prayer. Then they bade each other a *buenas noches,* each kissed the cura's hand, and then, with his petata, or straw hat, in his hand, came to us, bowing respectfully, and wishing each of us also the good night.

The cura still considered us on his hands, and, in order to entertain us, requested the major domo to get up a dance of the Indians. Very soon we heard the sound of the violins and the Indian drum. This latter consists of a hollow log about three feet long, with a piece of parchment stretched over the end, on which an Indian, holding it under his left arm, beats with his right hand. It is the same instrument known to the inhabitants at the time of the conquest by the name of *tunkúl* and is the favourite now. Going out into the back corridor, we saw the musicians sitting at one end, before the door of the chapel; on one side of the corridor were the women, and on the other the men. For some time there was no dancing, until, at length, at the instance of the cura, the major domo gave his directions, and a young man stood up in the middle of the corridor. Another, with a pocket-handkerchief in his hand having a knot tied in one end, walked along the line of women, threw the handkerchief at one, and then returned to his seat. This was considered a challenge or invitation; but, with a proper prudery, as if to show that she was not to be had for the asking, she waited some minutes, then rose, and slowly taking the shawl from her head, placed herself opposite the young man, at a distance of about ten feet, and commenced dancing. The dance was called the toros, or the bull. The movements were slow; occasionally the performers crossed over and changed places, and when the time ended the lady walked deliberately off, which either brought the young man to a standstill, or he went on dancing, as he liked. The manager or master of ceremonies, who was called the *bastonero,* again walked along the line, and touched another lady in the same way with the handkerchief. She again, after waiting a moment, removed her shawl and took her place on the floor; and in this way the dance continued, the dancing man being always the same, and taking the partner provided for him. Afterward the dance was changed to a Spanish one, in which, instead of castanets, the dancers from time to time snapped their fingers. This was more lively, and seemed to please them better than their own, but throughout there was nothing national or characteristic.

Early in the morning we were roused by loud bursts of music in the church. The cura was giving them the benefit of his accidental visit by an early mass. After this we heard music of a different kind. It was the lash on the back of an Indian. Looking out into the corridor, we saw the poor fellow on his knees on the pavement, with his arms clasped around the legs of another Indian, so as to present his back fair to the lash. At every blow he rose on one knee, and sent forth a piercing cry. He seemed struggling to restrain it, but it burst from him in spite of all his efforts. His whole bearing showed the subdued character of the present Indians, and with the last stripe the expression of his face seemed that of thankfulness for not getting more. Without uttering a word, he crept to the major domo, took his hand, kissed it, and walked away. No sense of degradation crossed his mind. Indeed, so humbled is this once fierce people, that they have a proverb of their own, "Los Indios no oigan si no por las nalgas"—"The Indians cannot hear except through their backs," and the cura related to us a fact which indicates an abasement of character perhaps never found in any other people. In a village not far distant, the name of which I have lost, they have a fiesta with a scenic representation called Shtol. The scene is laid at the time of the conquest. The Indians of the village gather within a large place enclosed by poles, and are supposed to be brought together by an invasion of the Spaniards. An old man rises and exhorts them to defend their country; if need be, to die for it.

The Indians are roused, but in the midst of his exhortations a stranger enters in the dress of a Spaniard and armed with a musket. The sight of this stranger throws them all into consternation; he fires the musket, and they fall to the ground. He binds the chief, carries him off captive, and the play is ended.

After breakfast the cura left us to return to his village, and we set out to continue our journey to Uxmal. Our luggage was sent off by Indians of the hacienda, and the major domo accompanied us on horseback. Our road was by a bridle path over the same stony country, through thick woods. The whole way it lay through the lands of the provisor, all wild, waste, and desolate, and showing the fatal effects of accumulation in the hands of large landed proprietors. In two hours we saw rising before us the gate

Fig. 4

of the hacienda of Mucuyché (Figure 4). To the astonishment of the gaping Indians, the doctor, as he wheeled his horse, shot a hawk that was hovering over the pinnacle of the gateway, and we rode up to the house.

I trust the reader has not forgotten this fine hacienda. It was the same to which, on our former visit, we had been borne on the shoulders of Indians, and in which we had taken a bath in a senote, never to be forgotten. We were once more on the hands of our old friend Don Simon Peon. The whole hacienda, horses, mules, and Indians, were at our disposal. It was but ten o'clock, and we intended to continue our journey to Uxmal, but first we resolved upon another bath in the senote. My first impression of the beauty of this fancy bathing place did not deceive me, and the first glance satisfied me that I incurred no risk in introducing to it a stranger. A light cloud of almost imperceptible dust, ascribed to the dripping of the waters of the rainy season, or

FIG. 5. Senote.

perhaps made visible by the rays of the midday sun, rested on the surface, but underneath were the same crystal fluid and the same clear bottom. Very soon we were in the water, and before we came out we resolved to postpone our journey till the next day, for the sake of an evening bath.

First Sight of the Ruins

As the reader is now on ground which I trust he has travelled before, I shall merely state that the next day we rode on to the hacienda of San José, where we stopped to make some preparations, and on the fifteenth, at eleven o'clock, we reached the hacienda of Uxmal.

It stood in its suit of sombre gray, with cattle-yard, large trees, and tanks, the same as when we left it, but there were no friends of old to welcome us: the Delmonico major domo had gone to Tobasco, and the other had been obliged to leave on account of illness. The mayoral remembered us, but we did not know him; and we determined to pass on and take up our abode immediately in the ruins. Stopping but a few minutes, to give directions about the luggage, we mounted again, and in ten minutes, emerging from the woods, came out upon the open field in which, grand and lofty as when we saw it before, stood the House of the Dwarf; but the first glance showed us that a year had made great changes. The sides of the lofty structure, then bare and naked, were now covered with high grass, bushes, and weeds, and on the top were bushes and young trees twenty feet high. The House of the Nuns was almost smothered, and the whole field was covered with a rank growth of grass and weeds, over which we could barely look as we rode through. The foundations, terraces, and tops of the buildings were overgrown, weeds and vines were rioting and creeping on the façades, and mounds, terraces, and ruins were a mass of destroying verdure. A strong and vigorous nature was struggling for mastery over art, wrapping the city in its suffocating enbraces, and burying it from sight. It seemed as if the grave was closing over a friend, and we had arrived barely in time to take our farewell.

Amid this mass of desolation, grand and stately as when we left it, stood the Casa del Gobernador, but with all its terraces covered, and separated from us by a mass of impenetrable verdure.

On the left of the field was an overgrown milpa, along the edge of which a path led in front of this building. Following this path, we turned the corner of the terrace, and on the farthest side dismounted, and tied our horses. The grass and weeds were above our heads, and we could see nothing. The mayoral broke a way through them, and we reached the foot of the terrace. Working our way over the stones with much toil, we reached the top of the highest terrace. Here, too, the grass and weeds were of the same rank growth. We moved directly to the wall at the east end, and entered the first open door. Here the mayoral wished us to take up our abode; but we knew the localities better than he did, and, creeping along the front as close to the wall as possible, cutting some of the bushes, and tearing apart and trampling down others, we reached the centre apartment. Here we stopped. Swarms of bats, roused by our approach, fluttered and flew through the long chamber, and passed out at the doors.

The appearance of things was not very promising for a place of residence. There were two salas, each sixty feet long; that in front had three large doors, opening upon the encumbered terrace, and the other had no windows and but one door. In both there was an extreme sensation of closeness and dampness, with an unpleasant smell, and in the back room was a large accumulation of dirt and rubbish. Outside, high grass and weeds were growing into the very doorway. We could not move a step, and all view was completely cut off. After the extreme heat of the sun out of doors, we were in a profuse perspiration from climbing up the terrace, and the dank atmosphere induced a feeling of chilliness which made us reflect seriously upon what we had not sufficiently regarded before.

Throughout Yucatan "el campo," or the country, is considered unhealthy in the rainy season. We had arrived in Yucatan counting upon the benefit of the whole dry season, which generally begins in November and lasts till May; but this year the rains had continued longer than usual, and they were not yet over. The proprietors of haciendas were still cautious about visiting them, and confined themselves to the villages and towns. Among all the haciendas, Uxmal had a reputation pre-eminent for its unhealthiness. Every person who had ever been at work among the ruins had been obliged by sickness to leave them. Mr. Catherwood had had sad experience, and this unhealthiness was not confined to strangers. The Indians suffered every season from fevers; many of them were at that time ill, and the major domo had been obliged to go away. All this we had been advised of in Merida, and had been urged to postpone our visit; but as this would have interfered materially with our plan, and as we had with us a "medico" who could cure "biscos," we determined to risk it. On the spot, however, perceiving the dampness of the apartments and the rankness of vegetation, we felt that we had been imprudent; but it was too late to draw back, even if we had wished to do so. We agreed that we were better on this high terrace than at the hacienda, which stood low, and had around it great tanks of water, mantled with green, and wearing a very fever-and-aguish aspect. We therefore set to work immediately to make the best of our condition.

The mayoral left us to take the horses back to the hacienda, and give directions about the luggage, and we had only a little Indian boy to help us. Him we employed to clear with his machete a space before the principal doorway, and in order to change as quickly as possible the damp, unwholesome atmosphere within, we undertook to kindle a fire ourselves. For this purpose we made a large collection of leaves and brush, which we placed in one corner of the back corridor, and, laying stones at the bottom, built up a pile several feet high, and set fire to it. The blaze crept through the pile, burning the light combustible stuff, and went out. We kindled it again, and the result was the same. Several times we thought we had succeeded, but the dampness of the place and of the materials baffled our efforts, and extinguished the flame. We exhausted all our odd scraps of paper and other availables, and were left with barely a spark of fire to begin anew. The only combustible we had left was gunpowder, of which we made what the boys call a squib, by wetting a quantity of it, and this, done up in a ball, we ignited under the pile. It did not answer fully, but gave us encouragement, and we made a larger ball of the same, which we ignited with a slow match. It blew our pile to atoms, and scattered the materials in all directions. Our ingenuity had now been taxed to the uttermost, and our resources were exhausted. In extremity we called in the boy.

He had, in the mean time, been more successful; for, continuing the work at which we had set him, with characteristic indifference taking no notice of our endeavours, he had cleared a space of several yards around the door. This admitted a sunbeam, which, like the presence of a good spirit, gladdened and cheered all within its reach. We intimated to him by signs that we wanted a fire, and, without paying any respect to what we had done, he began in his own way, with a scrap of cotton, which he picked up from the ground, and, lighting it, blew it gently in his folded hands till it was all ignited. He then laid it on the floor, and, throwing aside all the material we had been using, looked around carefully, and gathered up some little sticks, not larger than matches, which he laid against the ignited cotton, with one point on the ground and the other touching the fire. Then kneeling down, he encircled the nascent fire with his two hands, and blew gently on it, with his mouth so close as almost to touch it. A slight smoke rose above the palms of his hands, and in a few minutes he stopped blowing. Placing the little sticks carefully together, so that all their points touched the fire, he went about picking up others a little larger than the first, and laying them in order one by one. With the circumference of his hands a little extended, he again began blowing gently; the smoke rose a little stronger than before. From time to time he gently changed the position of the sticks, and resumed his blowing. At length he stopped, but whether in despair or satisfied with the result seemed doubtful. He had a few little sticks with a languishing fire at one end, which might be extinguished by dropping a few tears over it. We had not only gone beyond this, but had raised a large flame, which had afterward died away. Still there was a steadiness, an assurance in his manner that seemed to say he knew what he was about. At all events, we had nothing to do but watch him. Making a collection of larger sticks, and again arranging them in the same way as before, taking care not to put them so close together as to smother the fire, with a circumference too large for the space of his hands, but of materials so light as easily to be thrown into confusion, he again commenced blowing, so gently as not to disturb a single stick, and yet to the full power that the arrangement would bear. The wood seemed to feel the influence of his cherishing care, and a full body of smoke rose up to gladden us, and bring tears into his eyes. With the same imperturbable industry, unconscious of our admiration, he went on again, having now got up to sticks as large as the finger. These he coaxed along with many tears, and at the next size he saved his own wind and used his petata, or straw hat. A gentle blaze rose in the whole centre of the pile; still he coaxed it along, and by degrees brought on sticks as large as his arm, which, by a gentle waving of his hat, in a few minutes were all ignited. Our uncertainty was at an end. The whole pile was in a blaze, and all four of us went busily to work gathering fuel. There was no necessity for dry wood; we cut down bushes, and carried them in green; all burned together; the flames extended, and the heat became so great that we could not approach to throw on more. In our satisfaction with the result we did not stop to read the moral of the lesson taught us by the Indian boy. The flames were fast rectifying the damp, unwholesome atmosphere, and inducing more warm and genial sensations. Very soon, however, this bettering of our house's condition drove us out of doors. The smoke rolled through the long apartment, and, curling along the roof, passed into the front sala, where, dividing, it rushed through the doors in three dense bodies, and rolled up the front of the palace. We sat down outside, and watched it as it rolled away.

While this was going on, the mayoral crawled along the same path by which we had ascended, and told us that the luggage had arrived. How it could be got to us seemed a problem. The slight clearing on the upper terrace gave us a view of the lower one, which was an unbroken mass of bushes and weeds ten or twelve feet high. Perhaps half an hour elapsed, when we saw a single Indian ascend the platform of the second terrace, with his machete slowly working his way toward us. Very soon the top of a long box was seen rising above the same terrace, apparently tottering and falling back, but rising again and coming on steadily, with an Indian under it, visible from time to time through the bushes. Toward the foot of the terrace on which we were it disappeared, and after a few minutes rose to the top. Holding on with both hands to the strap across his forehead, with every nerve strung, and the veins of his forehead swelled almost to bursting, his face and his whole body dripping with sweat, he laid his load at our feet. A long line followed; staggering, panting, and trembling, they took the loads from their backs, and deposited them at the door. They had carried these loads three leagues, or nine miles, and we paid them eighteen and three quarter cents, being at the rate of a *medio,* or six and a quarter cents, per league. We gave them a medio extra for bringing the things up the terrace, and the poor fellows were thankful and happy.

In the mean time the fire was still burning, and the smoke rushing out. We set the Indians at work on the terrace with their machetes, and as the smoke rolled away we directed them to sweep out the apartments. For brooms they had merely to cut a handful of bushes, and to shovel out the dirt they had their hands. This over, we had our luggage carried in, set up our beds in the back sala, and swung our hammocks in the front. At nightfall the Indians left us, and we were again alone in the palace of unknown kings.

We had reached the first point of our journey; we were once more at the ruins of Uxmal. It was nearly two years since we originally set out in search of American ruins, and more than a year since we were driven from this place. The freshness and enthusiasm with which we had first come upon the ruins of an American city had perhaps gone, but our feelings were not blunted, and all the regret which we had felt in being obliged to leave was more than counterbalanced by the satisfaction of returning.

It was in this spirit that, as evening came on, we swung in our hammocks and puffed away all troubles. The bats, retiring to their nightly haunt, seemed startled by the blaze of our fire. Owls and other birds of darkness sent up their discordant cries from the woods, and as the evening waned we found ourselves debating warmly the great question of excitement at home, whether M'Leod ought to be hanged or not.

As a measure of precaution, and in order to have the full benefit of a medical man's company, we began immediately upon a course of preventive treatment, by way of putting ourselves on the vantage ground against fever. As we were all in perfect health, Dr. Cabot thought such a course could not hurt us. This over, we threw more wood upon the pile and went to bed.

Up to this time our course had been before the wind. Our journey from Merida had again been a sort of triumphal procession. We had been passed from hacienda to hacienda, till we fell into the hospitable hands of Don Simon Peon, and we were now in absolute possession of the ruins of Uxmal. But very soon we found that we had to encounter troubles from which neither Don Simon, nor the government, nor recommendations to the hospitality of citizens of the interior, could afford us protection. Early in the evening a few straggling moschetoes had given us notice of the existence of these free and independent citizens of Yucatan; but while we were swinging in our hammocks and the fire burned brightly, they had not troubled us much. Our heads, however, were hardly upon our pillows, before the whole population seemed to know exactly where they could have us, and, dividing into three swarms, came upon us as if determined to lift us up and eject us bodily from the premises. The flame and volumes of smoke which had rolled through the building, in ridding us of the damp, unwholesome atmosphere, seemed only to have started these torments from their cracks and crevices, and filled them with thirst for vengeance or for blood. I spare the reader farther details of our first night at Uxmal, but we all agreed that another such would drive us forever from the ruins.

CHAPTER VIII

Morning brought with it other perplexities. We
had no servant, and wanted breakfast, and altogether our prospects were not good. We did not expect to find the hacienda so
entirely destitute of persons with whom we could communicate.
The mayoral was the only one who spoke a word of Spanish,
and he had the business of the hacienda to attend to. He had received special orders from his master to do everything in his
power to serve us, but the power of his master had limits. He
could not make the Indians, who knew only the Maya, speak
Spanish. Besides this, the power of the master was otherwise re-
stricted. In fact, except as regards certain obligations which they
owed, the Indians were their own masters, and, what was worse
for us, their own mistresses, for one of our greatest wants was a
woman to cook, make tortillas, and perform those numerous do-
mestic offices without which no household can go on well. The
mayoral had given us no hope of being able to procure one; but
in the midst of our anxieties, and while we were preparing breakfast for ourselves, we perceived him coming across the terrace,
followed by a train of Indians, and closing the procession was
a woman, at that time really a welcome visiter. The mayoral said
that the evening before, on his return to the hacienda, he had
gone round to all the huts, and proposed to woman after woman,
promising liberal pay and good treatment, but they all refused

until he came to this one, and with her he had been obliged to stipulate that she should not remain at the ruins in the night, but should return home every evening. This was a great drawback, as we wanted to breakfast early, but we had no choice, and were glad to get her upon her own terms.

She was taller than most of the Indian women, and her complexion was somewhat darker. Her dress fitted more closely to her body, and she had more of it. Her character was unimpeached, her bearing would have kept presumption at a distance, and, as an additional safeguard, she had with her a little grandson, named José, whose complexion indicated that the descending line of her house had no antipathies to the white race. Her age might be a little over fifty, and her name was Chaipa Chi.

The preliminaries being settled, we immediately installed her as *chef de cuisine*, without assistants, and sent off the mayoral to direct the Indians in some clearings which we wished made immediately. The first essay of Chaipa Chi was in boiling eggs, which, according to the custom of the country, she boiled *para beber*, or to drink; that is, by breaking a small hole in the shell, into which a stick is inserted to mix together the white and yolk; the egg is to be disposed of through this hole in the primitive way which nature indicates to the new-born babe. This did not suit us, and we wished the process of cooking to be continued a little longer, but Chaipa Chi was impenetrable to hints or signs. We were obliged to stand over her, and, but for the name of the thing, we might as well have cooked them ourselves. This over, we gave up, and left our dinner to the mercies of our chef.

Before we were in a condition to begin an examination and exploration of the ruins, we had a serious business before us in making the necessary clearings. These were not required for picturesque effect; indeed, overgrown as the ruins were, they addressed themselves more powerfully to the imagination than if the whole field and every stone lay bare; but facilities of moving from place to place were indispensable, and for this purpose we determined first to clear the terrace of the Casa del Gobernador, and cut roads from ruin to ruin, until we had a complete line of communication; and that we might know exactly our whereabout, Mr. Catherwood took an observation, by which he found the latitude of Uxmal to be 20° 27′ 30″ N.

Our Indians made a good beginning, and by the afternoon we had the upper terrace cleared. Toward evening they all left us, including Chaipa Chi, and at night, while the moon was glimmering mournfully over the ruins, we had a stroll along the whole front of the Casa del Gobernador.

We were in no hurry to retire, and when we did so it was with some misgivings. Besides a little general attention to what was going on out of doors, the principle business of the day had been to prepare our moscheto-nets, and for this we grudged no time, labour, or ingenuity; but our success was complete. Throughout the whole long apartment there was a continued singing and whizzing, lower or louder as the musicians came near or retired, furious at being defrauded of their prey, but they could not touch us. Our satisfaction went beyond that of the mere prospect for the night, for we felt sure of rest after labour, and of being able to maintain our ground.

The next day we made a valuable addition to our household. Among the Indians who came out to work was a lad who spoke Spanish. He was the puniest, lankest, and leanest of any we had seen on the hacienda, and his single garment was the dirtiest. His name was Bernaldo. He was but fifteen, and he was already experiencing the vicissitudes of fortune. His education had been neglected; and for confounding some technical distinctions in the laws of property, he was banished from a hacienda near Merida to the deserts of Uxmal. We were in such straits for want of an interpreter, and, except during the short visit of the mayoral, so entirely destitute, that we overlooked entirely Bernaldo's moral weakness, withdrew him from the workmen, and led him to the sala of the palace, where, in the course of conveying some instructions to Chaipa Chi, he showed such an interest in the subject that Doctor Cabot immediately undertook to give him a lesson in cookery. In his first essay he was so apt that we forthwith inducted him as ruler over the three stones that composed our kitchen fireplace, with all the privileges and emoluments of sipping and tasting, and left Chaipa Chi to bestow all her energies upon the business that her soul loved, the making of tortillas.

Being now domesticated, I shall introduce the reader without preface to the ruins of Uxmal. In the account of my former visit I endeavoured to give a brief description of these ruins. Hurried away, however, without plans or drawings, it was impossible to present any definite idea of their character. Plate II represents the plan of this ancient city, as indicated by the remaining edifices. The ranges were all taken with the compass, and the distances measured, and the dimensions of the buildings and their

Plate II

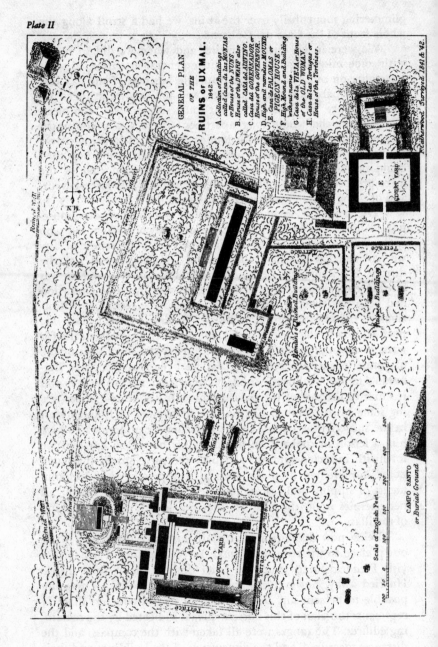

GENERAL PLAN
OF THE
RUINS or UXMAL.
1842.

A. Collection of Buildings
   called Casa de las MONJAS
   or House of the NUNS
B. House of the DWARF also
   called CASA del ADIVINO.
C. Casa del GOBERNADOR or
   House of the GOVERNOR.
D. High and narrow MOUND
E. Casa de PALOMAS or
   PIGEON HOUSE.
F. High Mound and Building
G. Casa de la Vieja or House
   of the OLD WOMAN
H. Casa de las Tortugas or
   House of the Tortoises.

Catherwood Surveyd 1841 & '42.

Scale of English Feet.

CAMPO SANTO
or Burial Ground

108

distances from each other can be ascertained by means of the scale at the foot of the plate.

The first ruin which I shall present is that in which we lived, called the Casa del Gobernador. The engraving which forms the frontispiece of this volume represents its front, with the three great terraces on which it stands. This front is three hundred and twenty-two feet long. Large as the engraving is, it can serve only to give some idea of the general effect; the detail of ornament cannot be shown.

The edifice is represented as it exists now, without any attempt at restoration, and the reader will perceive that over two of the doorways the façade has fallen. Don Simon Peon told us that in the year 1825 this fallen part was still in its place, and the whole front almost entire. The fragments now lie as they fell, forming, as appears in the engraving, a great mass of mortar, rude and sculptured stones, all imbedded together, which had never been disturbed until we dug into it for the purpose of disinterring and bringing to light some of the fallen ornaments.

This building was constructed entirely of stone. Up to the cornice, which runs round it the whole length and on all four of its sides, the façade presents a smooth surface; above is one solid mass of rich, complicated, and elaborately sculptured ornaments, forming a sort of arabesque.

The grandest ornament, which imparts a richness to the whole façade, is over the centre doorway. Around the head of the principal figure are rows of characters, which, in our first hurried visit, we did not notice as essentially different from the other incomprehensible subjects sculptured on the façade; but we now discovered that these characters were hieroglyphics. We had ladders made, by means of which Mr. Catherwood climbed up and made accurate drawings of them. They differ somewhat from the hieroglyphics before presented, and are more rich, elaborate, and complicated, but the general character is the same. From their conspicuous position, they no doubt contain some important meaning: probably they were intended as a record of the construction of the building, the time when and the people by whom it was built.

The full drawing of this rich and curious ornament cannot be presented with any effect on the scale adapted to these pages. All the other doorways have over them striking, imposing, and even elegant decorations, varying sometimes in the details, but corresponding in general character and effect with that represented in the accompanying engravings.

FIG. 6

Figure 6 represents the part immediately over the doorway. It shows the remaining portion of a figure seated on a kind of throne. This throne was formerly supported by a rich ornament, still forming part of similar designs over other doorways in this building. The head-dress is lofty, and from it proceed enormous plumes of feathers, dividing at the top, and falling symmetrically on each side, until they touch the ornament on which the feet of the statue rest. Each figure was perhaps the portrait of some cacique, warrior, prophet, or priest, distinguished in the history of this unknown people.

Plate III represents that part of the ornament immediately above the preceding; it occupies the whole portion of the wall from the top of the head-dress to the cornice along the top of the building. This ornament or combination appears on all parts of the edifice, and throughout the ruins is more frequently seen than any other. In the engraving the centre presents a long, flat, smooth surface. This indicates a projecting ornament, which cannot be exhibited in a front view; but, as seen in profile, consists of a stone projecting from the face of the wall, as shown in Figure 7; and the reader must suppose this stone projecting in order clearly to understand the character of the ornament last presented. It measures one foot seven inches in length from the stem by which it is fixed in the wall to the end of the curve, and resembles somewhat an elephant's trunk, which name has, perhaps not inaptly, been given to it by Waldeck, though it is not probable that as such the sculptor intended it, for the elephant was unknown on the Continent of America.

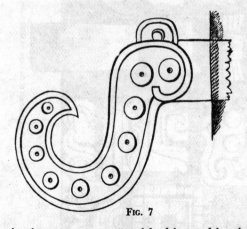

Fig. 7

This projecting stone appears with this combination all over the façade and at the corners; and throughout all the buildings it is met with, sometimes in a reversed position, oftener than any other design in Uxmal. It is a singular fact, that though entirely out of reach, the ends of nearly all of them have been broken off; and among the many remains in every part of the walls throughout the whole ruins, there are but three that now exist entire. Perhaps they were wantonly broken by the Spaniards; though at this day the Indians believe these old buildings are haunted, and that all the monefatos or ornaments are animated, and walk at

Plate III

Ornament of the Casa del Gobernador. Uxmal.

112

night. In the daytime, it is believed, they can do no harm, and for ages the Indians have been in the habit of breaking and disfiguring them with the machete, believing that by so doing they quiet their wandering spirits.

The combination of the last two engravings is probably intended to represent a hideous human face; the eyes and teeth appear in the first, and the projecting stone is perhaps intended for the nose or snout. It occupies a space in breadth equal to about five feet of the wall. To present the whole façade on the same scale would require an engraving sixty-four times as long as this. The reader will perceive how utterly unprofitable it would be to attempt a verbal description of such a façade, and the lines in the engraving show that, as I remarked in my former account, there is no tablet or single stone representing separately and by itself an entire subject, but every ornament or combination is made up of separate stones, each of which had carved on it part of the subject, and was then set in its place in the wall. Each stone by itself is an unmeaning fractional portion, but, placed by the side of others, makes part of a whole, which without it would be incomplete. Perhaps it may with propriety be called a species of sculptured mosaic; and I have no doubt that all these ornaments have a symbolical meaning; that each stone is part of a history, allegory, or fable.

The rear elevation of the Casa del Gobernador is a solid wall, without any doorways or openings of any kind. Like the front, above the cornice it was ornamented throughout its whole length with sculptured stone. The subjects, however, were less complicated, and the sculpture less gorgeous and elaborate; and on this side, too, a part of the façade has fallen.

The two ends are thirty-nine feet each. Figure 8 represents the southern end. It has but one doorway, and of this, too, the sculptured subjects were more simple.

The roof is flat, and had been covered with cement; but the whole is now overgrown with grass and bushes.

Such is the exterior of the Casa del Gobernador. To go into any description of details would extend these pages to an indefinite length. Its distinguishing features are, that it was long, low, and narrow; below the cornice plain, and above ornamented with sculpture all around. Mr. Catherwood made minute architectural drawings of the whole, and has in his possession the materials for erecting a building exactly like it; and I would remark that, as on our former expedition, he made all his drawings with the camera lucida, for the purpose of obtaining the utmost ac-

Fig. 8

curacy of proportion and detail. Besides which, we had with us a Daguerreotype apparatus, the best that could be procured in New-York, with which, immediately on our arrival at Uxmal, Mr. Catherwood began taking views; but the results were not sufficiently perfect to suit his ideas. At times the projecting cornices and ornaments threw parts of the subject in shade, while others were in broad sunshine; so that, while parts were brought out well, other parts required pencil drawings to supply their defects. They gave a general idea of the character of the buildings, but would not do to put into the hands of the engraver without copying the views on paper, and introducing the defective parts, which would require more labour than that of making at once complete original drawings. He therefore completed everything with his pencil and camera lucida, while Doctor Cabot and myself took up the Daguerreotype; and, in order to ensure the utmost accuracy, the Daguerreotype views were placed with the drawings in the hands of the engravers for their guidance.

114

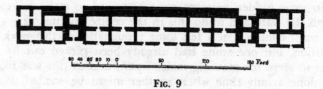

FIG. 9

The ground plan of the Casa del Gobernador is represented in Figure 9. It has eleven doorways in front and one at each end. The doors are all gone, and the wooden lintels over them have fallen. The interior is divided longitudinally by a wall into two corridors, and these again, by cross walls or partitions, into oblong rooms. Every pair of these rooms, the front and back, communicate by a doorway exactly opposite a corresponding doorway in front.

The principal apartments in the centre, with three doorways opening upon the terrace, are sixty feet long. The one in front is eleven feet six inches wide, and the inner one thirteen feet. The former is twenty-three feet high to the top of the arch, and the other twenty-two feet. The latter has but one door of entrance from the front room, and except this it has no door or aperture of any kind, so that at the ends it is dark and damp, as is the case with all the inner rooms. In these two apartments we took up our abode.

The walls are constructed of square, smooth blocks of stone, and on each side of the doorway are the remains of stone rings fixed in the walls with shafts, which no doubt had some connexion with the support of the doors. The floors were of cement, in some places hard, but, by long exposure, broken, and now crumbling under the feet.

The ceiling forms a triangular arch, as at Palenque, without the keystone. The support is made by stones overlapping, and bevilled so as to present a smooth surface, and within about a foot of the point of contact covered by a layer of flat stones. Across the arch were beams of wood, the ends built in the wall on each side, which had probably been used for the support of the arch while the building was in progress.

For the rest, I refer to the plan, mentioning only one circumstance. In working out the plan on the spot, it was found that the back wall, throughout its whole length of two hundred and seventy feet, was nine feet thick, which was nearly equal to the width of the front apartment. Such thickness was not necessary for the support of the building, and, supposing it might

115

contain some hidden passages, we determined to make a breach through the wall, and to do this in the centre apartment.

I must confess that I felt some repugnance to this work of demolition, but one stone had already been picked out by an Indian to serve for mashing maize upon; and as this was likely to be done at any time when another might be wanted, I got over my scruples.

Over the cavity left in the mortar by the removal of the stone were two conspicuous marks, which afterward stared us in the face in all the ruined buildings of the country. They were the prints of a red hand with the thumb and fingers extended, not drawn or painted, but stamped by the living hand, the pressure of the palm upon the stone. He who made it had stood before it alive as we did, and pressed his hand, moistened with red paint, hard against the stone. The seams and creases of the palm were clear and distinct in the impression. There was something lifelike about it that waked exciting thoughts, and almost presented the images of the departed inhabitants hovering about the building. And there was one striking feature about these hands; they were exceedingly small. Either of our own spread over and completely hid them; and this was interesting from the fact that we had ourselves remarked, and heard remarked by others, the smallness of the hands and feet as a striking feature in the physical conformation of the Indians at the present day.

The stones with this red hand upon them were the first that fell as we commenced our breach into the wall. There were two crowbars on the hacienda, and working nearly two days, the Indians made a hole between six and seven feet deep, but throughout the wall was solid, and consisted of large stones imbedded in mortar, almost as hard as rock. The reason of this immense back wall, where everything else had a certain degree of fitness and conformity, we did not discover, and we had this huge hole staring us reproachfully in the face during all the remainder of our residence.

A few words more, and I have done with this building. In the south end apartment, the façade of which has been presented, we found the sculptured beam of hieroglyphics which had so much interested us on our former visit. In some of the inner apartments the lintels were still in their places over the doorways, and some were lying on the floor sound and solid, which better condition was no doubt owing to their being more sheltered than those over the outer doorway. This was the only sculptured beam in Uxmal, and at that time it was the only piece of carved wood we had seen. We considered it interesting, as indicating a degree of proficiency in an art of which, in all our previous explorations, we had not discovered any evidence, except, perhaps, at Ocosingo, where we found a beam, not carved, but which had evidently been reduced to shape by sharp instruments of metal. This time I determined not to let the precious beam escape me. It was ten feet long, one foot nine inches broad, and ten inches thick, of Sapote wood, enormously heavy and unwieldly. To keep the sculptured side from being chafed and broken, I had it covered with costal or hemp bagging, and stuffed with dry grass to the thickness of six inches. It left Uxmal on the shoulders of ten Indians, after many vicissitudes reached this city uninjured, and was deposited in Mr. Catherwood's Panorama. I had referred to it as being in the National Museum at Washington, whither I intended to send it as soon as a collection of large sculptured stones, which I was obliged to leave behind, should arrive; but on the burning of that building, in the general conflagration of Jerusalem and Thebes, this part of Uxmal was consumed, and with it other beams afterward discovered, much more curious and interesting; as also the whole collection of vases, figures, idols, and other relics gathered upon this journey. The collecting, packing, and transporting of these things had given me more trouble and annoyance than any other circumstance in our journey, and their loss cannot be replaced; for, being first on the ground, and having all at my choice, I of course selected only those objects which were most curious and valuable; and if I were to go over the whole ground again, I could not find others equal to them. I had the melancholy satisfaction of seeing their ashes exactly as the fire had left them. We seemed doomed to be in the midst of ruins; but in all our explorations there was none so touching as this.

Next to the great building of the Casa del Gobernador, and hardly less extraordinary and imposing in character, are the three great terraces which hold it aloft, and give it its grandeur of position; all of them artificial, and built up from the level of the plain.

The lowest of these terraces is three feet high, fifteen feet broad, and five hundred and seventy-five feet long; the second is twenty feet high, two hundred and fifty feet wide, and five hundred and forty-five feet in length; and the third, on which the building stands, is nineteen feet high, thirty feet broad, and three hundred and sixty feet in front. They were all supported by substantial stone walls; that of the second terrace is still in a good state of preservation, and at the corners the stones which support it are still in their places, with their outer surfaces rounded, instead of presenting sharp angles.

The platform of this terrace is a noble terra plana, five hundred and forty-five feet long and two hundred and fifty feet wide, and, from the remains still visible upon it, once contained structures and ornaments of various kinds, the character of which it is now difficult to make out. On our first arrival the whole was covered with a rank growth of bushes and weeds ten or twelve feet high, on clearing which away these remains were brought to light.

Along the south end there is an oblong structure about three feet high, two hundred long, and fifteen feet wide, at the foot of which there is a range of pedestals and fragments of columns about five feet high and eighteen inches in diameter. There are no remains of a roof or of any other structure connected with them.

Near the centre of the platform, at a distance of eighty feet from the foot of the steps, is a square enclosure, consisting of two layers of stones, in which stands, in an oblique position, as if falling, or perhaps, as if an effort had been made to throw it down, a large round stone, measuring eight feet above the ground and five feet in diameter. This stone is striking for its uncouth and irregular proportions, and wants conformity with the regularity and symmetry of all around. From its conspicuous position, it doubtless had some important use, and, in connexion with other monuments found at this place, induces the belief that it was connected with the ceremonial rites of an ancient worship known to have existed among all Eastern nations. The Indians call this stone the Picote, or whipping-post.

At a distance of sixty feet in a right line beyond this was a rude circular mound, about six feet high. We had used it as a position from which to take a Daguerreotype view of the front of the building, and, at the instance of the Cura Carillo, who came to pay us a visit, we determined to open it. It was a mere mass of earth and stones; and, on digging down to the depth of three or four feet, a sculptured monument was discovered, which is represented in Figure 10. It was found standing on its feet, in the position represented in the engraving. It is carved out of a single block of stone, and measures three feet two inches in length and two feet in height. It seems intended to represent a doube-headed cat or lynx, and is entire with the exception of one foot, which is a little broken. The sculpture is rude. It was too

118

Catherwood. D.

Fig. 10

heavy to carry away. We had it raised to the side of the mound for Mr. Catherwood to draw, and probably it remains there still. The *picote*, or great stone, before referred to, appears in Figure 10 in the distance.

Why this monument had been consigned to the strange place in which it was discovered we were at a loss to conjecture. This could never have been its original destination. It had been formally and deliberately buried. In my opinion, there is but one way of accounting for it. It had been one of the many idols worshipped by the people of Uxmal; and the probability is, that when the inhabitants abandoned the city they buried it, that it might not be desecrated; or else the Spaniards, when they drove out the inhabitants and depopulated the city, in order to destroy all the reverential feeings of the Indians toward it, followed the example of Cortez at Cholula, and threw down and buried the idols.

At a distance of 130 feet from this mound was a square stone structure, six feet high and twenty feet at the base, in which we made an excavation, and discovered two sculptured heads, no doubt intended as portraits.

From the centre of this great platform a grand staircase 130 feet broad, which once contained 35 steps, rises to the third terrace, on which the building stands; besides this there is no staircase connected with either of the three terraces, and the only ascent to the platform of the second is by an inclined plane 100 feet broad, at the south end of the building, which makes it necessary for all approaching from the north to pass the whole length of the lower terrace, and, ascending by the inclined plane, go back to reach the steps. The probability is, that the labour of this was not regarded by the ancient inhabitants, and that all visiters or residents in the building passed in and out on the shoulders of Indians in coches, as the rich do now.

There remains to be noticed one important building on the grand platform of the second terrace. It stands at the northwest corner, and is represented in Plate IV. It is called the Casa de las Tortugas, or the House of the Turtles, which name was given to it by a neighbouring cura, from a bead or row of turtles which goes round the cornice, indicated in the engraving.

This building is 94 feet in front and 34 feet deep, and in size and ornaments contrasts strikingly with the Casa del Gobernador. It wants the rich and gorgeous decoration of the former, but is distinguished for its justness and beauty of proportions, and its chasteness and simplicity of ornament. Throughout there is nothing that borders on the unintelligible or grotesque, nothing that can shock a fastidious architectural taste; but, unhappily, it is fast going to decay. On our first visit Mr. Catherwood and myself climbed to the roof, and selected it as a good position from which to make a panoramic sketch of the whole field of ruins. It was then trembling and tottering, and within the year the whole of the centre part had fallen in. In front the centre of the wall is gone, and in the rear the wooden lintel, pressed down and broken in two, still supports the superincumbent mass, but it gave us a nervous feeling to pass under it. The interior is filled up with the ruins of the fallen roof.

Plate IV

UXMAL.
Front of the Casa de Las Tortugas.

This building, too, has the same peculiar feature, want of convenient access. It has no communication, at least by steps or any visible means, with the Casa del Gobernador, nor were there any steps leading to the terrace below. It stands isolated and alone, seeming to mourn over its own desolate and ruinous condition. With a few more returns of the rainy season it will be a mass of ruins, and perhaps on the whole continent of America there will be no such monument of the purity and simplicity of aboriginal art.

Such is a brief description of the Casa del Gobernador, with its three great terraces, and the buildings and structures upon the grand platform of the second. From the place which we had fixed upon as our residence, and the constant necessity of ascending and descending the terraces, it was with these that we became the soonest familiar. The reader will be able to form some idea of the subjects that engaged our attention, and the strange spectacle that we had constantly before our eyes.

CHAPTER IX

Having made such advances in the clearing that Mr. Catherwood had abundance of occupation, on Thursday, the 18th of November, I set out, under the guidance of the mayoral, on an excursion to meet Don Simon Peon at the fair of Jalacho, and visit some ruins on another hacienda of his in that neighbourhood. We started at half past six, our course being west by north. At ten minutes past seven we crossed a *serrania*, or range of hills, about a hundred and fifty feet high, and came down upon an extensive savanna of low, flat land, a mere canebrake. The road was the worst I had found in the country, being simply a wet and very muddy path for mules and horses to the fair. My horse sunk up to his saddle-girths, and it was with great exertion that he dragged himself through. Every moment I had fear of his rolling over in the mud, and in some places I was strongly reminded of the *malos pasos* in Central America. Occasionally the branches were barely high enough to allow mules to pass, and then I was obliged to dismount, and trudge through the mud on foot. At eight o'clock we came to an open savanna, and saw a high mound with ruins on the top, bearing south, about a mile distant. It was called, as the mayoral said, Senuisacal. I was strongly tempted to turn aside and examine it, but, on account of the thickness of the cane-brake and the mud, it would have been impossible to reach it, and the mayoral said that it was entirely in ruins.

In half an hour we came into a clear and open country, and at ten we entered the camino real for Jalacho, a broad and open road, passable for calesas. Up to this time we had not seen a single habitation or met a human being, and now the road was literally thronged with people moving on to the fair, with whose clean garments my mud-stained clothes contrasted very unfavourably. There were Indians, Mestizoes, and white people on horseback, muleback, and on foot, men, women, and children, many carrying on their backs things to sell, in petaquillas, or long baskets of straw; whole families, sometimes half a village moving in company; and I fell in behind a woman perched on a loaded horse, with a child in her arms, and a little fellow behind, his legs stretched out nearly straight to span the horse's flanks, and both arms clasping her substantial body to keep himself from slipping off. We passed parties sitting in the shade to rest or eat, and families lying down by the roadside to sleep, without any fear of molestation from the rest.

At half past eleven we reached the village of Becal, conspicuous, like all the others, for a large plaza and church with two towers. In the suburbs the mayoral and I interchanged sentiments about breakfast, and, after making a circle in the plaza, he struck off direct for the house of the cura. I do not think the cura could have been expecting me, but if so, he could not have provided a better breakfast, or at shorter notice. Besides the breakfast, the cura told me of ruins on his hacienda which he had never visited, but which he promised to have cleared away, and be ready to show me on my return. Circumstances occurred to prevent my returning by the same road, but the cura, having had the ruins cleared away, visited them himself, and I afterward heard that I had lost something by not seeing them. I took leave of him with the buoyancy of old times, breakfast secured, and a prospect of another ruined city.

In an hour I reached Jalacho, where I met Don Simon and two of his brothers, with whom I was not yet acquainted; Don Lorenzo, who had a hacienda in that neighbourhood, and Don Alonzo, then living in Campeachy, who was educated in New-York, and spoke English remarkably well.

The village of Jalacho lies on the main road from Merida to Campeachy, and, next to that of Yzamal, its fair is the greatest in Yucatan, while in some respects it is more curious. It is not attended by large merchants with foreign goods, nor by the better classes from Merida, but it is resorted to by all the Indians from the haciendas and villages. It is inferior in one respect: gambling is not carried on upon so large a scale as at Yzamal.

The time was when all countries had their periodical fairs; but the changed and improved condition of the world has almost abolished this feature of ancient times. Increased facilities of communication with foreign countries and different parts of the same country make opportunties for buying and selling an everyday thing; and at this day, in general throughout Europe, for all articles of necessity, and even of luxury, every man has, as it were, a fair every day at his own door. But the countries in America subject to the Spanish dominion have felt less sensibly, perhaps, than any others in the world, the onward impulse of the last two centuries, and in them many usages and customs derived from Europe, but there long since fallen into oblivion, are still in full force. Among them is this of holding fairs, of which, though several took place during the time of my journey in Central America, I had no opportunity of seeing any.

The fair of Jalacho was an observance of eight days, but the first two or three were marked only by the arrival of scattering parties, and the business of securing places to live in and to display wares. The great gathering or high change did not begin till Thursday, which was the day of my arrival, and then it was computed that there were assembled in the village ten thousand persons.

Of all this crowd the plaza was the grand point of concentration. Along the houses fronting it was a range of tables set out with looking-glasses in frames of red paper, rings and necklaces, cotton, and toys and trinkets for the Indians. On the opposite side of the street, along the square of the church, were rustic arbours, occupied by venders having similar commodities spread before them. The plaza was partitioned, and at regular intervals was a merchant, whose shop was a rude stick fixed upright in the ground, and having another crosswise at the top, covered with leaves and twigs, thus forming a sort of umbrella, to protect its sitting occupant from the sun. These were the merchants of dulces and other eatables. This part of the fair was constantly crowded, and perhaps nine tenths were Indians from the pueblos and haciendas around. Don Simon Peon told me that he had entered on his books a hundred and fifty *criados*, or servants, who had applied to him for money, and he did not know how many more were present.

It may be supposed that the church was not uninterested

in this great gathering. In fact, it was the fête of Santiago, and among the Indians this fiesta was identified with the fair. The doors of the church were constantly open, the interior was thronged with Indians, and a crowd continually pressing to the altar. In the doorway was a large table covered with candles and small figures of arms and legs in wax, which the Indians purchased as they entered at a medio apiece, for offerings to the saint. Near the altar, on the left, sat an unshaved ministro, with a table before him, on which was a silver waiter, covered with medios, reales, and two shilling pieces, showing to the backward what others had done, and inviting them to do the same. The candles purchased at the door had been duly blessed, and as the Indians went up with them, a strapping negro, with linen particularly dirty, received and lighted them at one burning on the altar, whence with his black hands he passed them on to a rusty white assistant, who arranged them upon a table, and, even before the backs of the offerers were turned, puffed out the light, and took the candles to be smoothed over, and resold at the door for another medio each.

High above the heads of the crowd, catching the eye on first entering the church, was the figure of Santiago, or Saint James, on horseback, holy in the eyes of all who saw it, and famed for its power of working miracles, healing the sick, curing the fever and ague, insuring to prospective parents a boy or girl as desired, bringing back a lost cow or goat, healing a cut of the machete, or relieving from any other calamity incident to an Indian's lot. The fore feet of the horse were raised in the air, and the saint wore a black cocked hat, with a broad gold band, a short mantle of scarlet velvet, having a broad gold edging round the cape and skirts, green velvet trousers, with a wide gold stripe down the sides, and boots and spurs. All the time I stood there, and every time I went into the church, men, women, and children were pressing forward, struggling with each other to kiss the foot of the saint. The simple Indian, as the first act of devotion, led up his whole family to do this act of obeisance. The mother lifted her sucking child, and pressed its lips, warm from her breast, against the foot of the bedizened statue.

In the afternoon commenced the first bull-fight. The *toreadores*, or bull-fighters, all lived at the house opposite ours, and from it the procession started. It was headed by a wrinkled, squint-eyed, bandy-legged Indian, carrying under his arm the old Indian drum, and dancing grotesquely to his own music;

126

then followed the band, and then the gallant picadores, a cut-throat looking set of scoundrels, who, imagining themselves the admiration, were the contempt of the crowd.

The Plaza de Toros was on one side of the square of the plaza, and, like that in the square of the church of San Cristoval, was constructed of poles and vines, upright, intwining and interlaced, tottering and yielding under pressure, and yet holding together firmly. In the centre was a pole, on the top of which flourished the Mexican eagle, with outspread wings, holding in his beak a scroll with the appropriate motto, "Viva la Republica de Yucatan," and strings extended like radii to different parts of the boxes, wrapped with cut and scolloped papers fluttering in the wind. On one side of the ring was a pole with a wooden beam, from which hung, by strings fastened to the crown of an old straw hat, two figures stuffed with straw, with grotesque masks and ludicrous dresses. One was very narrow in the shoulders and very broad below, and his trousers were buttoned behind.

The toros, fallen into disrepute in the capital, is still the favourite and national amusement in the pueblos. The animal tied to the post when we entered was from the hacienda of the senote, which was famed for the ferocity of its bulls. The picadores, too, were fiercer than those in the capital, and the contests were more sanguinary and fatal. Several times the bulls were struck down, and two, reeking with blood, were dragged off by the horns, dead; and this was in the presence of women, and greeted with their smiles and approbation: a disgusting and degrading spectacle, but as yet having too strong a hold upon popular feeling to be easily set aside. The entertainment was got up at the expense of the village, and all who could find a place had liberty to enter.

This over, there was an interval for business, and particularly for visiting the horse-market, or rather a particular section to which dealers sent their horses to be exhibited. I was more interested in this than any other branch of commerce carried on at the fair, as I wished to purchase horses for our journey. There were plenty of them, though, as in all other sections of the country, but few fine ones. Prices varied from ten dollars to two hundred, the value depending, not upon bone, blood, or muscle, but upon training and paces. The young hacienda horses, with nothing but the trot, or trotones, as they were called, were worth from ten dollars to twenty-five, but as they excelled in pace or easiness of movement their value increased. No one pretends to ride a trotting horse in Yucatan, for he who does labours under the imputation of not being able to purchase a pacer. The finest horses in the country in appearance are those imported; but the Yucatan horses, though small, are remarkably hardy, require no care, and endure an extraordinary degree of fatigue.

Night came on, and the plaza was alive with people and brilliant with lights. On one side, opposite the church, along the corridors of the houses and in front of them, were rows of tables, with cards and dice, which were very soon crowded with players, whites and Mestizoes; but the great scene of attraction was the gathering of Indians in the centre of the plaza. It was the hour of supper, and the small merchants had abundant custom for their eatables. Turkeys which had stood tied by one leg all day, inviting people to come and eat them, were now ready, of which for a medio two men had a liberal allowance; and I remarked, what I had heard of, but had not seen before, that grains of cacao circulated among the Indians as money. Every merchant or vender of eatables, the most of whom were women, had on the table a pile of these grains, which they were constantly counting and exchanging with the Indians. There is no copper money in Yucatan, nor any coin whatever under a medio, or six and a quarter cents, and this deficiency is supplied by these grains of cacao. The medio is divided into twenty parts, generally of five grains each, but the number is increased or decreased according to the quantity of the article in the market, and its real value. As the earnings of the Indians are small, and the articles they purchase are the mere necessaries of life, which are very cheap, these grains of cacao, or fractional parts of a medio, are the coin in most common use among them. The currency has always a real value, and is regulated by the quantity of cacao in the market, and the only inconvenience, economically speaking, that it has, is the loss of a certain public wealth by the destruction of the cacao, as in the case of bank notes. But these grains had an interest independent of all questions of political economy, for they indicate or illustrate a page in the history of this unknown and mysterious people. When the Spaniards first made their way into the interior of Yucatan, they found no circulating medium, either of gold, or silver, or any other species of metal, but only grains of cacao; and it seemed a strange circumstance, that while the manners and customs of the Indians have undergone an immense change, while their cities have been destroyed, their religion dishonoured, their princes swept away, and their whole government modified by foreign laws, no experiment has yet been made upon their currency.

In the midst of this strange scene, there was a stir at one end of the plaza, and an object presented itself that at once turned my thoughts and feelings homeward. It was a post-coach, from a Troy factory, exactly like those seen on every road in our country, but it had on the panel of the door "La Diligencia Campechana." It was one of the line of diligences between Campeachy and Merida, and just arrived from the former place. It came up on a run, drawn by wild, uncombed horses, not yet broken to the bit, and with their breasts galled and raw from the pressure of the collar. It had nine inside, and had an aspect so familiar that, as the door opened, I expected to see acquaintances get out; but all spoke a foreign tongue, and instead of being welcomed to supper or bed by an officious landlord and waiter, all inquired anxiously where they could get something to eat and a place to sleep in.

Leaving them to do as well as they could, we went to the baile or ball. In front of the quartel was a rustic arbour, enclosed by a temporary railing, with benches and chairs arranged around the sides, and the centre cleared for dancing. Until I saw them collected together, I did not suppose that so many white persons were present at the fair, and, like the men at the gambling-table, and the Indians in the plaza, these seeemed to forget that there was any other party present than themselves. In this obliviousness I sympathized, and slipping into an easy arm-chair, from the time of my drag through the mud in the morning I had not so quiet and comfortable a moment, in which condition I remained until awakened by Don Simon.

The next day was a repetition of the same scenes. In the afternoon, at the bull-fight, I fell into conversation with a gentleman who sat next to me, and who gave me information of some antiquities in Maxcanú, a village four leagues distant. That I might take this place on my return to Uxmal, it was advisable to visit the ruins on Don Simon's hacienda the next day. Don Simon could not go with me until after the fair, and amid the great concourse of Indians it was difficult to find one who could serve as a guide.

It was not till eleven o'clock the next day that I was able to set out, and I had as a guide a major domo of another hacienda, who, being, as I imagined, vexed at being obliged to leave the fiesta, and determined to get me off his hands as soon as possible, set out at a swinging trot. The sun was scorching, the road broad, straight, and stony, and without a particle of shade, but in forty minutes, both considerably heated, we reached the hacienda of Sijoh, two leagues distant.

This hacienda belonged to a brother of Don Simon, then resident in Vera Cruz, and was under the latter's charge. Here my guide passed me over into the hands of an Indian, and rode back as fast as he could to the fair. The Indian mounted another horse, and, continuing a short distance on the same road through the lands of the hacienda, we turned off to the right, and in five minutes saw in the woods to our left, near the road, a high mound of ruins of that distinctive character once so strange, but now so familiar to me, proclaiming the existence of another unknown, nameless, desolate, and ruined city.

We continued on to another mound nearer than the first, where we dismounted and tied our horses to the bushes. This mound was a solid mass of masonry, about thirty feet high, and nearly square. The stones were large, one at the corner measuring six feet in length by three in width, and the sides were covered with thorns and briers. On the south side was a range of steps still in good condition, each fifteen inches high, and in general three feet long. On the other sides the stones rose in a pyramidal form, but without steps. On the top was a stone building, with its wall as high as the cornice standing. Above this the façade had fallen, but the mass of stone and mortar which formed the roof remained, and within the apartment was precisely like the interior of the buildings at Uxmal, having the same distinctive arch. There were no remains of sculpture, but the base of the mound was encumbered with fallen stones, among which were some about three feet long, dug out so as to form a sort of trough, the same as we had seen at Uxmal, where they were called pilas or fountains.

Leaving this, we returned through the woods to the mound we had first seen. This was perhaps sixty feet high, and was a mere mass of fallen stone. Whatever it might have been, its features were entirely lost, and but for the structure I had just seen, and the waste of ruins in other parts of the country, it might have seemed doubtful whether it had ever been formed according to any plan or rules of art. The mass of stone was so solid that no vegetation could take root upon it; its sides were bare and bleached, and the pieces, on being disturbed, slid down with a metallic sound like the ringing of iron. In climbing up I received a blow from a sliding stone, which nearly carried me back to the bottom, for the moment completely disabled me, and from which I did not entirely recover until some time afterward.

From the top of this mound I saw two others of nearly the same height, and, taking their direction with the compass, I descended and directed my steps toward them. The whole ground was covered with trees and a thick undergrowth of brush and thorn-bushes. My Indian had gone to lead the horses round to another road. I had no machete, and though the mounds were not far distant, I was excessively scratched and torn in getting to them. They were all ruined, so that they barely preserved their form. Passing between these, I saw beyond three others, forming three angles of a patio or square; and in this patio, rising above the thorn-bushes and briers, were huge stones, which, on being first discovered, suddenly and unexpectedly, actually startled me. At a distance they reminded me of the monuments of Copan, but they were even more extraordinary and incomprehensible. They were uncouth in shape, and rough as they came from the quarry. Four of them were flat; the largest was fourteen feet high, and measured toward the top four feet in width, and one and a half in thickness. The top was broader than the bottom, and it stood in a leaning posture, as if its foundation had been loosened. The others were still more irregular in shape, and it seemed as if the people who erected them had just looked out for the largest stones they could lay their hands on, tall or short, thick or thin, square or round, without regard to anything except bulk. They had no beauty or fitness of design or proportion, and there were no characters upon them. But in that desolation and solitude they were strange and striking, and, like unlettered headstones in a churchyard, seemed to mark the graves of unknown dead.

On one of the mounds, looking down upon this patio, was a long building, with its front wall fallen, and leaving the whole interior exposed to view. I climbed up to it, but saw only the remains of the same narrow corridor and arch, and on the wall were prints of the red hand. The whole country was so overgrown that it was impossible to form any idea of what its extent had been, but one thing was certain, a large city had once stood here, and what its name was no man knew.

At this time my visit was merely intended as preliminary, for the purpose of judging whether there were any subjects for Mr. Catherwood's pencil, and it was now about one o'clock. The heat was intense, and sweating and covered with briers and burrs, which stuck to every part of my clothes, I came out into the open road, where my Indian was waiting for me with the horses. We mounted immediately, and continued on a gallop to the hacienda of Tankuché, two leagues distant.

This hacienda was a favourite with Don Simon, as he had created it out of the wilderness, and the entire road from the village he had made himself. It was a good logwood country, and here he had erected machinery for extracting the dye. In general, it was the most busy place of all his haciendas, but this day it seemed as if a desolating scourge had swept over it. The huts of the Indians were closed and locked up; no barebodied children were playing around them, and the large gate was locked. We tied our horses by one of the panels, and, ascending by a flight of stone steps, entered the lane and walked up to the house. Every door was locked, and not a person in sight. Moving on to the high stone structure forming the platform of the well, I saw a little boy, dressed in a straw hat, dozing on an old horse, which was creeping round with the well-beam, drawing in broken buckets a slow stream of water, for which no one came. At sight of me he rose from the neck of his horse, and tried to stop him, but the old animal seemed so used to going round that he could not stop, and the little fellow looked as if he expected to be going till some one came to take him off. All had gone to the fiesta, and were now swelling the great crowd I had left in the village. It was an immense change from the thronged fair to the solitude of this desolate hacienda. I sat down under a large seybo tree overshadowing the well, and ate a roll of bread and an orange, after which I strolled back to the gate, and, to my surprise, found only one horse. My guide had mounted his and returned to his hacienda. I walked into the factory, returned to the well, and attempted speech with the boy, but the old horse started forward and carried him away from me; I lay down on the platform of the well; the creaking of the beam served as a sort of lullaby, and I had made such progress that I was not very eager to be interrupted, when an Indian lad arrived, who had been hunted up by my missing guide, and directed to show me the ruins. This fact, however, he would not have been able to communicate, but, fortunately, he was accompanied by an Indian who spoke Spanish. The latter was an intelligent, middle-aged man, of highly respectable appearance, but Don Simon told me he was the worst fellow on the hacienda. He was desperately in love with a girl who did not live on the estate, and he was in the habit of running away to visit her, and of being brought back with his arms tied behind him; as a punishment for a late offence of this kind, he had been prohibited from going to the fiesta. Through him I had an understanding with my new guide, and set out again.

In five minutes after leaving the hacienda, we passed between two mounds of ruins, and, from time to time having glimpses of other vestiges in the woods, in twenty minutes we came to a mound about thirty feet high, on the top of which was a ruined building. Here we dismounted, tied our horses, and ascended the mound. The whole of the front wall had fallen, together with the front half of the arch; the interior chamber was filled with dirt and rubbish nearly up to the cornice, and the arch of the back wall was the only part above ground; but this, instead of being of smooth stones, like all the others we had seen in Yucatan, was plastered and covered with paintings, the colours of which were still bright and fresh. The principal colours were red, green, yellow, and blue, and at first the lines and figures seemed so distinct, that I thought I could make out the subjects. The apartment being filled up with dirt, I stood above the objects, and it was only by sitting, or rather lying down, that I could examine them. One subject at first sight struck me as being a representation of the mask found at Palenque. I was extremely desirous to get this off entire, but found, by experiments upon other parts of the plaster with the machete, that it would be impossible to do so, and left it untouched.

In the interest of the work, I did not discover that thousands of garrapatas were crawling over me. These insects are the scourge of Yucatan, and altogether they were a more constant source of annoyance and suffering than any we encountered in the country. I had seen something of them in Central America, but at a different season, when the hot sun had killed off the immensity of their numbers, and those left had attained such a size that a single one could easily be seen and picked off. These, in colour, size, and numbers, were like grains of sand. They disperse themselves all over the body, get into the seams of the clothes, and, like the insect known among us as the tick, bury themselves in the flesh, causing an irritation that is almost intolerable. The only way to get rid of them effectually is by changing all the clothes. In Uxmal we had not been troubled with them, for they are said to breed only in those woods where cattle pasture, and the grounds about Uxmal had been used as a milpa, or plantation of corn. It was the first time I had ever had them upon me in such profusion, and their presence disturbed most materially the equanimity with which I examined the paintings. In fact, I did not remain long on the ground.

It is particularly unfortunate that, while so many apartments have remained free, this most curious and interesting one has become filled up. It is probable that the walls, as well as the arch, are plastered and painted. It would have cost a week's labour to clear it out, and my impression was, that, in consequence of the dirt having been piled up against the walls for an unknown length of time, through a long succession of rainy seasons, the colours were so completely effaced that nothing would have been discovered to compensate for the labour.

It was now nearly dark. My day's work had been a severe one. I was tired and covered with garrapatas, but the next day was Sunday, the last of the fiesta, and I determined on returning to the village that night. There was a brilliant moonlight, and, hurrying on, at eleven o'clock I saw, at the end of a long straight road, the illuminated front of the church of Jalacho. Very soon, amid the shining lights and congregated thousands, I forgot desolations and ruins, and my sympathies once more moved with the living. I passed by the tables of the gamblers, worked my way through the plaza and through a crowd of Indians, who fell back in deference to the colour of my skin, and, unexpectedly to my friends, presented myself at the baile. This time I had no disposition to sleep. For the last night of the fiesta the neighbouring villages had sent forth their all; the ball was larger and gayer of whites and those in whose veins white blood ran, while outside, leaning upon the railing, looking in, but not presuming to enter, were close files of Indians, and beyond, in the plaza, was a dense mass of them—natives of the land and lords of the soil, that strange people in whose ruined cities I had just been wandering, submitting quietly to the dominion of strangers, bound down and trained to the most abject submission, and looking up to the white man as a superior being. Could these be the descendants of that fierce people who had made such bloody resistance to the Spanish conquerors?

At eleven o'clock the ball broke up, and fireworks were let off from the balustrade of the church. These ended with the national piece of El Castillo, and at twelve o'clock, when we went away, the plaza was as full of Indians as at midday. At no time since my arrival in the country had I been so struck with the peculiar constitution of things in Yucatan. Originally portioned out as slaves, the Indians remain as servants. Veneration for masters is the first lesson they learn, and these masters, the descendants of the terrible conquerors, in centuries of uninterrupted peace have lost all the fierceness of their ancestors. Gentle, and averse to labour themselves, they impose no heavy burdens upon the Indians, but understand and humour their ways, and the two races move on harmoniously together, with nothing to apprehend from each other, forming a simple, primitive, and almost patriarchal state of society; and so strong is the sense of personal security, that, notwithstanding the crowds of strangers, and although every day Don Simon had sat with doors open and piles of money on the table, so little apprehension was there of robbery, that we slept without a door or window locked.

CHAPTER X

The next day was Sunday. The church was thronged for grand mass; candles were burned, and offerings were made to the amount of many medios, and at nine o'clock the bells tolled for the procession, the crowning scene of the fiesta. The church was emptied of its votaries, and the plaza was alive with people hurrying to take a place in the procession, or to see it pass. I climbed up into the Plaza de Toros, and had a whole box to myself.

The space along the side of the bull-ring was thronged; and first came a long procession of Indians with lighted candles; then the ministro with the large silver salver, and money upon it, presenting it on either side to receive additional offerings. As it passed, a woman walked up and put upon it two reales, probably her all. Then came, borne on a barrow above the heads of the crowd, the figure which had attracted so much veneration in the church, Santiago on horseback, with his scarlet and embroidered mantle and green velvet pantaloons bordered with gold. This was followed by the cura, a fat, yellow-looking half-breed, with his two dirty-faced assistants. Directly under me the procession stopped, and the priests, turning toward the figure of the saint, set up a chant. This over, the figure moved on, and stopping from time to time, continued to work its way around the church, ùntil finally it was restored to its place on the altar. So ended the fair of Jalacho and the fête of Santiago, the second which I had seen since my arrival in the country, and both exhibiting the powerful influence of the ceremonials of the church over the minds of the Indians. Throughout the state, this class of the inhabitants pays annually a tax of twelve reales per head for the support of the cura; and it was said on the ground that the Indians at this fiesta had paid eight hundred dollars for salves, five hundred for aves, and six hundred for masses, which, if true, was an enormous sum out of their small earnings.

But the fiesta was over, and almost immediately the crowd was in motion, preparing to set out for home. At three o'clock every street was lined with people, some less and others more heavily laden than they came, and some carrying home the respectable head of a family in a state of brutal intoxication; and here I particularly remarked, what I had frequently observed before, that among all the intoxication of the Indians, it was a rare thing to see a woman in that state; it was really an interesting spectacle to see these poor women, with their children around them, supporting and conducting homeward their intoxicated husbands.

At four o'clock I set off with Don Lorenzo Peon, a brother of Don Simon, for Maxcanú. Our mode of conveyance, much used in Yucatan, but new to me, was called a caricoché. It was a long wagon, on two large wheels, covered with cotton cloth as a protection against the sun, and on the bottom was stretched a broad mattress, on which two persons could recline at full length. If they would sit up, it was large enough for three or four. It was drawn by one horse, with a driver riding as postillion, and another horse followed to change. The road was broad, even, and level. It was the camino real between Merida and Campeachy, and would pass in any country for a fair carriage-road. All along we passed parties of Indians returning from the fair. In an hour we came in sight of the sierra which traverses at that point the whole peninsula of Yucatan from east to west. The sight of hills was cheering, and with the reflection of the setting sun upon them, they presented almost the first fine scenery I had encountered in the country. In an hour and ten minutes we reached Maxcanú, twelve miles distant, being by far the greatest speed at which I ever travelled in Yucatan.

The hacienda of Don Lorenzo was in this neighbourhood, and he had a large house in the village, at which we stopped. My object in coming to this place was to visit La Cueva de Maxcanú, or the Cave of Maxcanú. In the evening, when notice was given of my intention, half the village was ready to join me, but in the morning my volunteers were not forthcoming, and I was reduced to the men procured for me by Don Lorenzo. From the time consumed in getting the men together and procuring torches, cord, &c., I did not get off till after nine o'clock. Our direction was due east till we reached the sierra, ascending which through a passage overgrown with woods, at eleven o'clock we arrived at the mouth, or rather door, of the cueva, about a league distant from the village.

I had before heard so much of caves, and had been so often disappointed, that I did not expect much from this; but the first view satisfied me in regard to the main point, viz., that it was not a natural cave, and that, as had been represented to me, it was hecha à mano, or made by hand.

La Cueva de Maxcanú, or the Cave of Maxcanú, has in that region a marvellous and mystical reputation. It is called by the Indians Satun Sat, which means in Spanish El Laberinto or El Perdedero, the Labyrinth, or place in which one may be lost. Notwithstanding its wonderful reputation, and a name which alone, in any other country, would induce a thorough exploration, it is a singular fact, and exhibits more strikingly than anything I can mention the indifference of the people of all classes to the antiquities of the country, that up to the time of my arrival at the door, this Laberinto had never been examined. My friend Don Lorenzo Peon would give me every facility for exploring it except joining me himself. Several persons had penetrated to some distance with a string held outside, but had turned back, and the universal belief was, that it contained passages without number and without end.

Under these circumstances, I certainly felt some degree of excitement as I stood in the doorway. The very name called up those stupendous works in Crete and on the shores of the Mœritic Lake which are now almost discredited as fabulous.

My retinue consisted of eight men, who considered themselves in my employ, besides three or four supernumeraries, and all together formed a crowd around the door. Except the mayoral of Uxmal, I had never seen one of them before, and as I considered it important to have a reliable man outside, I stationed him at the door with a ball of twine. I tied one end round my left wrist, and told one of the men to light a torch and follow me, but he refused absolutely, and all the rest, one after the other, did the same. They were all ready enough to hold the string; and I was curious to know, and had a conference with them on the interesting point, whether they expected any pay for their services in standing out of doors. One expected pay for showing me the place, others for carrying water, another for taking care of the horses, and so on, but I terminated the matter abruptly by declaring that I should not pay one of them a medio; and, ordering them all away from the door, which they were smothering, and a little infected with one of their apprehensions of starting some wild beast, which might be making his lair in the recesses of the cave, I entered with a candle in one hand and a pistol in the other.

The entrance faces the west. The mouth was filled up with rubbish, scrambling over which, I stood in a narrow passage or gallery, constructed, like all the apartments above ground, with smooth walls and triangular arched ceiling. This passage was about four feet wide, and seven feet high to the top of the arch. It ran due east, and at the distance of six or eight yards opened into another, or rather was stopped by another crossing it, and running north and south. I took first that on the right hand, running south. At the distance of a few yards, on the right side of the wall, I found a door, filled up, and at the distance of thirty-five feet the passage ended, and a door opened at right angles on the left into another gallery running due east. Following this, at the distance of thirteen feet I found another gallery on the left, running north, and beyond it, at the end, still another, also on the left, and running north, four yards long, and then walled up, with only an opening in it about a foot square.

Turning back, I entered the gallery which I had passed, and which ran north eight or ten yards; at the end was a doorway on the right, opening into a gallery that ran east. At the end of this were six steps, each one foot high and two wide, leading to another gallery, which ran north twelve yards. At the end there came another gallery on the left, which ran west ten yards, and at the end of this another on the right, running north about sixty feet. This passage was walled up at the north end, and at the distance of five yards from this end another doorway led into a passage running to the east. At the distance of four yards a gallery crossed this at right angles, running north and south, forty-five feet long, and walled up at both ends; and three or four yards farther on another gallery crossed it, also running north and south. This last was walled up at the south, and on the north led to still another gallery, which ran east, three yards long. This was stopped by another gallery crossing it, running to the south three yards, when it was walled up, and to the north eight yards, when it turned to the west.

In utter ignorance of the ground, I found myself turning and doubling along these dark and narrow passages, which seemed really to have no end, and justly to entitle the place to its name of El Laberinto.

I was not entirely free from the apprehension of starting some wild animal, and moved slowly and very cautiously. In the mean time, in turning the corners, my twine would be entangled, and the Indians, moved by the probability of getting no pay, entered to clear it, and by degrees all came up with me in a body. I got a glimpse of their torches behind me just as I was turning into a new passage, and at the moment I was startled by a noise which sent me back rather quickly, and completely routed them. It proceeded from a rushing of bats, and, having a sort of horror of these beastly birds, this was an ugly place to meet them in, for the passage was so low, and there was so little room for a flight over head, that in walking upright there was great danger of their striking the face. It was necessary to move with the head bent down, and protecting the lights from the flapping of their wings. Nevertheless, every step was exciting, and called up recollections of the Pyramids and tombs of Egypt, and I could not but believe that these dark and intricate passages would introduce me to some large saloon, or perhaps some royal sepulchre. Belzoni, and the tomb of Cephrenes and its alabaster sarcophagus, were floating through my brain, when all at once I found the passage choked up and effectually stopped. The ceiling had fallen in, crushed by a great mass of superincumbent earth, and farther progress was utterly impossible.

I was not prepared for this abrupt termination. The walls and ceiling were so solid and in such good condition that the possibility of such a result had not occurred to me. I was sure of going on to the end and discovering something, and I was arrested without knowing any better than when I entered to what point these passages led, or for what purposes they had been constructed. My first impulse was, not to turn back, but to begin immediately and dig a way through; but the impossibility of accomplishing anything in this way soon presented itself. For the Indians to carry out the earth on their backs through all these passages would be a never-ending work; besides, I had no idea how far the destruction extended, and, for the present at least, nothing could be done.

In a spirit of utter disappointment, I pointed out to the Indians the mass of earth that, as it were, maliciously cut off all my hopes, and told them to put an end to their lying stories about the Laberinto and its having no end; and in my disappointment I began to feel most sensibly the excessive heat and closeness of the place, which I had hardly perceived before, and which now became almost insufferable from the smoke of the torches and the Indians choking the narrow passage.

All that I could do, and that was very unsatisfactory, was to find out the plan of this subterraneous structure. I had with me a pocket compass, and, notwithstanding the heat and smoke, and the little help that the Indians afforded me, under all annoyances, and with the sweat dropping on my memorandum book, I measured back to the door.

I remained outside a few moments for fresh air, and entered again to explore the passage which branched off to the left of the door. I had just gone far enough to have my hopes revived by the prospect of some satisfactory result, when again I found the passage choked up by the falling in and burial of the arch.

I measured and took the bearings of this too. From the excessive heat and annoyance, this plan may not be very correct, and therefore I do not present it. The description will enable the reader to form some general idea of the character of the structure.

In exploring that part to the left of the door, I made an important discovery. In the walls of one of the passages was a hole eight inches square, which admitted light, and looking through it, I saw some plump and dusky legs, which clearly did not belong to the antiguos, and which I easily recognised as those of my worthy attendants.

Having heard the place spoken of as a subterraneous construction, and seeing, when I reached the ground, a half-buried door with a mass of overgrown earth above it, it had not occurred to me to think otherwise; but on examining outside, I found that what I had taken for an irregular natural formation, like a hill-side, was a pyramidal mound of the same general character with all the rest we had seen in the country. Making the Indians clear away some thorn-bushes, with the help of the branches of a tree growing near I climbed up it. On the top were the ruins of a building, the same as all the others. The door of El Laberinto, instead of opening into a hill-side, opened into this mound, and, as near as I could judge from the ruins along the base, was ten feet high, and the Laberinto, instead of being subterraneous, or, rather, under the surface of the earth, was in the body of this mound. Heretofore it had been our impression that these mounds were solid and compact masses of stone and earth, without any chambers or structures of any kind, and the discovery of this gave rise to the exciting idea that all the great mounds scattered over the country contained secret, unknown, and hidden chambers, presenting an immense field for exploration and discovery, and, ruined as the buildings on their summits were, perhaps the only source left for acquiring knowledge of the people by whom the cities were constructed.

I was really at a loss to know what to do. I was almost tempted to abandon everything else, send word to my companions, and not leave the spot till I had pulled down the whole mound, and discovered every secret it contained; but it was not a work to be undertaken in a hurry, and I determined to leave it for a future occasion. Unfortunately, in the multiplicity of other occupations in distant regions of the country, I never had an opportunity of returning to this mound. It remains with all its mystery around it, worthy the enterprise of some future explorer, and I cannot but indulge the hope that the time is not far distant when its mystery will be removed and all that is hidden brought to light.

In the account which I had received of this Labyrinth, no mention had been made of any ruins, and probably, when on the ground, I should have heard nothing of them, but from the top of this mound I saw two others, both of which, with a good deal of labour, I reached under the guidance of the Indians, crossing a patch of beans and milpa. I ascended them both. On the top of one was a building eighty or a hundred feet long. The front wall had fallen, and left exposed the inner part of the back wall, with half the arch, as it were, supporting itself in the air. The Indians then led me to a fourth mound, and told me that there were others in the woods, but all in the same ruinous condition; and, considering the excessive heat and the desperate toil of clambering, I did not think it worth while to visit them. I saw no sculptured stones, except those I have before mentioned, dug out like troughs, and called *pilas*, though the Indians persisted in saying that there were such all over, but they did not know exactly where to find them.

At three o'clock I resumed my journey toward Uxmal. For a short distance the road lay along the ridge of the sierra, a mere bed of rock, on which the horse's hoofs clattered and rang at every step. Coming out upon the brow of the sierra, we had one of those grand views which everywhere present themselves from this mountain range; an immense wooded plain, in this place broken only by a small spot like a square on a chess-board, the clearing of the hacienda of Santa Cruz. We descended the sierra, and at the foot of it struck the camino real.

About an hour before dark, and a league before reaching the village of Opocheque, I saw on the left, near the road, a high mound, with an edifice on its top, which at that distance, as seen through the trees, seemed almost entire. It stood in a corn-field. I was not looking out for anything of the kind, and but for the clearing made for the milpa, I could not have seen it at all. I threw the bridle of my horse to the major domo, and made for it, but it was not very easy of access. The field, according to the fashion of the country, was enclosed by a fence, which con-sisted of all the brush and briers collected on the clearing, six or eight feet high and as many wide, affording a sufficient bar-rier against wild cattle. In attempting to cross this, I broke through, sinking almost to my neck in the middle, and was con-siderably torn by thorns before I got over into the milpa.

The mound stood on one side of the milpa, isolated, and of the building upon it, the lower part, to the cornice, was standing. Above the cornice the outer wall had fallen, but the roof remained, and within all was entire. There was no view from the top; beyond the milpa all was forest, and what lay buried in it I had no means of ascertaining. The place was silent and desolate; there was no one of whom I could ask any ques-tions. I never heard of these ruins till I saw them from the back of my horse, and I could never learn by what name they are called.

At half past six we reached the village of Opocheque. In the centre of the plaza was a large fountain, at which women were drawing water, and on one side was a Mestizo family, with two men playing the guitar. We stopped for a cup of water, and then, pushing on by a bright moonlight, at nine o'clock reached the village of Moona, which the reader of my former volumes may remember was the first stage of our journey on leaving Uxmal for home.

Early the next morning we resumed our course. Immedi-ately behind the village we crossed the sierra, the same broken and stony range, commanding on both sides the same grand view of a boundless wooded plain. In an hour we saw at a dis-tance on our left the high mound of ruins visible from the House of the Dwarf, known under the Indian name of Xcoch. About five miles before arriving at Uxmal, I saw on the right another high mound. The intervening space was covered with trees and thorn-bushes, but I reached it without dismounting. On the top were two buildings about eighteen feet each, with the upper part of the outer walls fallen. Of both, the inner part was entire.

At twelve o'clock I reached Uxmal. The extent of my journey had been thirteen leagues, or thirty-nine miles; for though I had varied my route in returning, I had not increased the distance, and I had seen seven different places of ruins, memorials of cities which had been and had passed away, and such memorials as no cities built by the Spaniards in that country would present.

The ruins of Uxmal presented themselves to me as a home, and I looked upon them with more interest than before. I had found the wrecks of cities scattered more numerously than I expected, but they were all so shattered that no voice of instruction issued from them; here they still stood, tottering and crumbling, but living memorials, more worthy than ever of investigation and study, and as I then thought, not knowing what others more distant, of which we had heard, might prove, perhaps the only existing vestiges that could transmit to posterity the image of an American city.

As I approached, I saw on the terrace our beds, with moscheto-nets fluttering in the wind, and trunks and boxes all turned out of doors, having very much the appearance of a forcible ejectment or ouster for non-payment of rent; but on arriving I found that my companions were *moving*. In the great sala, with its three doors, they had found themselves too much exposed to the heavy dews and night air, and they were about removing to a smaller apartment, being that next to the last on the south wing, which had but one door, and could more easily be kept dry by a fire. They were then engaged in cleaning house, and at the moment of my arrival I was called in to consult whether the rooms should undergo another sweeping. After some deliberation, it was decided in the affirmative, and about two bushels more of dirt were carried out, which discouraged us from carrying the process of cleaning any farther.

During my absence an addition had been made to our household in a servant forwarded from Merida by the active kindness of the Doña Joaquina Peon. He was a dark Mestizo named Albino, short and thick, and so near being squint-eyed that at the first glance I thought him a subject for Doctor Cabot to practise on. Bernaldo was still on hand, as also Chaipa Chi, the former under the doctor's instructions, as chef de cuisine,

A Beautiful Scene

and Chaipa still devoting all her energies to the business in
which she shone, the making of tortillas.

In the afternoon we were comfortably settled in our new
quarters. We continued the precaution of kindling a fire in one
corner, to drive away malaria, and at night we had a bonfire
out of doors. The grass and bushes which had been cut down
on the terrace, parched and dried by the hot sun, were ready
for the fire; the flames lighted up the façade of the great palace,
and when they died away, the full moon broke upon it, mellow-
ing its rents and fissures, and presenting a scene mournfully
beautiful.

CHAPTER XI

The next day I resumed my occupation of superintending the Indians. It was, perhaps, the hardest labour I
had in that country to look on and see them work, and it was
necessary to be with them all the time; for if not watched, they
would not work at all.

The next day opened with a drizzling rain, the beginning
of the prevailing storm of the country, called El Norte. This
storm, we were told, rarely occurred at this season, and the
mayoral said that after it was over, the regular dry season would
certainly set in. The thermometer fell to fifty-two, and to our
feelings the change was much for the better. In fact, we had
begun to feel a degree of lassitude, the effect of the excessive
heat, and this change restored and reinvigorated us.

This day, too, with the beginning of the storm, Don Simon
arrived from Jalacho, according to promise, to pay us a visit. He
was not in the habit of visiting Uxmal at this season, and though
less fearful than other members of his family, he was not without apprehensions on account of the health of the place. In
fact, he had suffered much himself from an illness contracted
there. At the hacienda he found the mayoral, who had just returned with me from Jalacho, ill with calentura or fever. This,
with the cold and rain of the Norther, did not tend to restore
his equanimity. We insisted on his becoming our guest, but
agreed to let him off at night on account of the moschetoes. His

visit was a fortunate circumstance for us; his knowledge of localities, and his disposition to forward our views, gave us great
facilities in our exploration of the ruins, and at the same time
our presence and co-operation induced him to satisfy his own
curiosity in regard to some things which had not yet been
examined.

Throughout the ruins circular holes were found at different
places in the ground, opening into chambers underneath, which
had never been examined, and the character of which was entirely unknown. We had noticed them, at the time of our former visit, on the platform of the great terrace; and though this
platform was now entirely overgrown, and many of them were
hidden from sight, in opening a path to communicate with the
hacienda we had laid bare two. The mayoral had lately discovered another at some distance outside the wall, so perfect at
the mouth, and apparently so deep on sounding it with a stone,
that Don Simon wished to explore it.

The next morning he came to the ruins with Indians, ropes,
and candles, and we began immediately with one of those on
the platform before the Casa del Gobernador. The opening was
a circular hole, eighteen inches in diameter. The throat consisted of five layers of stones, a yard deep, to a stratum of solid
rock. As it was all dark beneath, before descending, in order to
guard against the effects of impure air, we let down a candle,
which soon touched bottom. The only way of descending was to
tie a rope around the body, and be lowered by the Indians. In
this way I was let down, and almost before my head had passed
through the hole my feet touched the top of a heap of rubbish,
high directly under the hole, and falling off at the sides. Clambering down it, I found myself in a round chamber, so filled
with rubbish that I could not stand upright. With a candle in
my hand, I crawled all round on my hands and knees. The
chamber was in the shape of a dome, and had been coated with
plaster, most of which had fallen, and now encumbered the
ground. The depth could not be ascertained without clearing
out the interior. In groping about I found pieces of broken pottery, and a vase of terra cotta, about one foot in diameter, of
good workmanship, and having upon it a coat of enamel, which,
though not worn off, had lost some of its brightness. It had three
feet, each about an inch high, one of which is broken. In other
respects it was entire.

The discovery of this vase was encouraging. Not one of
these places had ever been explored. Neither Don Simon nor any

of the Indians knew anything about them, and, entering them now for the first time, we were excited by the hope that we had discovered a rich mine of curious and interesting fabrics wrought by the inhabitants of this ruined city. Besides this, we had already ascertained one point in regard to which we were doubtful before. This great terrace was not entirely artificial. The substratum was of natural rock, and showed that advantage had been taken of a natural elevation, so far as it went, and by this means some portion of the immense labour of constructing the terrace had been saved.

On the same terrace, directly at the foot of the steps, was another opening of the same kind, and, on clearing around, we found near by a circular stone about six inches in thickness, which fitted the hole, and no doubt had served as a cover. This hole was filled up with dirt to within two feet of the mouth, and setting some Indians at work to clear it out, we passed on in search of another.

Descending the terrace, and passing behind the high and nameless mound which towers between the Casa del Gobernador and Casa de Palomos, the Indians cleared away some bushes, and brought us to another opening, but a few feet from the path we had cut through, entirely hidden from view until the clearing was made. The mouth was similar to that of the first; the throat about a yard deep, and the Indians lowered me down, without any obstruction, to the bottom.

The Indians looked upon our entering these places as senseless and foolhardy, and, besides imaginary dangers, they talked of snakes, scorpions, and hornets, the last of which, from the experience we had had of them in different parts of the ruins, were really objects of fear; for a swarm of them coming upon a man in such a place, would almost murder him before he could be hauled out.

It did not, however, require much time to explore this vault. It was clear of rubbish, perfect and entire in all its parts, without any symptoms of decay, and to all appearances, after the lapse of unknown years, fit for the uses to which it was originally applied. Like the one on the terrace, it was dome-shaped, and the sides fell in a little toward the bottom, like a well-made haystack. The height was ten feet and six inches directly under the mouth, and it was seventeen feet six inches in diameter. The walls and ceiling were plastered, still in a good state of preservation, and the floor was of hard mortar. Don Simon and Dr. Cabot were lowered down, and we examined every part thoroughly.

Leaving this, we went on to a third, which was exactly the same, except that it was a little smaller, being only five yards in diameter.

The fourth was the one which had just been discovered, and which had excited the curiosity of the mayoral. It was a few feet outside of a wall which, as Don Simon said, might be traced through the woods, broken and ruined, until it met and enclosed within its circle the whole of the principal buildings. The mouth was covered with cement, and in the throat was a large stone filling it up, which the mayoral, on discovering it, had thrown in to prevent horses or cattle from falling through. A rope was passed under the stone, and it was hauled out. The throat was smaller than any of the others, and hardly large enough to pass the body of a man. In shape and finish it was exactly the same as the others, with perhaps a slight shade of difference in the dimensions. The smallness of this mouth was, to my mind, strong proof that these subterraneous chambers had never been intended for any purposes which required men to descend into them. I was really at a loss how to get out. The Indians had no mechanical help of any kind, but were obliged to stand over the hole and hoist by dead pull, making, as I had found before, a jerking, irregular movement. The throat was so small that there was no play for the arms, to enable me to raise myself up by the rope, and the stones around the mouth were insecure and tottering. I was obliged to trust to them, and they involuntarily knocked my head against the stones, let down upon me a shower of dirt, and gave me such a severe rasping that I had no disposition at that time to descend another. In fact, they too were tired out, and it was a business in which, on our own account at least, it would not do to overtask them.

We were extremely disappointed in not finding any more vases or relics of any kind. We could not account for the one found in the chamber under the terrace, and were obliged to suppose that it had been thrown in or got there by accident.

These subterraneous chambers are scattered over the whole ground covered by the ruined city. There was one in the cattle-yard before the hacienda, and the Indians were constantly discovering them at greater distances. Dr. Cabot found them continually in his hunting excursions, and once, in breaking through bushes in search of a bird, fell into one, and narrowly escaped a serious injury; indeed, there were so many of them, and in places where they were so little to be expected, that they made rambling out of the cleared paths dangerous, and to the last day of our visit we were constantly finding new ones.

That they were constructed for some specific purpose, had some definite object, and that that object was uniform, there was no doubt, but what it was, in our ignorance of the habits of the people, it was difficult to say. Don Simon thought that the cement was not hard enough to hold water, and hence that they were not intended as cisterns or reservoirs, but for granaries or store-houses of maize, which, from our earliest knowledge of the aborigines down to the present day, has been the staff of life to the inhabitants. In this opinion, however, we did not concur, and from what we saw afterward, believe that they were intended as cisterns, and had furnished, in part at least, a supply of water to the people of the ruined city.

We returned to our apartments to dine, and in the afternoon accompanied Don Simon to see the harvest of the maize crop. The great field in front of the Casa del Gobernador was planted with corn, and on the way we learned a fact which may be interesting to agriculturists in the neighbourhood of those numerous cities throughout our country which, being of premature growth, are destined to become ruins. The debris of ruined cities fertilize and enrich land. Don Simon told us that the ground about Uxmal was excellent for milpas or corn-fields. He had never had a better crop of maize than that of the last year; indeed, it was so good that he had planted a part of the same land a second time, which is a thing unprecedented under their system of agriculture; and Don Simon had another practical view of the value of these ruins, which would have done for the meridian of our own city. Pointing to the great buildings, he said that if he had Uxmal on the banks of the Mississippi, it would be an immense fortune, for there was stone enough to pave every street in New-Orleans, without sending to the North for it, as it was necessary to do; but, not to be outdone in sensible views of things, we suggested that if he had it on the banks of the Mississippi, easy of access, preserved from the rank vegetation which is now hurrying it to destruction, it would stand like Herculaneum and Pompeii, a place of pilgrimage for the curious; and that it would be a much better operation to put a fence around it and charge for admission, than to sell the stone for paving streets.

By this time we had reached the foot of the terrace, and a few steps brought us into the corn-field. The system of agriculture in Yucatan is rather primitive. Besides hemp and sugar, which the Indians seldom attempt to raise on their own account, the principal products of the country are corn, beans, and calabazas, like our pumpkins and squashes, camotes, which are perhaps the parent of our Carolina potatoes, and chili or pepper, of which last an inordinate quantity is consumed, both by the Indians and Spaniards. Indian corn, however, is the great staple, and the cultivation of this probably differs but little now from the system followed by the Indians before the conquest. In the dry season, generally in the months of January and February, a place is selected in the woods, from which the trees are cut down and burned. In May or June the corn is planted. This is done by making little holes in the ground with a pointed stick, putting in a few grains of corn and covering them over. Once in the ground, it is left to take care of itself, and if it will not grow, it is considered that the land is not worth having. The corn has a fair start with the weeds, and they keep pace amicably together. The hoe, plough, and harrow are entirely unknown; indeed, in general neither of the last two could be used, on account of the stony face of the country: the machete is the only instrument employed.

The milpa around the ruins of Uxmal had been more than usually neglected; the crop turned out badly, but such as it was, the Indians from three of Don Simon's adjoining haciendas, according to their obligation to the master, were engaged in getting it in. They were distributed in different parts of the field; and of those we came upon first, I counted a small group of fifty-three. As we drew near, all stopped working, approached Don Simon, bowed respectfully to him, and then to us as his friends. The corn had been gathered, and these men were engaged in threshing it out. A space was cleared of about a hundred feet square, and along the border of it was a line of small hammocks hanging on stakes fixed in the ground, in which the Indians slept during the whole time of the harvest, each with a little fire underneath to warm him in the cool night air, and drive away the moschetoes.

Don Simon threw himself into one of the hammocks, and held out one of his legs, which was covered with burrs and briers. These men were free and independent electors of the State of Yucatan; but one of them took in his hand Don Simon's foot, picked off the burrs, pulled off the shoe, cleaned the stocking, and restoring the shoe, laid the foot back carefully in the hammock, and then took up the other. It was all done as a matter of course, and no one bestowed a thought upon it except ourselves.

On one side of the clearing was a great pile or small mountain of corn in the ear, ready to be threshed, and near by was the threshing machine, which certainly could not be considered an infringement of any Yankee patent right. It was a rude scaffold about eighteen or twenty feet square, made of four untrimmed upright posts for corners, with poles lashed to them horizontally three or four feet from the ground, and across these was a layer of sticks, about an inch thick, side by side; the whole might have served as a rude model of the first bedstead ever made.

The parallel sticks served as a threshing floor, on which was spread a thick layer of corn. On each side a rude ladder of two or three rounds rested against the floor, and on each of these ladders stood a nearly naked Indian, with a long pole in his hand, beating the corn. The grains fell through, and at each corner under the floor was a man with a brush made of bushes, sweeping off the cobs. The shelled corn was afterward taken up in baskets and carried to the hacienda. The whole process would have surprised a Genesee farmer; but perhaps, where labour was so little costly, it answered as well as the best threshing machine that could be invented.

The next day we had another welcome visiter in our fellow-passenger, Mr. Camerden, who was just from Campeachy, where he had seen New-York papers to the third of November. Knowing our deep interest in the affairs of our country, and postponing his own curiosity about the ruins, he hastened to communicate to us the result of the city elections, viz., a contest in the sixth ward and entire uncertainty which party was uppermost.

Unfortunately, Mr. Camerden, not being in very good health at the time, was also infected with apprehensions about Uxmal, and as El Norte still continued, the coldness and rain made him uneasy in a place of such bad reputation. Having no ill feelings against him and no spare moscheto-net, we did not ask him to remain at night, and he accompanied Don Simon to the hacienda to sleep.

The next day Doctor Cabot had a professional engagement at the hacienda. In both my expeditions into that region of country our medical department was incomplete. On the former occasion we had a medicine-chest, but no doctor, and this time we had a doctor, but no medicine-chest. This necessary appendage had been accidentally left on board the ship, and did not come to our hands till some time afterward. We had only a small stock purchased in Merida, and on this account, as well as because it interfered with his other pursuits, the doctor had avoided entering into general practice. He was willing to attend to cases that might be cured by a single operation, but the principle diseases were fevers, which could not be cut out with a knife. The day before, however, a young Indian came to the ruins on an errand to Don Simon, who had a leg swollen with varicose veins. He had a mild expression, meek and submissive manners, and was what Don Simon called, in speaking of his best servants, muy docil, or very docile. He stood at that time in an interesting position, being about to be married. Don Simon had had him at Merida six months, under the care of a physician, but without any good result, and the young man was taking his chance for better or worse, almost with the certainty of becoming in a few years disabled, and a mass of corruption. Doctor Cabot undertook to perform an operation, for which purpose it was necessary to go to the hacienda; and, that we might return with Mr. Camerden, we all went there to breakfast.

Under the corridor was an old Indian leaning against a pillar, with his arms folded across his breast, and before him a row of little Indian girls, all, too, with arms folded, to whom he was teaching the formal part of the church service, giving out a few words, which they all repeated after him. As we entered the corridor, he came up to us, bowed, and kissed our hands, and all the little girls did the same.

Don Simon had breakfast ready for us, but we found some deficiencies. The haciendas of that country never have any surplus furniture, being only visited by the master once or twice a year, and then only for a few days, when he brings with him whatever he requires for his personal comfort. Uxmal was like the rest, and at that moment it was worse off, for we had stripped it of almost every movable to enlarge our accommodations at the ruins. Our greatest difficulty was about seats. All contrived to be provided for, however, except Don Simon, who finally, as it was an extreme case, went into the church and brought out the great confessional chair.

Breakfast over, the doctor's patient was brought forward. He was not consulted on the subject of the operation, and had no wish of his own about it, but did as his master ordered him. At the moment of beginning, Doctor Cabot asked for a bed. He had not thought of asking for it before, supposing it would be ready at a moment's notice; but he might almost as well have asked for a steamboat or a locomotive engine. Who ever thought of wanting a bed at Uxmal? was the general feeling of the Indians. They were all born in hammocks, and expected to die in them, and who wanted a bed when he could get a hammock? A bed, however (which means a bedstead), was indispensable, and the Indians dispersed in search, returning, after a long absence, with tidings that they had heard of one on the hacienda, but it had been taken apart, and the pieces were in use for other purposes. They were sent off again, and at length we received notice that the bed was coming, and presently it appeared advancing through the gate of the cattle-yard in the shape of a bundle of poles on the shoulder of an Indian. For purposes of immediate use, they might as well have been on the tree that produced them, but, after a while, they were put together, and made a bedstead that would have astonished a city cabinet-maker.

In the mean time the patient was looking on, perhaps with somewhat the feeling of a man superintending the making of his own coffin. The disease was in his right leg, which was almost as thick as his body, covered with ulcers, and the distended veins stood out like whipcords. Doctor Cabot considered it necessary to cut two veins. The Indian stood up, resting the whole weight of his body on the diseased leg, so as to bring them out to the fullest, and supporting himself by leaning with his hands on a bench. One vein was cut, the wound bound up, and then the operation was performed on the other by thrusting a stout pin into the flesh under the vein, and bringing it out on the other side, then winding a thread round the protruding head and point, and leaving the pin to cut its way through the vein and fester out. The leg was then bound tight, and the Indian laid upon the bed. During the whole time not a muscle of his face moved, and, except at the moment when the pin was thrust under the vein, when his hand contracted on the bench, it could not have been told that he was undergoing an operation of any kind.

This over, we set out on our return with Mr. Camerden to the ruins, but hardly left the gate of the cattle-yard, when we met an Indian with his arm in a sling, coming in search of Doctor Cabot. A death-warrant seemed written in his face. His little wife, a girl about fourteen years old, soon to become a mother, was trotting beside him, and his case showed how, in those countries, human life is the sport of accident and ignorance. A few days before, by some awkwardness, he had given his left arm a severe cut near the elbow with a machete. To stop the bleeding, his wife had tied one string as tightly as possible around the wrist, and another in the hollow of the arm, and so it had remained three days. The treatment had been pretty effectual in stopping the bleeding, and it had very nearly stopped the circulation of his blood forever. The hand was shrunken to nothing, and seemed withered; the part of the arm between the two ligatures was swollen enormously, and the seat of the wound was a mass of corruption. Doctor Cabot took off the fastenings, and endeavoured to teach her to restore the circulation by friction, or rubbing the arm with the palm of the hand, but she had no more idea of the circulation of the blood than of the revolution of the planets.

The wound, on being probed, gave out a foul and pestilential discharge, and, when that was cleared away, out poured a stream of arterial blood. The man had cut an arterial vein. Doctor Cabot had no instruments with him with which to take it up, and, grasping the arm with a strong pressure on the vein, so as to stop the flow of blood, he transferred the arm to me, fixing my fingers upon the vein, and requesting me to hold it in that position while he ran to the ruins for his instruments. This was by no means pleasant. If I lost the right pressure, the man might bleed to death; and, having no regular diploma warranting people to die on my hands, not willing to run the risk of any accident, and knowing the imperturbable character of the Indians, I got the arm transferred to one of them, with a warning that the man's life depended upon him. Doctor Cabot was gone more than half an hour, and during all that time, while the patient's head was falling on his shoulder with fainting fits, the Indian looked directly in his face, and held up the arm with a fixedness of attitude that would have served as a model for a sculptor. I do not believe that, for a single moment, the position of the arm varied a hair's breadth.

Doctor Cabot dressed the wound, and the Indian was sent away, with an even chance, as the doctor considered, for life or death. The next that we heard of him, however, he was at work in the fields; certainly, but for the accidental visit of Doctor Cabot, he would have been in his grave.

After this there were some delicate cases among the women of the hacienda; and these multifarious occupations consumed the whole of the morning, which we had intended to devote to Mr. Camerden and the ruins. It was a cold and cheerless day; the

Norther was increasing in force, and he saw malaria and sickness all around him. In the afternoon he left us to return to New-York by the same vessel which had brought us out. Unfortunately, he carried away with him the seeds of a dangerous illness, from which he did not recover in many months.

The next day Don Simon left us, and we were again alone. Sickness was increasing on the hacienda, and two days afterward we received notice that Doctor Cabot's leg patient was ill with fever, and also that a woman had died that day of the same disease, and was to be buried the next morning. We ordered horses to be sent up to the ruins, and early in the morning Dr. Cabot and myself rode to the hacienda, he to visit his patient, and I to attend the funeral, in the expectation that such an event, on a retired hacienda, without any priest or religious ceremonies, would disclose some usage or custom illustrative of the ancient Indian character. Leaving my horse in the cattle-yard, in company with the mayoral I walked to the campo santo. This was a clearing in the woods at a short distance from the house, square, and enclosed by a rude stone fence. It had been consecrated with the ceremonies of the church, and was intended as a burial-place for all who died on the estate; a rude place, befitting the rude and simple people for whom it was designed. When we entered we saw a grave half dug, which had been abandoned on account of the stones, and some Indians were then occupied in digging another.

Only one part of the cemetery had been used as a burial-place, and this was indicated by little wooden crosses, one planted at the head of each grave. In this part of the cemetery was a stone enclosure about four feet high, and the same in diameter, which was intended as a sort of charnel-house, and was then filled with skulls and bones, whitening in the sun. I moved to this place, and began examining the skulls.

The Indians, in digging the grave, used a crowbar and machete, and scooped out the loose earth with their hands. As the work proceeded, I heard the crowbar enter something with a cracking, tearing sound: it had passed through a human skull. One of the Indians dug it out with his hands, and, after they had all examined and commented upon it, handed it to the mayoral, who gave it to me. They all knew whose skull it was. It was that of a woman who had been born and brought up, and who had died among them, and whom they had buried only the last dry season, but little more than a year before. The skull was laid upon the pile, and the Indians picked out the arms and legs, and all the smaller bones. Below the ribs, from the back downward, the flesh had not decayed, but dried up and adhered to the bones, which, all hanging together, they lifted out and laid upon the pile. All this was done decently and with respect.

As I stood by the enclosure of bones, I took up different skulls, and found that they were all known and identified. The campo santo had been opened but about five years, and every skull had once sat upon the shoulders of an acquaintance.

The graves were all on one side, and on the other no dead had been buried. I suggested to the mayoral, that by beginning on the farther side, and burying in order, every corpse would have time to decay and become dust before its place was wanted for another, which he seemed to think a good idea, and communicated it to the Indians, who stopped their work, looked at him and at me, and then went on digging. I added, that in a few years the bones of the friend they were about burying, and his own, and those of all the rest of them, would be pulled and handled like those on the pile, which, also, he communicated to them, and with the same effect. In the mean time I had overhauled the skulls, and placed on the top two which I ascertained to be those of full-blooded Indians, intending to appropriate and carry them off at the first convenient opportunity.

The Indians worked as slowly as if each was digging his own grave, and at length the husband of the deceased came out, apparently to hurry them. He was bare-headed, had long black hair hanging down over his eyes, and, dressed in a clean blue flannel shirt, he seemed what he really was, one of the most respectable men on the hacienda. Sitting down by the side of the grave, he took two sticks which were there for that purpose, with one of which he measured the length, and with the other the breadth. This, to say the least of it, was cool, and the expression of his face was of that stolid and unbending kind, that no idea could be formed of his feelings; but it was not too much to suppose that a man in the early prime of life, who had fulfilled well all the duties of his station, must feel some emotion in measuring the grave of one who had been his companion when the labours of the day were over, and who was the mother of his children.

The grave was not large enough, and he took his seat at the foot, and waited while the Indians enlarged it, from time to time suggesting an improvement. In the mean time Doctor Cabot arrived on the ground with his gun, and one of the gravediggers pointed out a flock of parrots flying over. They were too

far off to kill, but as the Indians were always astonished at seeing a shot on the wing, and all seemed anxious to have him
shoot, he fired, and knocked out some feathers. The Indians
laughed, watched the feathers as they fell into the graveyard,
and then resumed their work. At length the husband again took
the sticks, measured the grave, and finding all right, returned to
the house. The Indians picked up a rude barrow made of two
long poles with crosspieces, which had been thrown down by the
side of the last corpse it had carried, and went off for the dead
body. They were gone so long that we thought they wished to
wear out our patience, and told the mayoral to go and hurry
them; but presently we heard a shuffling of feet, and the sound
of female voices, heralding a tumultuous procession of women.
On reaching the fence of the cemetery they all stopped, and, seeing us, would not come in, except one old Beelzebub, who
climbed over, walked directly to the foot of the grave, leaned
down, and, looking into it, made some exclamation which set
all the women outside laughing. This so incensed the old woman
that she picked up a handful of stones, and began pelting them
right and left, at which they all scattered with great confusion
and laughter, and in the midst of this, the corpse, attended by
an irregular crowd of men, women, and children, made its
appearance.

The barrow was lifted over the fence and laid down beside
the grave. The body had no coffin, but was wrapped from head
to foot in a blue cotton shawl with a yellow border. The head
was uncovered, and the feet stuck out, and had on a pair of
leather shoes and white cotton stockings, probably a present
from her husband on his return from some visit to Merida,
which the poor woman had never worn in life, and which he
thought he was doing her honour by placing in her grave.

The Indians passed ropes under the body; the husband himself supported the head, and so it was lowered into the grave.
The figure was tall, and the face was that of a woman about
twenty-three or twenty-four years old. The expression was painful, indicating that in the final struggle the spirit had been reluctant to leave its mortal tenement. There was but one present
who shed tears, and that was the old mother of the deceased,
who doubtless had expected this daughter to lay her own head
in the grave. She held by the hand a bright-eyed girl, who looked
on with wonder, happily unconscious that her best friend on
earth was to be laid under the sod. The shawl was opened, and
showed a white cotton dress under it; the arms, which were

folded across the breast for the convenience of carrying the body, were laid down by the sides, and the shawl was again wrapped round. The husband himself arranged the head, placed under it a cotton cloth for a pillow, and composed it for its final rest as carefully as if a pebble or a stone could hurt it. He brushed a handful of earth over the face; the Indians filled up the grave, and all went away. No romance hangs over such a burial scene, but it was not unnatural to follow in imagination the widowed Indian to his desolate hut.

We had been disappointed in not seeing any relic of Indian customs, and, as it was now eleven o'clock and we had not breakfasted, we did not consider ourselves particularly indemnified for our trouble.

159

CHAPTER XII

In the account of my former visit to the ruins of Uxmal, I mentioned the fact that this city was entirely destitute of apparent means for obtaining water. Within the whole circumference there is no well, stream, or fountain, and nothing which bears the appearance of having been used for supplying or obtaining water, except the subterraneous chambers before referred to; which, supposing them to have been intended for that purpose, would probably not have been sufficient, however numerous, to supply the wants of so large a population.

All the water required for our own use we were obliged to procure from the hacienda. We felt the inconvenience of this during the whole of our residence at the ruins, and very often, in spite of all our care to keep a supply on hand, we came in, after hard work in the sun, and, parched with thirst, were obliged to wait till we could send an Indian to the hacienda, a distance, going and returning, of three miles.

Very soon after our arrival our attention and inquiries were directed particularly to this subject, and we were not long in satisfying ourselves that the principal supply had been drawn from aguadas, or ponds, in the neighbourhood. These aguadas are now neglected and overgrown, and perhaps, to a certain extent, are the cause of the unhealthiness of Uxmal. The principal of them we saw first from the top of the House of the Dwarf,

Fig. 11

bearing west, and perhaps a mile and a half distant. We visited it under the guidance of the mayoral, with some Indians to clear the way. The whole intervening space was overgrown with woods, the ground was low and muddy, and, as the rains still continued, the aguada was at that time a fine sheet of water. It was completely imbosomed among trees, still and desolate, with tracks of deer on its banks; a few ducks were swimming on its surface, and a kingfisher was sitting on the bough of an over-hanging tree, watching for his prey. The mayoral told us that this aguada was connected with another more to the south, and that they continued, one after the other, to a great distance; to use his own expression, which, however, I did not understand literally, there were a hundred of them.

The general opinion with regard to these aguadas is the same with that expressed by the cura of Tekoh respecting that near Mayapan; viz., that they were "hechas á mano," artificial formations or excavations made by the ancient inhabitants as reservoirs for holding water. The mayoral told us that in the dry season, when the water was low, the remains of stone embankments were still visible in several places. As yet we were incredulous as to their being at all artificial, but we had no difficulty in believing that they had furnished the inhabitants of Uxmal with water. The distance, from what will be seen hereafter, in that dry and destitute country amounts to but little.

At the time of our first visit to it, however, this aguada had in our eyes a more direct and personal interest. From the difficulty of procuring water at the ruins, we were obliged to economize in the use of it, while, from the excessive heat and toil of working among the ruins, covered with dust and scratched with briers, there was nothing we longed for so much as the refreshment of a bath, and it was no unimportant part of our business at the aguada to examine whether it would answer as a bathing-place. The result was more satisfactory than we expected. The place was actually inviting. We selected a little cove shaded by a large tree growing almost out of the water, had a convenient space cleared around it, a good path cut all the way through the woods to the terrace of the Casa del Gobernador, and on the first of December we consecrated it by our first bath. The mayoral, shrunken and shattered by fever and ague, stood by protesting against it, and warning us of the consequences; but we had attained the only thing necessary for our comfort at Uxmal, and in the height of our satisfaction had no apprehensions for the result.

Up to this time our manner of living at the ruins had been very uniform, and our means abundant. All that was on the hacienda belonging to the master was ours, as were also the services of the Indians, so far as he had a right to command them. The property of the master consisted of cattle, horses, mules, and corn, of which only the last could be counted as provisions. Some of the Indians had a few fowls, pigs, and turkeys of their own, which they were in general willing to sell, and every morning those who came out to work brought with them water, fowls, eggs, lard, green beans, and milk. Occasionally we had a haunch of venison, and Doctor Cabot added to our larder several kinds of ducks, wild turkeys, chachalachas, quails, pigeons, doves, parrots, jays, and other smaller birds. Besides these, we received from time to time a present from the Doña Joaquina or Don Simon, and altogether our living was better than we had ever known in exploring ruins. Latterly, however, on account of the thickness of the woods, Doctor Cabot had become disgusted with sporting; having no dog, it was sometimes impossible to find one bird out of six, and he confined his shooting to birds which he wanted for dissection. At this time, too, we received intelligence that the fowls at the hacienda were running short, and the eggs gave out altogether.

There was no time to be lost, and we forthwith despatched Albino with an Indian to the village of Moona, twelve miles distant, who returned with a back-load of eggs, beans, rice, and sugar, and again the sun went down upon us in the midst of plenty. A pig arrived from Don Simon, sent from another hacienda, the cooking of which enlisted the warmest sympathies of all our heads of departments, Albino, Bernaldo, and Chaipa Chi. They had their own way of doing it, national, and derived from their forefathers, being the same way in which those respectable people cooked men and women, as Bernal Dias says, "dressing the bodies in their manner, which is by a sort of oven made with heated stones, which are put under ground." They made an excavation on the terrace, kindled a large fire in it, and kept it burning until the pit was heated like an oven. Two clean stones were laid in the bottom, the pig (not alive) was laid upon them, and covered over with leaves and bushes, packed down with stones so close as barely to leave vent to the fire, and allow an escape for the smoke.

While this bake was going on I set out on a business close at hand, but which, in the pressure of other matters, I had postponed from day to day. On a line with the back of the Casa del Gobernador rises the high and nameless mound represented in the frontispiece, forming one of the grandest and most imposing structures among all the ruins of Uxmal. It was at that time covered with trees and a thick growth of herbage, which gave a gloominess to its grandeur of proportions, and, but for its regularity, and a single belt of sculptured stones barely visible at the top, it would have passed for a wooded and grass-grown hill. Taking some Indians with me, I ascended this mound, and began clearing it for Mr. Catherwood to draw. I found that its vast sides were all incased with stone, in some places richly ornamented, but completely hidden from view by the foliage.

The height of this mound was sixty-five feet, and it measured at the base three hundred feet on one side and two hundred on the other. On the top was a great platform of solid stone, three feet high and seventy-five feet square, and about fifteen feet from the top was a narrow terrace running on all four of the sides. The walls of the platform were of smooth stone, and the corners had sculptured ornaments. The area consisted entirely of loose rough stones, and there are no remains or other indications of any building. The great structure seemed raised only for the purpose of holding aloft this platform. Probably it had been the scene of grand religious ceremonies, and stained with the blood of human victims offered up in sight of the assembled people. Near as it was, it was the first time I had ascended this mound. It commanded a full view of every building. The day was overcast, the wind swept mournfully over the desolate city, and since my arrival I had not felt so deeply the solemnity and sublimity of these mysterious ruins.

Around the top of the mound was a border of sculptured stone ten or twelve feet high. The principal ornament was the Grecque, and in following it round, and clearing away the trees and bushes, on the west side, opposite the courtyard of the Casa de Palomos, my attention was arrested by an ornament, the lower part of which was buried in rubbish fallen from above. It was about the centre of this side of the mound, and from its position, and the character of the ornament, I was immediately impressed with the idea that it was over a doorway, and that underneath was an entrance to an apartment in the mound. The Indians had cleared beyond it, and passed on, but I called them back, and set them to excavating the earth and rubbish that buried the lower part of the ornament. It was an awkward place to work in: the side of the mound was steep, and the stones composing the ornament were insecure and tottering. The Indians, as usual, worked as if they had their lifetime for the job. They were at all times tedious and trying, but now, to my impatient eagerness, more painfully so than ever. Urging them, as well as I could, and actually making them comprehend my idea, I got them to work four long hours without any intermission, until they reached the cornice. The ornament proved to be the same hideous face, with the teeth standing out, before presented, varying somewhat in detail, and upon a grander scale. Throwing up the dirt upon the other side of them, the Indians had made a great pile outside, and stood in a deep hole against the face of the ornament. At this depth the stones seemed hanging loosely over their heads, and the Indians intimated that it was dangerous to continue digging, but by this time my impatience was beyond control. I had from time to time assisted in the work, and, urging them to continue, I threw myself into the hole, and commenced digging with all my strength. The stones went rolling and crashing down the side of the mound, striking against roots and tearing off branches. The perspiration rolled from me in a stream, but I was so completely carried away by the idea that had taken possession of me, so sure of entering some chamber that had been closed for ages, that I stopped at nothing; and with all this I considered myself cool and calm, and with great method resolved, as soon as I reached the doorway, to stop and send for Mr. Catherwood and Doctor Cabot, that we might all enter together, and make a formal note of everything exactly as it was found; but I was doomed to a worse disappointment than at El Laberinto de Maxcanú. Before getting below the cornice I thrust the machete through the earth, and found no opening, but a solid stone wall. The ground of my hope was gone, but still I kept the Indians digging, unconsciously, and without any object. In the interest of the moment I was not aware that the clouds had disappeared, and that I had been working in this deep hole, without a breath of air, under the full blaze of a vertical sun. The disappointment and reaction after the high excitement, co-operating with the fatigue and heat, prostrated all my strength. I felt a heaviness and depression, and was actually sick at heart, so that, calling off the Indians, I was fain to give over and return to our quarters. In descending the mound my limbs could scarcely support me. My strength and elasticity were gone. With great difficulty I dragged myself to our apartments. My thirst was unquenchable. I threw myself into my hammock, and in a few moments a fiery fever was upon me. Our household was thrown into consternation. Disease had stalked all around us, but it was the first time it had knocked at our door.

On the third day, while in the midst of a violent attack, a gentleman arrived whose visit I had expected, and had looked forward to with great interest. It was the cura Carillo of Ticul, a village seven leagues distant. A week after our arrival at the ruins, the mayoral had received a letter from him, asking whether a visit would be acceptable to us. We had heard of him as a person who took more interest in the antiquities of the country than almost any other, and who possessed more knowledge on the subject. He had been in the habit of coming to Uxmal alone to wander among the ruins, and we had contemplated an excusion to Ticul on purpose to make his acquaintance. We were, therefore, most happy to receive his overture, and advised him that we should anxiously expect his visit. His first words to me were, that it was necessary for me to leave the place and go with him to Ticul. I was extremely reluctant to do so, but it was considered advisable by all. He would not consent to my going alone, or with his servant, and the next morning, instead of a pleasant visit to the ruins, he found himself trotting home with a sick man at his heels. In consequence of some mis-understanding, no coché was in readiness, and I set out on horseback. It was my interval day, and at the moment the bare absence of pain was a positively pleasant sensation. In this humour, in the beginning of our ride, I listened with much interest to the cura's exposition of different points and localities, but by degrees my attention flagged, and finally my whole soul was fixed on the sierra, which stood out before us at a distance of two leagues from San José. Twice before I had crossed that sierra, and had looked upon it almost with delight, as relieving the monotony of constant plains, but now it was a horrible prospect. My pains increased as we advanced, and I dismounted at the hacienda in a state impossible to be described. The mayoral was away, the doors were all locked, and I lay down on some bags in the corridor. Rest tranquillized me. There was but one Indian to be found, and he told the cura that there were none to make a coché. Those in the neighbourhood were sick, and the others were at work more than a league away. It was impossible to continue on horseback, and, fortunately, the mayoral came, who changed the whole face of things and in a few minutes had men engaged in making a coché. The cura went on before to prepare for my reception. In an hour my coché was ready, and at five o'clock I crawled in. My carriers were loth to start, but, once under way, they took it in good part, and set off on a trot. Changing shoulders frequently, they never stopped till they carried me into Ticul, three leagues or nine miles distant, and laid me down on the floor of the convent. The cura was waiting to receive me. Albino had arrived with my catre, which was already set up, and in a few minutes I was in bed. The bells were ringing for a village fiesta, rockets and fire-works were whizzing and exploding, and from a distance the shrill voice of a boy screeching out the numbers of the loteria pierced my ears. The sounds were murderous, but the kind-ness of the cura, and the satisfaction of being away from an infected atmosphere, were so grateful that I fell asleep.

For three days I did not leave my bed; but on the fourth I breathed the air from the balcony of the convent. It was fresh, pure, balmy, and invigorating.

In the afternoon of the next day I set out with the cura for a stroll. We had gone but a short distance, when an Indian came running after us to inform us that another of the caballeros had arrived sick from the ruins. We hurried back, and found Doctor Cabot lying in a coché on the floor of the corridor at the door of the convent. He crawled out labouring under a violent fever, increased by the motion and fatigue of his ride, and I was startled by the extraordinary change a few days had made in his appearance. His face was flushed, his eyes were wild, his figure lank; and he had not strength to support himself, but pitched against me, who could barely keep myself up, and both nearly came down together. He had been attacked the day after I left, and the fever had been upon him, with but little intermission, ever since. All night, and all the two ensuing days, it continued rising and decreasing, but never leaving him. It was attended with constant restlessness and delirium, so that he was hardly in bed before he was up again, pitching about the room.

The next day Mr. Catherwood forwarded Albino, who, with two attacks, was shaken and sweated into a dingy-looking white man. Mr. Catherwood wrote that he was entirely alone at the ruins, and should hold out as long as he could against fever and ghosts, but with the first attack should come up and join us.

Our situation and prospects were now gloomy. If Mr. Catherwood was taken ill, work was at an end, and perhaps the whole object of our expedition frustrated; but the poor cura was more to be pitied than any of us. His unlucky visit to Uxmal had brought upon him three infermos, with the prospect every day of a fourth. His convent was turned into a hospital; but the more claims we made upon him, the more he exerted himself to serve us. I could not but smile, when speaking to Doctor Cabot of his kindness, as the latter, rolling and tossing with fever, replied, that if the cura had any squint-eyed friends, he could cure them.

The cura watched the doctor carefully, but without venturing to offer advice to a medico who could cure biscos, but the third day he alarmed me by the remark that the expression of the doctor's face was *fatál*. In Spanish this only means very bad, but it had always in my ears an uncomfortable sound. The cura added that there were certain indices of this disease which were mortal, but, happily, these had not yet exhibited themselves in the doctor. The bare suggestion, however, alarmed me. I inquired of the cura about the mode of treatment in the country, and whether he could not prescribe for him. Doctor Cabot had never seen anything of this disease, particularly as affected by climate. Besides, he was *hors de combat* on account of the absence of our medicine-chest, and in such constant pain and delirium that he was in no condition to prescribe for himself.

The cura was the temporal as well as spiritual physician of the village; there were daily applications to him for medicine, and he was constantly visiting the sick. Doctor Cabot was willing to put himself entirely into his hands, and he administered a preparation which I mention for the benefit of future travellers who may be caught without a medicine-chest. It was a simple decoction of the rind of the sour orange flavoured with cinnamon and lemon-juice, of which he administered a tumblerful warm every two hours. At the second draught the doctor was thrown into a profuse perspiration. For the first time since his attack the fever left him, and he had an unbroken sleep. On waking, copious draughts of tamarind water were given; when the fever came on again the decoction was repeated, with tamarind water in the intervals. The effect of this treatment was particularly happy, and it is desirable for strangers to know it, for the sour orange is found in every part of the country, and from what we saw of it then and afterward, it is, perhaps, a better remedy for fever in that climate than any known in foreign pharmacy.

The village of Ticul, to which we were thus accidentally driven, was worthy of the visit, once in his life, of a citizen of New-York. The first time I looked upon it from the balcony of the convent, it struck me as the perfect picture of stillness and repose. The plaza was overgrown with grass; a few mules, with their fore feet hoppled, were pasturing upon it, and at long intervals a single horseman crossed it. The balcony of the convent was on a level with the tops of the houses, and the view was of a great plain, with houses of one story, flat roofs, high garden walls, above which orange, lemon, and plantain trees were growing, and, after the loud ringing of the matin and vesper bell was over, the only noise was the singing of birds. All business or visiting was done early in the morning or toward evening; and through the rest of the day, during the heat, the inhabitants were within doors, and it might almost have passed for a deserted village.

Like all the Spanish villages, it was laid out with its plaza and streets running at right angles, and was distinguished among the villages of Yucatan for its casas de piedra, or stone houses. These were on the plaza and streets adjoining; and back, extending more than a mile each way, were the huts of the Indians. These huts were generally plastered, enclosed by stone fences, and imbowered among trees, or, rather, overgrown and concealed by weeds. The population was about five thousand, of which about three hundred families were vecinos, or white people, and the rest Indians. Fresh meat can be procured every day; the tienda grande, or large store of Guzman, would not disgrace Merida. The bread is better than at the capital. Altogether, for appearance, society, and conveniences of living, it is perhaps the best village in Yucatan, and famous for its bull-fights and the beauty of its Mestiza women.

The church and convent occupy the whole of one side of the plaza. Both were built by the Franciscan monks, and they are among the grandest of those gigantic buildings with which that powerful order marked its entrance into the country. They stand on a stone platform about four feet high and several hundred feet in front. The church was large and sombre, and adorned with rude monuments and figures calculated to inspire the Indians with reverence and awe. In one place, in a niche in the wall, was a funeral urn, painted black, with a white streak around the top, which contains the ashes of a lady of the village. Under it was a monument with this inscription:

¡Hombres!
He aqui el termino de nuestros afanes;
La muerte, tierra, nada.

———

En esta urna reposan los restos de Dña Loretta Lara,
Muger caritativa, y esposa fiel, madre tierna,
prudente y virtuosa.

———

¡Mortales!
Al Senor dirigamos por ella nuestras preces.
Falleció
El 29 de Novembre del año 1830, á los 44 de su edad.

———

¡O Man!
Behold the end of our troubles—
Death, Earth, Nothing.

———

In this urn repose the remains of Dña Loretta Lara,
A charitable woman, faithful wife, and tender mother,
prudent and virtuous.

———

¡Mortals!
To the Lord let us direct our prayers for her.
She died
The 29th of November, in the year 1830, aged 44.

One of the altars was decorated with human skulls and cross-bones, and in the rear of the church was a great charnel-house. It was enclosed by a high stone wall, and was filled with a collection of skulls and bones, which, after the flesh had decayed, had been dug up from the graves in the cemetery of the church.

The convent is connected with the church by a spacious corridor. It is a gigantic structure, built entirely of stone, with massive walls, and four hundred feet in length. The entrance is under a noble portico, with high stone pillars, from which ascends a broad stone staircase to a spacious corridor twenty feet wide. This corridor runs through the whole length of the building, with a stone pavement, and is lighted in two places by a dome. On each side are cloisters, once occupied by a numerous body of Franciscan friars. The first two and principal of these cloisters on the left are occupied by the cura, and were our home. Another is occupied by one of his ministros, and in the fourth was an old Indian making cigars. The rest on this side are unoccupied, and on the right, facing the great garden of the convent, all the cloisters are untenanted, dismantled, and desolate; the doors and windows are broken, and grass and weeds are growing out of the floors. The garden had once been in harmony with the grandeur and style of the convent, and now shares its fortunes. Its wells and fountains, parterres and beds of flowers, are all there, but neglected and running to waste, weeds, oranges, and lemons growing wildly together, and our horses were turned into it loose, as into a pasture.

Associated in my mind with this ruined convent, so as almost to form part of the building, is our host, the pride and love of the village, the cura Carillo. He was past forty, tall and thin, with an open, animated, and intelligent countenance, manly, and at the same time mild, and belonged to the once powerful order of Franciscan friars, now reduced in this region to himself and a few companions. After the destruction of the convent at Merida, and the scattering of the friars, his friends procured for him the necessary papers to enable him to secularize, but he would not abandon the brotherhood in its waning fortunes, and still wore the long blue gown, the cord, and cross of the Franciscan monks. By the regulations of his order, all the receipts of his curacy belonged to the brotherhood, deducting only forty dollars per month for himself. With this pittance, he could live and extend hospitality to strangers. His friends urged him to secularize, engaging to procure for him a better curacy, but he steadily refused; he never expected to be rich, and did not wish to be; he had enough for his wants, and did not desire more. He was content with his village and with the people; he was the friend of everybody, and everybody was his friend; in short, for a man not indolent, but, on the contrary, unusually active both in mind and body, he was, without affectation or parade, more entirely contented with his lot than any man I ever knew. The quiet and seclusion of his village did not afford sufficient employment for his active mind, but, fortunately for science and for me, and strangely enough as it was considered, he had turned his attention to the antiquities of the country. He could neither go far from home, nor be absent long, but he had visited every place within his reach, and was literally an enthusiast in the pursuit. His friends smiled at this folly, but, in consideration of his many good qualities, excused it. There was no man in the country whom we were so well pleased to meet, and as it was a rare thing for him to associate with persons who took the slightest interest in his hobby, he mourned that he could not throw up all his business and accompany us in our exploration of the ruins.

It is worthy of remark, that even to a man so alive to all subjects of antiquarian interest, the history of the building of this convent is entirely unknown. In the pavement of the great corridor, in the galleries, walls, and roof, both of the church and convent, are stones from ancient buildings, and no doubt both were constructed with materials furnished by the ruined edifices of another race, but when, or how, or under what circumstances, is unknown. On the roof the cura had discovered, in a situation which would hardly have attracted any eyes but his own, a square stone, having roughly engraved on it this inscription:

26
Marzo,
1625.

Perhaps this had reference to the date of the construction, and if so, it is the only known record that exists in relation to it; and the thought almost unavoidably occurs, that where such obscurity exists in regard to a building constructed by the Spaniards but little more than two hundred years ago, how much darker must be the cloud that hangs over the ruined cities of the aborigines, erected, if not ruined, before the conquest.

During the first days of my convalescence I had a quiet and almost mournful interest in wandering about this venerable convent. I passed, too, some interesting hours in looking over the archives. The books had a time-worn aspect, with parchment covers, tattered and worm-eaten. In some places the ink had faded, and the writing was illegible. They were the records of the early monks, written by their own hands, and contained a register of baptisms and marriages, including, perhaps, the first Indian who assented to these Christian rites. It was my hope to find in these archives some notice, however slight, of the circumstances under which the early fathers set up the standard of the cross in this Indian town, but the first book has no preamble or introduction of any kind, commencing abruptly with the entry of a marriage.

This entry bears date in 1588, but forty or fifty years after the Spaniards established themselves in Merida. This is thirty-eight years anterior to the date on the stone before referred to, but it is reasonable to suppose that the convent was not built until some time after the beginning of the archives. The monks doubtless commenced keeping a register of baptisms and marriages as soon as there were any to record, but as they were distinguished for policy and prudence as well as zeal, it is not likely that they undertook the erection of this gigantic building until they had been settled in the country long enough to understand thoroughly its population and resources, for these buildings had not only to be erected, but to be kept up, and their ministers supported by the resources of the district. Besides, the great churches and convents found in all parts of Spanish America were not built by means of funds sent from Spain, but by the labour of the Indians themselves, after they were completely subdued and compelled to work for the Spaniards, or, more generally, after they had embraced Christianity, when they voluntarily erected buildings for the new worship and its ministers. It is not probable that either of these events occurred in this interior village so early as 1588.

These first entries are of the marriage, or rather marriages, of two widowers and two widows—X. Diego Chuc with Maria Hu, and Zpo-Bot with Cata Keul. In running over the archives, it appeared, I found, that there was in those days an unusual number of widowers and widows disposed to marry again, and, in fact, that the business of this kind was in a great measure confined to them; but probably, as the relation of husband and wife was not very clearly defined among the Indians, these candidates for Christian matrimony had only parted from former companions, and, through the charity or modesty of the monks, were called widowers and widows.

172

The first baptisms are on the twentieth of November, 1594, when considerable business seems to have been done. There are four entries on that day, and, in looking over the pages, from my acquaintance with the family I was struck with the name of Mel Chi, probably an ancestor of our Chaipa Chi. This Mel seems to have been one of the pillars of the padres, and a standing godfather for Indian babies.

There was no instruction to be derived from these archives, but the handwriting of the monks, and the marks of the Indians, seemed almost to make me a participator in the wild and romantic scenes of the conquest; at all events, they were proof that, forty or fifty years after the conquest, the Indians were abandoning their ancient usages and customs, adopting the rites and ceremonies of the Catholic Church, and having their children baptized with Spanish names.

CHAPTER XIII

Another ruined City.—Relics.—Ruins of San Francisco.—Proved to be those of the Aboriginal City of the name Ticul.—A beautiful Vase.—Search for a Sepulchre.—Discovery of a Skeleton and Vase.—An Indian Needle.—These Cities not built by Descendants of Egyptians.—Their Antiquity not very great.—Examination of the Skeleton by Doctor Morton, and his Opinion.—Mummies from Peru.—These Cities built by the Ancestors of the present Race of Indians.—The Seybo Tree.—The Campo Santo.—A quiet Village.

It was fortunate for the particular objects of our expedition that, go where we would in this country, the monuments of its ancient inhabitants were before our eyes. Near the village of Ticul, almost in the suburbs, are the ruins of another ancient and unknown city. From the time of our arrival the memorials of it had been staring us in the face. The cura had some sculptured stones of new and exceedingly pretty design; and heads, vases, and other relics, found in excavating the ruins, were fixed in the fronts of houses as ornaments. My first stroll with the cura was to these ruins.

At the end of a long street leading out beyond the campo santo we turned to the right by a narrow path, overgrown with bushes covered with wild flowers, and on which birds of beautiful plumage were sitting, but so infested with garrapatas that we had to keep brushing them off continually with the bough of a tree.

This path led us to the hacienda of San Francisco, the property of a gentleman of the village, who had reared the walls of a large building, but had never finished it. There were fine shade trees, and the appearance of the place was rural and picturesque, but it was unhealthy. The deep green foliage was impregnated with the seeds of death. The proprietor never visited it except in the daytime, and the Indians who worked on the milpas returned to the village at night.

A short distance in the rear of the hacienda were the ruins

of another city, desolate and overgrown, having no name except that of the hacienda on which they stand. At this time a great part of the city was completely hidden by the thick foliage of the trees. Near by, however, several mounds were in full sight, dilapidated, and having fragments of walls on the top. We ascended the highest, which commanded a magnificent view of the great wooded plain, and at a distance the towers of the church of Ticul rising darkly above. The cura told me that in the dry season, when the trees were bare of foliage, he had counted from this point thirty-six mounds, every one of which had once held aloft a building or temple, and not one now remained entire. In the great waste of ruins it was impossible to form any idea of what the place had been, except from its vastness and the specimens of sculptured stone seen in the village, but beyond doubt it was of the same character as Uxmal, and erected by the same people. Its vicinity to the village had made its destruction more complete. For generations it had served as a mere quarry to furnish the inhabitants with building-stone. The present proprietor was then excavating and selling, and he lamented to me that the piedra labrada, or worked stone, was nearly exhausted, and his profit from this source cut off.

A few words toward identifying these ruins. The plan for reducing Yucatan was to send a small number of Spaniards, who were called *vecinos* (the name still used to designate the white population), into the Indian towns and villages where it was thought advisable to make settlements. We have clear and authentic accounts of the existence of a large Indian town called Ticul, certainly in the same neighbourhood where the Spanish village of that name now stands. It must have been either on the site now occupied by the latter, or on that occupied by the ruins of San Francisco. Supposing the first supposition to be correct, not a single vestige of the Indian city remains. Now it is incontestible that the Spaniards found in the Indian towns of Yucatan, mounds, temples, and other large buildings of stone. If those on the hacienda of San Francisco are of older date, and the work of races who have passed away, as vast remains of them still exist, though subject to the same destroying causes, why has every trace of the stone buildings in the Indian city disappeared?

And it appears in every page of the history of the Spanish conquest, that the Spaniards never attempted to occupy the houses and villages of the Indians as they stood. Their habits of life were inconsistent with such occupation, and, besides, their policy was to desolate and destroy them, and build up others after their own style and manner. It is not likely that at the early epoch at which they are known to have gone to Ticul, with their small numbers, they would have undertaken to demolish the whole Indian town, and build their own upon its ruins. The probability is, that they planted their own village on the border, and erected their church as an antagonist and rival to the heathen temples; the monks, with all the imposing ceremonies of the Catholic Church, battled with the Indian priests; and, gradually overthrowing the power of the caciques, or putting them to death, they depopulated the old town, and drew the Indians to their own village. It is my belief that the ruins on the hacienda of San Francisco are those of the aboriginal city of Ticul.

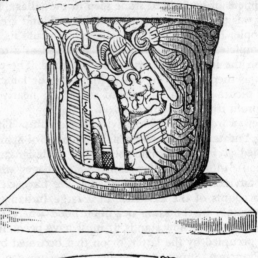

FIG. 12.   Front and back of Ticul vase.

From the great destruction of the buildings, I thought it unprofitable to attempt any exploration of these ruins, especially considering the insalubrity of the place and our own crippled state. In the excavations constantly going on, objects of interest were from time to time discovered, one of which, a vase, was fortunately only loaned to us to make a drawing of, or it would have shared the fate of the others, and been burned up by *that* fire. Figure 12 represents two sides of the vase; on one side is a border of hieroglyphics, with sunken lines running to the bottom, and on the other the reader will observe that the face portrayed bears a strong resemblance to those of the sculptured and stuccoed figures at Palenque: the headdress, too, is a plume of feathers, and the hand is held out in the same stiff position. The vase is four and a half inches high, and five inches in diameter. It is of admirable workmanship, and realizes the account given by Herrera of the markets at the Mexican city of Tlascala. "There were goldsmiths, feather-men, barbers, baths, and *as good earthenware as in Spain.*"

It was not yet considered safe for me to return to Uxmal, and the sight of these vases induced me to devote a few days to excavating among the ruins. The cura took upon himself the whole burden of making arrangements, and early in the morning we were on the ground with Indians. Amid the great waste of ruins it was difficult to know what to do or where to begin. In Egypt, the labours of discoverers have given some light to subsequent explorers, but here all was dark. My great desire was to discover an ancient sepulchre, which we had sought in vain among the ruins of Uxmal. These were not to be looked for in the large mounds, or, at all events, it was a work of too much labour to attempt opening one of them. At length, after a careful examination, the cura selected one, upon which we began.

It was a square stone structure, with sides four feet high, and the top was rounded over with earth and stones bedded in it. It stood in a small milpa, or corn-field, midway between two high mounds, which had evidently been important structures, and from its position seemed to have some direct connexion with them. Unlike most of the ruined structures around, it was entire, with every stone in its place, and probably had not been disturbed since the earth and stones had been packed down on the top.

The Indians commenced picking out the stones and clearing away the earth with their hands. Fortunately, they had a crowbar, an instrument unknown in Central America, but indispensable here on account of the stony nature of the soil, and for the first and only time in the country I had no trouble in superintending the work. The cura gave them directions in their own language, and under his eye they worked actively.

177

Nevertheless, the process was unavoidably slow. In digging down, they found the inner side of the outer wall, and the whole interior was loose earth and stones, with some layers of large flat stones, the whole very rough. In the mean time the sun was beating upon us with prodigious force, and some of the people of the village, among others the proprietor of the hacienda, came down to look on and have an inward smile at our folly. The cura had read a Spanish translation of the Antiquary, and said that we were surrounded by Edie Ochiltrees, though he himself, with his tall, thin figure and long gown, presented a lively image of that renowned mendicant. We continued the work six hours, and the whole appearance of things was so rude that we began to despair of success, when, on prying up a large flat stone, we saw underneath a skull. The reader may imagine our satisfaction. We made the Indians throw away crowbar and machete, and work with their hands. I was exceedingly anxious to get the skeleton out entire, but it was impossible to do so. It had no covering or envelope of any kind; the earth was thrown upon it as in a common grave, and as this was removed it all fell to pieces. It was in a sitting posture, with its face toward the setting sun. The knees were bent against the stomach, the arms doubled from the elbow, and the hands clasping the neck or supporting the head. The skull was unfortunately broken, but the facial bone was entire, with the jaws and teeth, and the enamel on the latter still bright, but when the skull was handed up many of them fell out. The Indians picked up every bone and tooth, and handed them to me. It was strangely interesting, with the ruined structures towering above us, after a lapse of unknown ages, to bring to light these buried bones. Whose were they? The Indians were excited, and conversed in low tones. The cura interpreted what they said; and the burden of it was, "They are the bones of our kinsman," and "What will our kinsman say at our dragging forth his bones?" But for the cura they would have covered them up and left the sepulchre.

In collecting the bones, one of the Indians picked up a small white object, which would have escaped any but an Indian's eye. It was made of deer's horn, about two inches long, sharp at the point, with an eye at the other end. They all called it a needle, and the reason of their immediate and unhesitating opinion was the fact that the Indians of the present day use needles of the same material, two of which the cura procured for me on our return to the convent. One of the Indians, who had acquired some confidence by gossiping with the cura, jocosely said that the skeleton was either that of a woman or a tailor.

The position of this skeleton was not in the centre of the sepulchre, but on one side, and on the other side of it was a very large rough stone or rock firmly imbedded in the earth, which it would have taken a long time to excavate with our instruments. In digging round it and on the other side, at some little distance from the skeleton we found a large vase of rude pottery, resembling very much the cantaro used by the Indians now as a water-jar. It had a rough flat stone lying over the mouth, so as to exclude the earth, on removing which we found, to our great disappointment, that it was entirely empty, except some little hard black flakes, which were thrown out and buried before the vase was taken up. It had a small hole worn in one side of the bottom, through which liquid or pulverized substances could have escaped. It may have contained water or the heart of the skeleton. This vase was got out entire, and is now ashes.

One idea presented itself to my mind with more force than it had ever possessed before, and that was the utter impossibility of ascribing these ruins to Egyptian builders. The magnificent tombs of the kings at Thebes rose up before me. It was on their tombs that the Egyptians lavished their skill, industry, and wealth, and no people, brought up in Egyptian schools, descended from Egyptians, or deriving their lessons from them, would ever have constructed in so conspicuous a place so rude a sepulchre. Besides this, the fact of finding these bones in so good a state of preservation, at a distance of only three or four feet from the surface of the earth, completely destroys all idea of the extreme antiquity of these buildings; and again there was the universal and unhesitating exclamation of the Indians, "They are the bones of our kinsman."

But whosesoever they were, little did the pious friends who placed them there ever imagine the fate to which they were destined. I had them carried to the convent, thence to Uxmal, and thence I bore them away forever from the bones of their kindred. In their rough journeys on the backs of mules and Indians they were so crumbled and broken that in a court of law their ancient proprietor would not be able to identify them, and they left me one night in a pocket-handkerchief to be carried to Doctor S. G. Morton of Philadelphia.

Known by the research he has bestowed upon the physical features of the aboriginal American races, and particularly by his late work entitled "Crania Americana," which is acknowledged, in the annual address of the president of the Royal Geographical Society of London, as "a welcome offering to the lovers of comparative physiology," this gentleman, in a communication on that subject, for which I here acknowledge my obligations, says that this skeleton, dilapidated as it is, has afforded him some valuable facts, and has been a subject of some interesting reflections.

The purport of his opinion is as follows: In the first place, the needle did not deceive the Indian who picked it up in the grave. The bones are those of a female. Her height did not exceed five feet three or four inches. The teeth are perfect, and not appreciably worn, while the *epiphyses*, those infallible indications of the growing state, have just become consolidated, and mark the completion of adult age.

The bones of the hands and feet are remarkably small and delicately proportioned, which observation applies also to the entire skeleton. The skull was crushed into many pieces, but, by a cautious manipulation, Doctor Morton succeeded in reconstructing the posterior and lateral portions. The occiput is remarkably flat and vertical, while the lateral or parietal diameter measures no less than five inches and eight tenths.

A chemical examination of some fragments of the bones proves them to be almost destitute of animal matter, which, in the perfect osseous structure, constitutes about thirty-three parts in the hundred.

On the upper part of the left tibia there is a swelling of the bone, called, in surgical language, a *node*, an inch and a half in length, and more than half an inch above the natural surface. This morbid condition may have resulted from a variety of causes, but possesses greater interest on account of its extreme infrequency among the primitive Indian population of the country.

On a late visit to Boston I had the satisfaction of examining a small and extremely interesting collection of mummied bodies in the possession of Mr. John H. Blake, of that city, dug up by himself from an ancient cemetery in Peru. This cemetery lies on the shore of the Bay of Chacota, near Arica, in latitude 18° 20′ south. It covers a large tract of ground. The graves are all of a circular form, from two to four feet in diameter, and from four to five feet deep. In one of them Mr. Blake found the mummies of a man, a woman, a child twelve or fourteen years old, and an infant. They were all closely wrapped in woollen garments of various colours and degrees of fineness, secured by needles of thorn thrust through the cloth. The skeletons are saturated with some bituminous substance, and are all in a remarkable state of preservation. The woollen cloths, too, are well preserved, which no doubt is accounted for, in a great degree, by the extreme dryness of the soil and atmosphere of that part of Peru.

Mr. Blake visited many other cemeteries between the Andes and the Pacific Ocean as far south as Chili, all of which possess the same general features with those found in the elevated valleys of the Peruvian Andes. No record or tradition exists in regard to these cemeteries, but woollen cloths similar to those found by Mr. Blake are woven at this day, and probably in the same manner, by the Indians of Peru; and in the eastern part of Bolivia, to the southward of the place where these mummies were discovered, he found, on the most barren portion of the Desert of Atacama, a few Indians, who, probably from the difficulty of access to their place of abode, have been less influenced by the Spaniards, and for this reason retain more of their primitive customs, and their dress at this day resembles closely that which envelops the bodies in his possession, both in the texture and the form.

Doctor Morton says that these mummies from Peru have the same peculiarities in the form of the skull, the same delicacy of the bones, and the same remarkable smallness of the hands and feet, with that found in the sepulchre at San Francisco. He says, too, from an examination of nearly four hundred skulls of individuals belonging to older nations of Mexico and Peru, and of skulls dug from the mounds of our western country, that he finds them all formed on the same model, and conforming in a remarkable manner to that brought from San Francisco; and that this cranium has the same *type* of physical conformation which has been bestowed with amazing uniformity upon all the tribes on our continent, from Canada to Patagonia, and from the Atlantic to the Pacific Ocean. He adds, that it affords additional support to the opinion which he has always entertained, that, notwithstanding some slight variation in physical conformation, and others of a much more remarkable character in intellectual attainments, all the aboriginal Americans of all known epochs belong to the same great and distinctive race.

If this opinion is correct, and I believe it—if this skeleton does present the same *type* of physical conformation with all the tribes of our continent—then, indeed, do these crumbling bones declare, as with a voice from the grave, that we cannot go back to any ancient nation of the Old World for the builders of these cities; they are not the works of people who have passed away, and whose history is lost, but of the same great *race* which, changed, miserable, and degraded, still clings around their ruins.

To return to the ruins of San Francisco. We devoted two days more to excavating, but did not make any farther discoveries.

Among the ruins were circular holes in the ground like those at Uxmal. The mouth of one was broken and enlarged, and I descended by a ladder into a dome-shaped chamber, precisely the same as at Uxmal, but a little larger. At Uxmal the character of these was mere matter of conjecture; but at this short distance, the Indians had specific notions in regard to their objects and uses, and called them chultunes, or wells. In all directions, too, were seen the oblong stones hollowed out like troughs, which at Uxmal were called pilas, or fountains, but here the Indians called them hólcas or piedras de molir, stones for grinding, which they said were used by the ancients to mash corn upon; and the proprietor showed us a round stone like a bread roller, which they called kabtum, brazo de piedra, or arm of stone, used, as they said, for mashing the corn. The different names they assigned in different places to the same thing, and the different uses ascribed to it, show, with many other facts, the utter absence of all traditionary knowledge among the Indians; and this is perhaps the greatest difficulty we have to encounter in ascribing to their ancestors the building of these cities.

The last day we returned from the ruins earlier than usual, and stopped at the campo santo. In front stood a noble seybo tree. I had been anxious to learn something of the growth of this tree, but had never had an opportunity of doing it before. The cura told me that it was then twenty-three years old. There could be no doubt or mistake on this point. Its age was as well known as his own, or that of any other person in the village. Figure 13 represents this tree. The trunk at the distance of five feet from the ground measured 17½ feet in circumference, and its great branches afforded on all sides a magnificent shade. We had found trees like it growing on the tops of the ruined structures at Copan and Palenque, and many had for that reason ascribed to the buildings a very great antiquity. This tree completely removed all doubts which I might have entertained, and confirmed me in the opinion I had before expressed, that no correct judgment could be formed of the anti-

Fig. 13. Seybo Tree.

quity of these buildings from the size of the trees growing upon them. Remarkable as I considered this tree at that time, I afterward saw larger ones, in more favourable situations, not so old.

The campo santo was enclosed by a high stone wall. The interior had some degree of plan and arrangement, and in some places were tombs, built above ground, belonging to families in the village, hung with withered wreaths and votive offerings. The population tributary to it was about five thousand; it had been opened but five years, and already it presented a ghastly spectacle. There were many new-made graves, and on several of the vaults were a skull and small collection of bones in a box or tied up in a napkin, being the remains of one buried within and taken out to make room for another corpse. On one of them were the skull and bones of a lady of the village, in a basket; an old acquaintance of the cura, who had died within two years. Among the bones was a pair of white satin shoes, which she had perhaps worn in the dance, and with which on her feet she had been buried.

At one corner of the cemetery was a walled enclosure, about

183

twenty feet high and thirty square, within which was the charnel-house of the cemetery. A flight of stone steps led to the top of the wall, and on the platform of the steps and along the wall were skulls and bones, some in boxes and baskets, and some tied up in cotton cloths, soon to be thrown upon the common pile, but as yet having labels with the names written on them, to make known yet a little while longer the individuals to whom they had once belonged. Within the enclosure the earth was covered several feet deep with the promiscuous and undistinguishable bones of rich and poor, high and low, men, women, and children, Spaniards, Mestizoes, and Indians, all mingled together as they happened to fall. Among them were fragments of bright-coloured dresses, and the long hair of women still clinging to the skull. Of all the sad mementoes declaring the end to which all that is bright and beautiful in this world is doomed, none ever touched me so affectingly as this—the ornament and crowning charm of woman, the peculiar subject of her taste and daily care, loose, dishevelled, and twining among dry and mouldering bones.

We left the campo santo, and walked up the long street of the village, the quiet, contented character of the people impressing itself more strongly than ever upon my mind. The Indians were sitting in the yards, shrouded by cocoanut and orange trees, weaving hammocks and platting palm leaves for hats; the children were playing naked in the road, and the Mestiza women were sitting in the doorways sewing. The news of our digging up the bones had created a sensation. All wanted to know what the day's work had produced, and all rose up as the cura passed; the Indians came to kiss his hand, and, as he remarked, except when the crop of maize was short, all were happy. In a place of such bustle and confusion as our own city, it is impossible to imagine the quiet of this village.

CHAPTER XIV

The next day was Sunday, which I passed in making preparations for returning to Uxmal. I had, however, some distraction. In the morning the quiet of the village was a little disturbed by intelligence of a revolution in Tekax, a town nine leagues distant. Our sojourn in the country had been so quiet that it seemed unnatural, and a small revolution was necessary to make me feel at home. The insurgents had deposed the alcalde, appointed their own authorities, and laid contributions upon the inhabitants, and the news was that they intended marching three hundred men against Merida, to extort an acknowledgment of independence. Ticul lay in their line of march, but as it was considered very uncertain whether they would carry this doughty purpose into execution, I determined not to change my plan.

Doctor Cabot's presence in the village was, of course, generally known, and though it was rather prejudicial to his reputation as a medical man to be ill himself, he did not fail to have patients. His fame as a curer of biscos had reached this place, but, fortunately for his quiet, there was only one squinter among the inhabitants, though his was violent enough for a whole village. In the afternoon this man applied for relief. Doctor Cabot told him that his hand was not yet steady enough to perform the operation, and that I was going away the next day; but this by no means satisfied him. It happened, however, that a gentleman present, who was consulting the doctor on some ailment of his own, mentioned incidentally that one of the doctor's patients at Merida had lost the eye, though he added that the loss was not ascribed to the operation, but to subsequent bad treatment. This story, as we afterward learned, was entirely without foundation, but it had its effect upon the bisco, who rolled his eye toward the door so violently that the rest of him followed, and he never came near the doctor again. His only operation that day was upon the wife of the proprietor of San Francisco, whose head he laid open, and took out a hideous wen.

I have mentioned the extraordinary stillness of this place. Every night, however, since my arrival, this stillness had been broken by the canting, singing tones of a boy calling out the numbers of the loteria. Preparations were making for a village fête in February; the ground was already marked out in front of the convent for the Plaza de Toros, and the loteria was adopted as the means of raising money to pay the expenses. I had not yet attended, and on the last night of my stay in Ticul I determined to go. It was held in the corridor of the audiencia, along which hung branches of palm leaves to protect the lights. It was Sunday evening, and, consequently, the attendance was more numerous than usual. At the entrance sat the boy, whose voice is even now ringing in my ears, rattling a bag of balls, drawing them out, and calling off the numbers. Along the corridor was a rough table with a row of candles in the centre, and benches on each side were occupied by the villagers, without distinction of persons, with papers and grains of corn before them, the same as at Merida. The largest sum called off was twenty-nine reals. One real was deducted from every dollar for the particular object of the lottery, and the fund which the boy had obtained by such a potent use of his voice then amounted to sixty-three dollars. There were several performers giving out somewhat equivocal music, without which nothing in that country could go on long, and occasionally two reals were drawn from the purse for them. All entered who pleased. There was no regulation of dress or etiquette, but much quiet courtesy of manner, and it was regarded a mere converzatione, or place for passing the evening. I remained about an hour. As we crossed the plaza, the moon lighted up the venerable front of the convent, and for the last time I slept within its walls.

The next morning I bade farewell to the cura, with an

understanding, that as soon as Doctor Cabot was able to return, the good padre would accompany him to finish his interrupted visit to us at Uxmal. My time at Ticul had not been lost. Besides exploring the ruins of San Francisco, I had received accounts of others from the cura, which promised to add greatly to the interest of our expedition.

That I might take a passing view of one of these places on my return to Uxmal, I determined to go back by a different road, across the sierra, which rises a short distance from the village of Ticul. The ascent was steep, broken, and stony. The whole range was a mass of limestone rock, with a few stunted trees, but not enough to afford shade, and white under the reflection of the sun. In an hour I reached the top of the sierra, Looking back, my last view of the plain presented, high above everything else, the church and convent which I had left. I was an hour crossing the sierra, and on the other side my first view of the great plain took in the church of Nohcacab, standing like a colossus in the wilderness, the only token to indicate the presence of man. Descending to the plain, I saw nothing but trees, until, when close upon the village, the great church again rose before me, towering above the houses, and the only object visible.

The village was under the pastoral charge of the cura of Ticul, and in the suburbs I met his ministro on horseback, waiting, according to the directions of the former, to escort me to the ruins of Nohpat. At a league's distance we turned off from the main road, and, following a narrow path leading to some milpas, in fifteen minutes we saw towering before us lofty but shattered buildings, the relics of another ruined city. I saw at a glance that it would be indispensable for Mr. Catherwood to visit them. Nevertheless, I passed three hours on the ground, toiling in the hot sun, and at four o'clock, with strong apprehensions of another attack of fever, I mounted to continue my journey.

A little before dark I emerged from the woods, and saw Mr. Catherwood standing on the platform of the Casa del Gobernador, the sole tenant of the ruins of Uxmal. His Indians had finished their day's work, Bernaldo and Chaipa Chi had gone, and since Doctor Cabot left he had slept alone in our quarters. He had a feeling of security from the tranquil state of the country, the harmless character of the Indians, their superstitions in regard to the ruins, and a spring pistol with a cord across the door, which could not fail to bring down any one who might attempt to enter at night.

It had happened most fortunately for our operations that Mr. Catherwood had held out. Without any resources or anything to occupy him except work, he had accomplished an enormous deal, and from being so much better provided with the comforts of living than at any former time while exploring ruins, he had continued in good health and spirits.

At dark the Indian arrived with my luggage, sweating at every pore, having carried it twenty-one miles, for which I paid him three shillings and sixpence. As he was going away we gave him a roll of bread, and he asked by signs if he was to carry it to the cura. Being made to comprehend that he was to eat it himself, he sat down and commenced immediately, having probably never eaten so much bread before in his life. We then gave him half a cup of Habanero, some plantains and a cigar, and, as the dew was heavy, told him to sit by the fire. When he had finished these we repeated the portion, and he seemed hardly to believe his good fortune real, but he had an idea that he was well off, and either from being a stranger, and free from the apprehensions felt by the Indians at Uxmal, or else from a fancy he had taken to us, he asked for a costal, a piece of hemp bagging, to sleep upon. We gave him one, and he lay down by the fire; for a while he endeavoured to protect his naked body against the moschetoes, and kept up a continued slapping, lighter or heavier according to the aggravation, changed his position, and tried the back corridor, but it was all in vain; and, finally, with a sad attempt at a smile, he asked for another drink of Habanero and a cigar, and went away.

On the twenty-fourth of December Doctor Cabot returned from Ticul, bringing back with him Albino, who was still in a rueful plight. Unfortunately, the cura Carillo was unwell, and unable to accompany him, but had promised to follow in a few days. On Christmas eve we were all once more together, and Christmas Day, in spite of ourselves, was a holyday. No Indians came out to work. Chaipa Chi, who had moved regularly as the sun, for the first time failed. We had, however, as visiters, a number of women from the village of Moona. From the top of the House of the Dwarf we saw them moving toward that of the Nuns, and went down to receive them. The only males who accompanied them were a lad about fourteen attending his newly-married wife, and the husband of the woman I had seen buried, who either had not the spirit for joining in the festivities at the hacienda, or was putting himself in the way of repairing his loss.

Unable to do anything at the ruins, I walked down to the hacienda to see one of our horses which had a sore back. The hacienda was deserted, but the sound of violins led me to the place where the Indians were congregated. Preparations were making on a large scale for the evening feast. The place looked like a butcher's shambles, for they had cut up what had once composed eight turkeys, two hogs, and I do not know how many fowls. The women were all busy; Chaipa Chi was lady-patroness, and up to her elbows in tortillas.

I walked on to the campo santo, for the purpose of carrying away two skulls which I had selected and laid aside on the charnel pile at the time of the funeral. I had taken some precautions, for the news of the carrying off the bones from San Francisco had created some excitement among the Indians all over the country; and as I had to pass a long row of huts, I had procured two calabazas, or gourds, for drinking cups, which I carried in a pocket-handkerchief, and intended to throw away in the grave-yard, and substitute the skulls. On reaching the pile, however, I found that other hands had been upon it. The skulls I had selected had been displaced and mingled with the others, so that I could not identify them. I examined the whole heap, but could recognise only the huge skull of an African and that of the woman I had seen dug up. The latter was the skull of a full-blooded Indian, but it had been damaged by the crowbar; besides, I had seen all her bones and her very flesh taken piece-meal out of the grave; I had heard so much of her that she seemed an acquaintance, and I had some qualms of conscience about carrying her skull away. In fact, alone in the stillness and silence of the place, something of a superstitious feeling came over me about disturbing the bones of the dead and robbing a graveyard. I should nevertheless, perhaps, have taken up two skulls at random, but, to increase my wavering feeling, I saw two Indian women peeping at me through the trees, and, not wishing to run the risk of creating a disturbance on the hacienda, I left the graveyard with empty hands. The mayoral afterward told me that it was fortunate I had done so, for that if I had carried any away, it would have caused an excitement among the Indians, and perhaps led to mishchief.

The account of our residence at Uxmal is now drawing to a close, and it is time to bring before the reader the remainder of the ruins; but before doing so I shall make one remark in regard to the work of Mr. Waldeck, which was published in folio at Paris in 1835, and, except my own hurried notice, is the only account that has ever been published of the ruins at Uxmal. I had this work with me on our last visit. It will be found that our plans and drawings differ materially from his, but Mr. Waldeck was not an architectural draughtsman, and he complains that his drawings were taken from him by the Mexican government. I differ from him, too, in the statement of some facts, and almost entirely in opinions and conclusions; but these things occur of course, and the next person who visits these ruins will perhaps differ in many respects from both of us. It is proper to say, moreover, that Mr. Waldeck had much greater difficulties to encounter than we, for at the time of his visit the ground had not been cleared for a milpa, and the whole field was overgrown with trees; besides, he is justly entitled to the full credit of being the first stranger who visited these ruins, and brought them to the notice of the public.

To return. I have already mentioned the Casa del Gobernador and the Casa de las Tortugas, or House of the Turtles, the latter of which stands on the grand platform of the second terrace of the Casa del Gobernador, at the northwest corner.

Descending from this building, and on a line with the doorway of the Casa de las Monjas, going north, at the distance of two hundred and forty feet are two ruined edifices facing each other, and seventy feet apart, as laid down on the general plan of the ruins. Each is one hundred and twenty-eight feet long, and thirty feet deep, and, so far as they can be made out, they appear to have been exactly alike in plan and ornament. The sides facing each other were embellished with sculpture, and there remain on both the fragments of entwined colossal serpents, which ran the whole length of the walls.

In the centre of each façade, at points directly opposite each other, are the fragments of a great stone ring. Each of these rings was four feet in diameter, and secured in the wall by a stone tenon of corresponding dimensions. They appear to have been broken wilfully; of each, the part nearest the stem still projects from the wall, and the outer surface is covered with sculptured characters. We made excavations among the ruins along the base of the walls, in hope of discovering the missing parts of these rings, but without success.

These structures have no doorways or openings of any kind, either on the sides or at the ends. In the belief that they must have interior chambers, we made a breach in the wall of the one on the east to the depth of eight or ten feet, but we found only rough stones, hanging so loosely together as to make it dangerous for the Indians to work in the holes, and they were obliged to discontinue.

This excavation, however, carried us through nearly one third of the structure, and satisfied us that these great parallel edifices did not contain any interior apartments, but that each consisted merely of four great walls, filled up with a solid mass of stones. It was our opinion that they had been built expressly with reference to the two great rings facing each other in the façades, and that the space between was intended for the celebration of some public games, in which opinion we were afterward confirmed.

Passing between these buildings, and continuing in the same direction, we reach the front of the Casa de las Monjas, or House of the Nuns.

This building is quadrangular, with a courtyard in the centre. It stands on the highest of three terraces. The lowest is three feet high and twenty feet wide; the second, twelve feet high and forty-five feet wide; and the third, four feet high and five feet wide, extending the whole length of the front of the building.

The front is two hundred and seventy-nine feet long, and above the cornice, from one end to the other, it is ornamented with sculpture. In the centre is a gateway ten feet eight inches wide, spanned by the triangular arch, and leading to the courtyard. On each side of this gateway are four doorways with wooden lintels, opening to apartments averaging twenty-four feet long, ten feet wide, and seventeen feet high to the top of the arch, but having no communication with each other.

The building that forms the right or eastern side of the quadrangle is one hundred and fifty-eight feet long; that on the left is one hundred and seventy-three feet long, and the range opposite or at the end of the quadrangle measures two hundred and sixty-four feet.

These three ranges of buildings have no doorways outside, but the exterior of each is a dead wall, and above the cornice all are ornamented with the same rich and elaborate sculpture. On the exterior of the range last mentioned, the designs are simple, and among them are two rude, naked figures, which have been considered as indicating the existence of that same Eastern worship before referred to among the people of Uxmal.

Such is the exterior of this building. Passing through the arched gateway, we enter a noble courtyard, with four great façades looking down upon it, each ornamented from one end

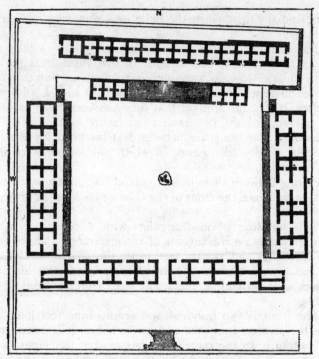

Fig. 14. Plan of the Courtyard.

to the other with the richest and most intricate carving known in the art of the builders of Uxmal; presenting a scene of strange magnificence, surpassing any that is now to be seen among its ruins. This courtyard is two hundred and fourteen feet wide, and two hundred and fifty-eight feet deep. At the time of our first entrance it was overgrown with bushes and grass, quails started up from under our feet, and, with a whirring flight, passed over the tops of the buildings. Whenever we went to it, we started flocks of these birds, and throughout the whole of our residence at Uxmal they were the only disturbers of its silence and desolation.

Among my many causes of regret for the small scale on which I am obliged to present these drawings, none is stronger than the consequent inability to present, with all their detail of ornament, the four great façades fronting this courtyard. There is but one alleviating circumstance; which is, that the side most richly ornamented is so ruined that, under any circumstances, it could not be presented entire.

This façade is on the left of the visiter entering the courtyard. It is one hundred and seventy-three feet long, and is distinguished by two colossal serpents entwined, running through and encompassing nearly all the ornaments throughout its whole length. Plates V and VI represent the only parts remaining.

Plate V exhibits that portion of the façade toward the north end of the building. The tail of one serpent is held up nearly over the head of the other, and has an ornament upon it like a turban, with a plume of feathers. The marks on the extremity of the tail are probably intended to indicate a rattlesnake, with which species of serpent the country abounds. The lower serpent has its monstrous jaws wide open, and within them is a human head, the face of which is distinctly visible on the stone, and appears faintly in the drawing. From the ruin to which all was hurrying, Don Simon cared only to preserve this serpent's head. He said that we might tear out and carry away every other ornament, but this he intended to build into the wall of a house in Merida as a memorial of Uxmal.

Plate VI represents the two entwined serpents enclosing and running through the ornaments over a doorway. The principal feature in the ornament enclosed is the figure of a human being, standing, but much mutilated. The bodies of the serpents, according to the representations of the same design in other parts of the sculpture, are covered with feathers.

Plates V and VI represent about one fifth of the whole façade; the other four fifths were enriched with the same mass of sculptured ornaments, and toward the south end the head and tail of the serpents corresponded in design and position with the portion still existing at the other. Had it been our fortune to reach this place a few years sooner, we might have seen the whole entire. Don Simon told us that in 1835 the whole front stood, and the two serpents were seen encircling every ornament in the building. In its ruins it presents a lively idea of the "large and very well constructed buildings of lime and stone" which Bernal Dias saw on landing at Campeachy, "with figures of serpents and of idols painted on the walls."

At the end of the courtyard, and fronting the gate of entrance, is the façade of a lofty building, two hundred and sixty-four feet long, standing on a terrace twenty feet high. The ascent is by a grand but ruined staircase, ninety-five feet wide, flanked on each side by a building with sculptured front, and having three doorways, each leading to apartments within.

The height of this building to the upper cornice is twenty-

Plate V

PORTION OF WESTERN BUILDING, MONJAS, UXMAL.

Plate VI

PORTION OF THE WESTERN RANGE OF BUILDING, MONJAS, UXMAL.

Plate VII

F. Catherwood

VIEW FROM LA CASA DE LAS MONJAS, UXMAL, LOOKING SOUTH.

Jordan & Halpin

five feet. It has thirteen doorways, over each of which rose a perpendicular wall ten feet wide and seventeen feet high above the cornice, making the whole height forty-two feet from the ground. These lofty structures were no doubt erected to give grandeur and effect to the building, and at a distance they appear to be turrets, but only four of them now remain. The whole great façade, including the turrets, is crowded with complicated and elaborate sculpture, among which are human figures rudely executed: two are represented as playing on musical instruments, one being not unlike a small harp, and the other in the nature of a guitar; a third is in a sitting posture, with his hands across his breast, and tied by cords, the ends of which pass over his shoulders. Of the rest there is nothing which stands out distinct and intelligible like the serpent, and the whole, loaded as it is with ornament, conveys the idea of vastness and magnificence rather than that of taste and refinement.

This building has one curious feature. It is erected over, and completely encloses, a smaller one of older date. The doorways, walls, and wooden lintels of the latter are all seen, and where the outer building is fallen, the ornamented cornice of the inner one is visible.

From the platform of the steps of this building, looking across the courtyard, a grand view presents itself, embracing all the principal buildings that now tower above the plain, except the House of the Dwarf. Plate VII represents this view. In the foreground is the inner façade of the front range of the Monjas, with a portion of the range on each side of the courtyard. To the left, in the distance, appears the Casa de la Vieja, or of the Old Woman, and, rising grandly above the front of the Monjas, are the House of the Turtles, that of the Governor, and the Casa de Palomos, or the House of the Pigeons.

The last of the four sides of the courtyard, standing on the right of the entrance, is represented in Plate VIII. It is the most entire of any, and, in fact, wants but little more than its wooden lintels, and some stones which have been picked out of the façade below the cornice, to make it perfect. It is, too, the most chaste and simple in design and ornament, and it was always refreshing to turn from the gorgeous and elaborate masses on the other façades to this curious and pleasing combination.

The ornament over the centre doorway is the most important, the most complicated and elaborate, and of that marked and peculiar style which characterizes the highest efforts of these ancient builders. The ornaments over the other doorways are

Plate VIII

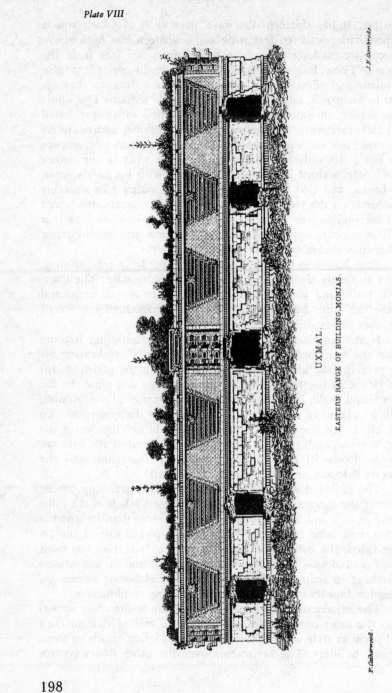

J.H. Cambralt.

UXMAL.

EASTERN RANGE OF BUILDING, MONJAS.

F. Catherwood.

less striking, more simple, and more pleasing. In all of them there is in the centre a masked face with the tongue hanging out, surmounted by an elaborate headdress; between the horizontal bars is a range of diamond-shaped ornaments, in which the remains of red paint are still distinctly visible, and at each end of these bars is a serpent's head, with the mouth wide open.

Plate IX represents the southeast corner of this building. The angle exhibits the great face before presented, with the stone curving upward at the projecting end. On each side is a succession of compartments, alternately plain, and presenting the form of diamond lattice-work. In both there is an agreeable succession of plain and ornamented, and, in fact, it would be difficult, in arranging four sides facing a courtyard, to have more variety, and at the same time more harmony of ornament. All these façades were painted; the traces of the colour are still visible, and the reader may imagine what the effect must have been when all this building was entire, and according to its supposed design, in its now desolate doorways stood noble Maya maidens, like the vestal virgins of the Romans, to cherish and keep alive the sacred fire buring in the temples.

I omit a description of the apartments opening upon this courtyard. We made plans of all of them, but they are generally much alike, except in the dimensions. The number in all is eighty-eight.

In the range last presented, however, there is one suite different from all the rest. The entrance to this suite is by the centre and principal doorway, and Plate X represents the interior. It consists of two parallel chambers, each thirty-three feet long and thirteen wide; and at each end of both chambers is a doorway communicating with other chambers nine feet long and thirteen wide. The doorways of all these are ornamented with sculpture, and they are the only ornaments found in the interior of any buildings in Uxmal. The whole suite consists of six rooms; and there is a convenience in the arrangements not unsuited to the habits of what we call civilized life; opening as they do upon this noble courtyard, in the dry season, with nothing to apprehend from vegetation and damp, they would be by far the most comfortable residence for any future explorer of the ruins of Uxmal; and every time I went to them I regretted that we could not avail ourselves of the facilities they offered.

With these few words I take leave of the Casa de las Monjas, remarking only that in the centre is the fragment of a large stone like that on the terrace of the Casa del Gobernador, called

Plate IX

Catherwood Del

Prudhomme S.

SOUTH EAST ANGLE OF MONJAS, UXMAL

Plate X

the Picote, and also that, induced by the account of Waldeck that the whole was once paved with sculptured turtles, I passed a morning digging all over the courtyard below the slight accumulation of earth, and found nothing of the kind. The substratum consisted of rude stones, no doubt once serving as a foundation for a floor of cement, which, from long exposure to the rainy seasons, has now entirely disappeared.

At the back of the last-mentioned range of the Monjas is another, or rather there are several ranges of buildings, standing lower than the House of the Nuns, in irregular order, and much ruined.

To the first portion of these we gave the name of the House of the Birds, from the circumstance of its being ornamented on

Fig. 15

the exterior with representations of feathers and birds rudely sculptured. Figure 15 represents a part of these ornaments.

The remaining portion consists of some very large rooms, among which are two fifty-three feet long, fourteen wide, and about twenty high, being the largest, or at least the widest in Uxmal. In one of them are the remains of painting well preserved, and in the other is an arch, which approaches nearer to the principle of the keystone than any we had yet met with in our whole exploration of ruins. It is very similar to the earliest arches, if they may be so called, of the Etruscans and Greeks, as seen at Arpino in the kingdom of Naples, and Tiryns in Greece. (See engravings in the Appendix.)

From this range of buildings we descend to the House of the Dwarf, also known by the name of la Casa del Adivino, or the House of the Diviner, from its overlooking the whole city, and enabling its occupant to be cognizant of all that was passing around him.

The courtyard of this building is one hundred and thirty-five feet by eighty-five. It is bounded by ranges of mounds from twenty-five to thirty feet thick, now covered with a rank growth of herbage, but which, perhaps, once formed ranges of buildings. In the centre is a large circular stone, like those seen in the other courtyards, called the Picote.

Plate XI represents the west front of this building, with the mound on which it stands. The base is so ruined and encumbered with fallen stones that it is difficult to ascertain its precise dimensions, but, according to our measurement, it is two hundred and thirty-five feet long, and one hundred and fifty-five wide. Its height is eighty-eight feet, and to the top of the building it is one hundred and five feet. Though diminishing as it rises, its shape is not exactly pyramidal, but its ends are rounded. It is encased with stone, and apparently solid from the plain.

A great part of the front presented in the engraving has fallen, and now lies a mass of ruins at the foot of the mound. Along the base, or rather about twenty feet up the mound, and probably once reached by a staircase, now ruined, is a range of curious apartments, nearly choked up with rubbish, and with the sapote beams still in their places over the door.

At the height of sixty feet is a solid projecting platform, on which stands a building loaded with ornaments more rich, elaborate, and carefully executed, than those of any other edifice in Uxmal. A great doorway opens upon the platform. The sapote

Plate XI

WEST FRONT OF THE HOUSE OF THE DWARF UXMAL.

Plate XII

beams are still in their places, and the interior is divided into two apartments; the outer one fifteen feet wide, seven feet deep, and nineteen feet high, and the inner one twelve feet wide, four feet deep, and eleven feet high. Both are entirely plain, without ornament of any kind, and have no communication with any part of the mound.

The steps or other means of communication with this building are all gone, and at the time of our visit we were at a loss to know how it had been reached; but, from what we saw afterward, we are induced to believe that a grand staircase upon a different plan from any yet met with, and supported by a triangular arch, led from the ground to the door of the building, which, if still in existence, would give extraordinary grandeur to this great mound.

The crowning structure is a long and narrow building, measuring seventy-two feet in front, and but twelve feet deep.

The front is much ruined, but even in its decay presents the most elegant and tasteful arrangement of ornaments to be seen in Uxmal, of which no idea could be given in any but a large engraving. The emblems of life and death appear on the wall in close juxta-position, confirming the belief in the existence of that worship practised by the Egyptians and all other Eastern nations, and before referred to as prevalent among the people of Uxmal.

The interior is divided into three apartments, that in the centre being twenty-four feet by seven, and those on each side nineteen feet by seven. They have no communication with each other; two have their doors opening to the east and one to the west.

A narrow platform five feet wide projects from all the four sides of the building. The northern end is decayed, and part of the eastern front, and to this front ascends a grand staircase one hundred and two feet high, seventy feet wide, and containing ninety steps.

Plate XII represents this front. The steps are very narrow, and the staircase steep; and after we had cleared away the trees, and there were no branches to assist us in climbing, the ascent and descent were difficult and dangerous. The padre Cogolludo, the historian referred to, says that he once ascended these steps, and "that when he attempted to descend he repented; his sight failed him, and he was in some danger." He adds, that in the apartments of the building, which he calls "small chapels," were the "idols," and that there they made sacrifices of men, women,

and children. Beyond doubt this lofty building was a great Teocalis, "El grande de los Kues," the great temple of idols worshipped by the people of Uxmal, consecrated by their most
mysterious rites, the holiest of their holy places. "The High
Priest had in his Hand a large, broad, and sharp Knife made of
Flint. Another Priest carried a wooden collar wrought like a
snake. The persons to be sacrificed were conducted one by one
up the Steps, stark naked, and as soon as laid on the Stone, had
the Collar put upon their Necks, and the four priests took hold
of the hands and feet. Then the high Priest with wonderful
Dexterity ripped up the Breast, tore out the Heart, reeking, with
his Hands, and showed it to the Sun, offering him the Heart and
Steam that came from it. Then he turned to the Idol, and threw
it in his face, which done, he kicked the body down the steps,
and it never stopped till it came to the bottom, because they
were *very upright;*" and "one who had been a Priest, and had
been converted, said that when they tore out the Heart of the
wretched Person sacrificed, it did beat so strongly that he took
it up from the Ground three or four times till it cooled by Degrees, and then he threw the Body, still moving, down the
Steps." In all the long catalogue of superstitious rites that
darkens the page of man's history, I cannot imagine a picture
more horribly exciting than that of the Indian priest, with his
white dress and long hair clotted with gore, performing his
murderous sacrifices at this lofty height, in full view of the
people throughout the whole extent of the city.

From the top of this mound we pass over the Casa del
Gobernador to the grand structure marked on the general plan
as the Casa de Palomos, or the House of the Pigeons, the front
of which is represented in Plate XIII. It is two hundred and
forty feet long; the front is much ruined, the apartments are
filled, and along the centre of the roof, running longitudinally,
is a range of structures built in a pyramidal form, like the fronts
of some of the old Dutch houses that still remain among us, but
grander and more massive. These are nine in number, built of
stone, about three feet thick, and have small oblong openings
through them. These openings give them somewhat the appearance of pigeon-houses, and from this the name of the building
is derived. All had once been covered with figures and ornaments in stucco, portions of which still remain. The view presented is in profile, as the full front could not be exhibited on
this scale.

In the centre of this building is an archway ten feet wide,

Plate XIII

UXMAL.
Casa de los Palomos.

which leads into a courtyard one hundred and eighty feet long and one hundred and fifty feet deep. In the centre of the courtyard, and thrown down, is the same large stone so often mentioned. On the right is a range of ruined buildings, on the left a similar range, and rising behind it the high mound represented in the frontispiece; and in front, at the end of the courtyard, is a range of ruined buildings, with another archway in the centre. Crossing the courtyard, and passing through this archway, we ascend a flight of steps, now ruined, and reach another courtyard, one hundred feet long by eighty-five deep. On each side of this courtyard, too, is a range of ruined buildings, and at the other end is a great Teocalis, two hundred feet in length, one hundred and twenty deep, and about fifty feet high. A broad staircase leads to the top, on which stands a long narrow building, one hundred feet by twenty, divided into three apartments.

There was a mournful interest about this great pile of ruins. Entering under the great archway, crossing two noble courtyards, with ruined buildings on each side, and ascending the great staircase to the building on the top, gave a stronger impression of departed greatness than anything else in this desolate city. It commanded a view of every other building, and stood apart in lonely grandeur, seldom disturbed by human footsteps. On going up to it once Mr. Catherwood started a deer, and at another time a wild hog.

At the northeast angle of this building is a vast range of high, ruined terraces, facing east and west, nearly eight hundred feet long at the base, and called the Campo Santo. On one of these is a building of two stories, with some remains of sculpture, and in a deep and overgrown valley at the foot, the Indians say, was the burial-place of this ancient city; but, though searching for it ourselves, and offering a reward to them for the discovery, we never found in it a sepulchre.

Besides these there was the Casa de la Vieja, or the House of the Old Woman, standing in ruins. Once, when the wind was high, I saw the remains of the front wall bending before its force. It is four or five hundred feet from the Casa del Gobernador, and has its name from a mutilated statue of an old woman lying before it.

Near by are other monuments lying on the ground, overgrown and half buried (referred to in the Appendix), which were pointed out to us by the Indians on our first visit. North of this there is a circular mound of ruins, probably of a circular building like that of Mayapan. A wall which was said to encompass the city is laid down on the plan so far as it can be traced; and beyond this, for a great distance in every direction, the ground is strewed with ruins; but with this brief description I close. I might extend it indefinitely, but I have compressed it within the smallest possible limits. We made plans of every building and drawings of every sculptured stone, and this place alone might furnish materials for larger volumes than these; but I have so many and such vast remains to present that I am obliged to avoid details as much as possible. These it is my hope at some future day to present with a minuteness that shall satisfy the most craving antiquary, but I trust that what I have done will give the reader some definite idea of the ruins of Uxmal. Perhaps, as we did, he will imagine the scene that must have been presented when all these buildings were entire, occupied by people in costumes strange and fanciful as the ornaments on their buildings, and possessing all those minor arts which must have been coexistent with architecture and sculpture, and which the imperishable stone has survived.

The historic light which beamed upon us at Merida and Mayapan does not reach this place; it is not mentioned in any record of the conquest. The cloud again gathers, but even through it a star appears.

The padre Cogolludo says, that on the memorable occasion when his sight failed as he was going down the steps of the great Teocalis, he found in one of the apartments, or, as he calls it, one of the chapels, offerings of cacao and marks of copal, used by the Indians as incense, *burned there but a short time before;* an evidence, he says, *of some superstition or idolatry recently committed by the Indians of that place*. He piously adds, "God help those poor Indians, for the devil deceives them very easily."

While in Merida I procured from Don Simon Peon the title papers to this estate. They were truly a formidable pile, compared with which the papers in a protracted chancery or ejectment suit would seem a billet-doux, and, unfortunately, a great portion of them was in the Maya language; but there was one folio volume in Spanish, and in this was the first formal conveyance ever made of these lands by the Spanish government. It bears date the twelfth day of May, 1673, and is entitled a testimonial of royal favour made to the Regidor Don Lorenzo de Evia, of four leagues of land (desde los edificios de Uxmal) from the buildings of Uxmal to the south, one to the east, another to the west, and another to the north, for his distinguished merits and services therein expressed. The preamble sets forth that the Regidor Don Lorenzo de Evia, by a writing that he presented to his majesty, made a narrative showing that at sixteen leagues from Merida, and three from the sierra of the village of Ticul, were certain meadows and places named Uxmalchecaxek, Tzemchan - Cemin - Curea - Kusultzac, Exmuue-Hixmon-nec, uncultivated and belonging to the crown, which the Indians could not profit by for tillage and sowing, and which could only serve for horned cattle; that the said regidor had a wife and children whom it was necessary for him to maintain for the service of the king in a manner conforming to his office, and that he wished to stock the said places and meadows with horned cattle, and praying a grant of them for that purpose in the name of his majesty, since no injury could result to any third person, but, "*on the contrary, very great service to God our Lord, because with that establishment it would prevent the Indians in those places from worshipping the devil in the ancient buildings which are there, having in them their idols, to which they burn copal, and performing other detestable sacrifices, as they are doing every day notoriously and publicly.*"

Following this is a later instrument, dated the third of December, 1687, the preamble of which recites the petition of the Captain Lorenzo de Evia, setting forth the grant above referred to, and that an Indian named Juan Can had importuned him with a claim of right to the said lands on account of his being a descendant of the ancient Indians, to whom they belonged; that the Indian had exhibited some confused papers and maps, and that, although it was not possible for him to justify the right that he claimed, to avoid litigation, he, the said Don Lorenzo de Evia, agreed to give him seventy-four dollars for the price and value of the said land. The petition introduces the deed of consent, or quit-claim, of Juan Can, executed with all the formalities required in the case of Indians (the original of which appears among the other title papers), and prays a confirmation of his former grant, and to be put in real and corporeal possession. The instrument confirms the former grant, and prescribes the formal mode of obtaining possession.

Under the deed of confirmation appears the deed of livery of seisin, beginning, "In the place called the edifices of Uxmal and its lands, the third day of the month of January, 1688," &c., &c., and concluding with these words: "In virtue of the power and authority which by the same title is given to me by the said governor, complying with its terms, I took by the hand the said Lorenzo de Evia, and he walked with me all over Uxmal and its buildings, *opened and shut some doors* that had several rooms, cut within the space some trees, picked up fallen stones and threw them down, drew water from one of the aguadas of the said place of Uxmal, and performed other acts of possession."

The reader will perceive that we have here two distinct, independent witnesses testifying that, one hundred and forty years after the foundation of Merida, the buildings of Uxmal were regarded with reverence by the Indians; that they formed the nucleus of a dispersed and scattered population, and were resorted to for the observance of religious rites at a distance from the eyes of the Spaniards. Cogolludo saw in the House of the Dwarf the "marks of copal recently burned," "the evidence of some idolatry recently committed;" and the private title papers of Don Simon, never intended to illustrate any point in history, besides showing incidentally that it was the policy of the government, and "doing God service," to break up the Indian customs, and drive the natives away from their consecrated buildings, are proofs, which would be good evidence in a court of law, that the Indians were, at the time referred to, openly and notoriously worshipping El Demonio, and performing other detestable sacrifices in these ancient buildings. Can it be supposed that edifices in which they were thus worshipping, and to which they were clinging with such tenacity as to require to be driven away, were the buildings of another race, or did they cling to them because they were adapted to the forms and ceremonies received from their fathers, and because they were the same in which their fathers had worshipped? In my mind there is but little question as to the fair interpretation to be put upon these acts, and I may add that, according to the deed of the notary, but one hundred and fifty-four years ago the ruined buildings of Uxmal had "doors" which could be "opened" and "shut."

CHAPTER XV

The reader, perhaps, is now anxious to hurry away from Uxmal, but he cannot be more anxious to do so than we were. We had finished our work, had resolved on the day for our departure, and had determined to devote the intermediate time to getting out of the wall and collecting together some ornaments for removal, and, having got the Indians fairly at work, we set about making some farewell Daguerreotype views. While working the camera under a blazing sun in the courtyard of the Monjas, I received a note from Mr. Catherwood advising me that his time had come, that he had a chill, and was then in bed. Presently a heavy rain came down, from which I took refuge in a damp apartment, where I was obliged to remain so long that I became perfectly chilled. On my return, I had a severe relapse, and in the evening Dr. Cabot, depressed by the state of things, and out of pure sympathy, joined us. Our servants went away, we were all three pinned to our beds together, and determined forthwith to leave Uxmal.

The next day it rained again, and we passed the hours in packing up, always a disagreeable operation, and then painfully so. The next day we departed, perhaps forever, from the Casa del Gobernador.

As we descended the steps, Mr. C. suggested that it was New-year's Day. It was the first time this fact had presented itself; it called up scenes strikingly contrasted with our own miscrable condition, and for the moment we would have been glad to be at home. Our cochés were in readiness at the foot of the terrace, and we crawled in; the Indians raised us upon their shoulders, and we were in motion from Uxmal. There was no danger of our incurring the penalty of Lot's wife; we never looked back; all the interest we had felt in the place was gone, and we only wanted to get away. Silent and desolate as we found them, we left the ruins of Uxmal, again to be overgrown with trees, to crumble and fall, and perhaps, in a few generations, to become, like others scattered over the country, mere shapeless and name-less mounds.

Our housekeeping and household were again broken up. Albino and Bernaldo followed us, and as we passed along the edge of the milpa, half hidden among the cornstalks was the stately figure of Chaipa Chi. She seemed to be regarding us with a mournful gaze. Alas! poor Chaipa Chi, the white man's friend! never again will she make tortillas for the Ingleses in Uxmal! A month afterward she was borne to the campo santo of the ha-cienda. The sun and rain are beating upon her grave. Her bones will soon bleach on the rude charnel pile, and her skull may perhaps one day, by the hands of some unscrupulous traveller, be conveyed to Doctor S. G. Morton of Philadelphia.

Our departure from Uxmal was such a complete rout, that it really had in it something of the ludicrous, but we were not in condition to enjoy it at the time. Notwithstanding the com-paratively easy movement of the coché, both Mr. C. and I suf-fered excessively, for, being made of poles hastily tied together, the vehicle yielded under the irregular steps of the carriers. At the distance of two leagues they laid us down under a large seybo tree, opposite the hacienda of Chetulish, part of the do-main of Uxmal. As if in mockery of us, the Indians were all out of doors in holyday dresses, celebrating the opening of the new year. We remained a short time for our carriers to rest, and in two hours we reached the village of Nohcacab, and were laid down at the door of the casa real. When we crawled out, the miserable Indians who had borne us on their shoulders were happy compared with us.

The arrival of three Ingleses was an event without precedent in the history of the village. There was a general curiosity to see us, increased by knowledge of the extraordinary and unaccountable purpose for which we were visiting the country. The circumstance of its being a fête day had drawn together into the plaza all the people of the village, and an unusual concourse of Indians from the suburbs, most of whom gathered round our door, and those who dared came inside to gaze upon us as we lay in our hammocks. These adventurous persons were only such as were particularly intoxicated, which number, however, included on that day a large portion of the respectable community of Nohcacab. They seemed to have just enough of reason left, or rather of instinct, to know that they might offend by intruding upon white men, and made up for it by exceeding submissiveness of manner and good nature.

We were at first excessively annoyed by the number of visiters and the noise of the Indians without, who kept up a contineud beating on the tunkul, or Indian drum; but by degrees our pains left us, and, with the comfortable reflection that we had escaped from the pernicious atmosphere of Uxmal, toward evening we were again on our feet.

The casa real is the public building in every village, provided by the royal government for the audienzia and other public offices, and, like the cabildo of Central America, is intended to contain apartments for travellers. In the village of Nohcacab, however, the arrival of strangers was so rare an occurrence that no apartment was assigned expressly for their accommodation. That given to us was the principal room of the building, used for the great occasions of the village, and during the week it was occupied as a public schoolroom; but, fortunately for us, being Newyear's Day, the boys had holyday.

It was about forty feet long and twenty-five wide. The furniture consisted of a very high table and some very low chairs, and in honour of the day the doors were trimmed with branches of cocoanut tree. The walls were whitewashed, and at one end was an eagle holding in his beak a coiled serpent, tearing it also with his claws. Under this were some indescribable figures, and a sword, gun, and cannon, altogether warlike emblems for the peaceful village which had never heard the sound of hostile trumpet. On one side of the eagle's beak was a scroll with the words "Sala Consistorial Republicana, Año 1828." The other had contained the words "El Systema Central," but on the triumph of the Federal party the brush had been drawn over it, and nothing was substituted in its place, so that it was all ready to be restored in case the Central party returned to power. On the wall hung a paper containing a "notice to the public" in

Spanish and the Maya language, that his Excellency the Governor of the State had allowed to this village the establishment of a school of first letters for teaching children to read, write, count, and the doctrines of the holy Catholic religion; that fathers and other heads of families should send their children to it, and that, being endowed by the public funds, it should not cost a medio real to any one. It was addressed to vecinos, or white people, indigenos, or Indians, and other classes, meaning Mestizoes.

On one side of this principal room was the quartel, with the garrison, which consisted of seven soldiers, militia, three or four of whom were down with fever and ague. On the other was the prison with its grated door, and one gentleman in misfortune looking through the grating.

This building occupied all one side of the plaza. The village was the only one I had seen that gave any indications of "improvement;" and certainly I had not seen any that needed it more. The plaza was the poorest in appearance, and at that time was worse than usual. It had been laid out on a hillside, and the improvement then going on was making it level. There was a great pile of earth thrown up in the centre, and the houses on one side had their foundations laid bare, so that they could only be entered by means of ladders; and it was satisfactory to learn that the alcaldes who had planned the improvement had got themselves into as much trouble as our aldermen sometimes do in laying out new streets.

From the door of the casa real two striking objects were in sight, one of which, grand in proportions and loftily situated, was the great church I had seen from the top of the sierra in coming from Ticul; the other was the noria, or well. This was an oblong enclosure with high stone walls, and a roof of palm leaves at one end, under which a mule was going round continually with a beam, drawing water into a large oblong basin cemented, from which the women of the village were filling their water-jars.

In our stroll out of doors our Indian carriers espied us, and came staggering toward us in a body, giving us to understand that they were overjoyed at seeing us, and congratulating us upon our recovery. They had not had a fair start with the Indians of the village, but they had been expeditious, and, by making good use of their time and the money we paid them, were as thoroughly intoxicated as the best in Nohcacab. Still they were good-natured as children, and, as usual, each one concluded his little speech with begging a medio.

The North American Indian is by drinking made insolent, ferocious, and brutal, and with a knife in his hand he is always a dangerous character; but the Indians of Yucatan when intoxicated are only more docile and submissive. All wear machetes, but they never use them to do harm.

We endeavoured to persuade our bearers to return to the hacienda before their money was all spent, and at length, giving us to understand that it was in obedience to us, they went away. We watched them as they reeled down the road, which they seemed to find hardly wide enough for one abreast, turning to look back and make us another reverence, and at length, when out of our reach, they all stopped, sat down in the road, and again took to their bottles.

We had arrived at Nohcacab at an interesting and exciting moment. The village had just gone through the agony of a contested election. During the administration of the last alcalde, various important causes, among which were the improvements in the plaza, had roused the feelings of the whole community, and a strong notion prevailed, particularly among the aspirants to office, that the republic was in danger unless the alcaldes were changed. This feeling extended through all classes, and, through the interposition of Providence, as it was considered by the successful party, the alcaldes were changed, and the republic saved.

Fig. 16

The municipal elections of Nohcacab are, perhaps, more important than those of any other village in the state. The reader is aware of the great scarcity of water in Yucatan; that there are no rivers, streams, or fountains, and, except in the neighbourhood of aguadas, no water but what is obtained from wells. Nohcacab has three public wells, and it has a population of about six thousand entirely dependant upon them. Two of these wells are called norias, being larger and more considerable structures, in which the water is drawn by mules, and the third is simply a poso, or well, having merely a cross-beam over the mouth, at which each comer draws with his own bucket and rope. For leagues around there is no water except that furnished by these wells. All the Indians have their huts or places of residence in the village, within reach of the wells; and when they go to work on their milpas, which are sometimes several miles distant, they are obliged to carry a supply with them. Every woman who goes to the noria for a cantaro of water carries a handful of corn, which she drops in a place provided for that purpose: this tribute is intended for the maintenance of the mules, and we paid two cents for the drinking of each of our horses.

The custody and preservation of these wells are an important part of the administration of the village government. Thirty Indians are elected every year, who are called alcaldes of the wells, and whose business it is to keep them in good order, and the tanks constantly supplied with water. They receive no pay, but are exempted from certain obligations and services, which makes the office desirable; and no small object of the political struggle through which the village had passed, was to change the alcaldes of the wells. Buried among the ruins of Uxmal, the news of this important election had not reached us.

Though practically enduring, in some respects, the appendages of an aristocratic government, the Indians who carried us on their shoulders, and our loads on their backs, have as good votes as their masters; and it was painful to have lost the opportunity of seeing the democratic principle in operation among the only true and real *native American* party; the spectacle being, as we were told, in the case of the hacienda Indians, one of exceeding impressiveness, not to say sublimity. These, being criados, or servants, in debt to their masters and their bodies mortgaged, go up to the village unanimous in opinion and purpose, without partiality or prejudice, either in favour of or against particular men or measures; they have no bank questions, nor questions of internal improvement, to consider; no angry discussions about the talents, private characters, or public services of candidates; and, above all, they are free from the degrading imputation of man worship, for in general they have not the least idea for whom they are voting. All they have to do is to put into a box a little piece of paper given to them by the master or major domo, for which they are to have a holyday. The only danger is that, in the confusion of greeting acquaintances, they may get their papers changed; and when this happens, they are almost invariably found soon after committing some offence against hacienda discipline, for which these independent electors are pretty sure to get flogged by the major domo.

In the villages the indifference to political distinctions, and the discrimination of the public in rewarding unobtrusive merit, are no less worthy of admiration, for Indian alcaldes are frequently elected without being aware that they have been held up for the suffrages of their fellow-citizens; they pass the day of election on the ground, and go home without knowing anything about it. The night before their term is to commence the retiring functionaries go round the village and catch these unconscious favourites of the people, put them into the cabildo, and keep them together all night, that they may be at hand in the morning to receive the staves and take the oath of office.

These little peculiarities were told to us as facts, and of such a population I can believe them to be true. At all events, the term of the incumbent officers was just expiring; the next morning the grand ceremony of the inauguration was to take place, and the Indians going out of office were actively engaged in hunting up their successors and bringing them together in the cabildo. Before retiring we went in with the padrecito to look at them. Most of them had been brought in, but some were still wanting. They were sitting round a large table, on which lay the record of their election; and, to beguile the tediousness of their honourable imprisonment, they had instruments by them, called musical, which kept up a terrible noise all night. Whatever were the circumstances of their election, their confinement for the night was, no doubt, a wise precaution, to ensure their being sober in the morning.

When we opened our door the next day, the whole village was in commotion, preparatory to the august ceremony of installing the new alcaldes. The Indians had slept off the debauch of the Newyear, and in clean dresses thronged the plaza; the great steps ascending to the church and the platform in front were filled with Indian women dressed in white, and near the door was a group of ladies, with mantas and veils, and the costume of the señoras in the capital. The morning air was fresh and invigorating; there were no threatening clouds in the sky, and the sun was pouring its early beams upon the scene of rejoicing. It was a great triumph of principle, and the humble mules which trod their daily circle with the beam of the noria, had red ribands round their necks, hung with half dollar and two shilling pieces, in token of rejoicing at the change of the alcaldes of the wells.

At seven o'clock the old alcaldes took their seats for the last time, and administered the oath of office to their successors, after which a procession formed for the church. The padrecito led the way, accompanied by the new alcaldes. They were dressed in black body-coats and black hats, which, as we had not seen such things since we left Merida, among the white dresses and straw hats around seemed a strange costume. Then followed the Indian officials, each with his staff of office, and the rest of the crowd in the plaza. Grand mass was said, after which the padrecito sprinkled the new alcaldes with holy water, and withdrew into his room in the convent to take chocolate. We followed him, and about the same time the whole body of new officers entered. The white alcaldes all came up and shook hands with us, and while the padrecito was raising his chocolate to his lips, the Indians went one by one and kissed his hand without disturbing his use of it. During this time he asked us what we thought of the muchachas, or girls of the village, whether they would compare with those of our country, and, still sipping his chocolate, made an address to the Indians, telling them that, although they were great in respect to the other Indians, yet in respect to the principal alcaldes they were but small men; and, after much other good advice, he concluded by telling them that they were to execute the laws and obey their superiors.

At nine o'clock we returned to our quarters, where, either by reason of our exertion, or from the regular course of the disease, we all had a recurrence of fever, and were obliged to betake ourselves to our hammocks. While in this condition the padrecito came in with a letter he had just received from Ticul, bringing intelligence that the cura had passed a fatál night, and was then dying. His ministro had written to us at the ruins, advising us of his continued indisposition and inability to join us, but, until our arrival at Nohcacab, we had no intimation that his illness was considered dangerous. The intelligence was sudden and most afflicting. It was so short a time since we had parted with him to meet again at Uxmal, his kindness was so fresh in our recollection, that we would have gone to him immediately, but we were fastened to our hammocks.

His illness had created a great sensation among the Indians of Ticul. They said that he was going to die, and that it was a visitation of God for digging up the bones in San Francisco; this rumour became wilder as it spread, and was not confined to the Indians. An intelligent Mestizo lad belonging to the village came over with the report, which he repeated to gaping listeners, that the poor cura lay on his back with his hands clasped on his breast, crying out, in a deep, sepulchral voice, every ten minutes by the watch, "Devuelve esos huesos." "Restore those bones."

We heard that he had with him accidentally an English physician, though we could not make any English of the name. Our fever might leave us in a few hours, and with the desperate hope that we might arrive in time for Doctor Cabot's skill to be of some use to him, or, if not, to bid him a last farewell, we requested the padrecito to procure cochés and Indians by two o'clock in the afternoon.

Two fête days in succession were rather too much for the Indians of Nohcacab. In about an hour one of the new alcaldes came to tell us that, in celebrating the choice of their new officers, the independent electors had all become so tipsy that competent men could be found for only one coché. Perhaps it would have been difficult for the alcaldes to know whether their immediate condition was really the fruit of that day's celebration or a holding over from Newyear's Day, but the effect was the same so far as we were concerned.

The alcaldes and the padrecito, however, appreciated our motives, and knew it was utterly impossible for us to go on horseback, so that, with great exertions, by two o'clock the requisite number came reeling and staggering into the room. We were still in our hammocks, uncertain whether it would be possible to go at all, and their appearance did not encourage us, for they seemed unable to carry themselves on their feet, much less us on their shoulders. However, we got them out of the room, and told them to get the cochés ready. At three o'clock we crawled into the vehicles, and in the mean time our carriers had taken another drink. It seemed foolhardy to trust ourselves to such men, particularly as we had to cross the sierra, the most dangerous road in the country; but the alcaldes said they were hombres de bien, men of good character and conduct; that they would be sober before the first league was passed; and with this encouragement we started. The sun was still scorching hot, and came in directly upon the back of my head. My carriers set off on a full run, which they continued for perhaps a mile, when they moderated their pace, and, talking and laughing all the time, toward evening they set me down on the ground. I scrambled out of the coché; the freshness of the evening air was reviving, and we waited till Doctor Cabot came up. He had had a much worse time than I, his carriers happening to be more intoxicated.

It was nearly dark when we reached the foot of the sierra, and, as we ascended, the clouds threatened rain. Before, it had been an object to leave the coché as open and airy as possible, on account of the heat, but now it was a greater object to avoid getting wet, and I had everything fastened down on the sides. On the top of the sierra the rain came on, and the Indians hurried down as fast as the darkness and the ruggedness of the road would permit. This road required care on horseback and by daylight; but as the Indians were now sober, and I had great confidence in their sureness of foot, I had no apprehensions, when all at once I felt the coché going over, and pinned in as I was, unable to help myself, with a frightful crash it came down on its side. My fear was that it would go over a precipice; but the Indians on the upper side held on, and I got out with considerable celerity. The rain was pouring, and it was so dark that I could see nothing. My shoulder and side were bruised, but, fortunately, none of the Indians were missing, and they all gathered round, apparently more frightened than I was hurt. If the accident had been worse, I could not have blamed them; for in such darkness, and on such a road, it was a wonder how they could get along at all. We righted the coché, arranged things as well as we could, and in due season I was set down at the door of the convent. I stumbled up the steps and knocked at the door, but the good cura was not there to welcome me. Perhaps we had arrived too late, and all was over. At the extreme end of the long corridor I saw a ray of light, and, groping my way toward it, entered a cloister, in which a number of Indians were busily employed making fireworks. The cura had been taken to the house of his sister-in-law, and we sent one of them over to give notice of our arrival. Very soon we saw a lantern crossing the plaza, and recognised the long gown of the padre Brizeño, whose letter to the padrecito had been the occasion of our coming. It had been written early in the morning, when there was no hope; but within the last six hours a favourable change had taken place, and the crisis had passed. Perhaps no two men were ever more glad than the doctor and myself at finding their journey bootless. Doctor Cabot was even more relieved than I; for, besides the apprehension that we might arrive too late, or barely in time to be present at the cura's death, the doctor had that of finding him under the hands of one from whom it would be necessary to extricate him, and still his interference might not be effectual.

As a matter of professional etiquette, Doctor Cabot proposed to call upon the English physician. His house was shut up, and he was already in his hammock, being himself suffering from calentura, for which he had just taken a warm bath; but before the door was opened we were satisfied that he was really an Ingles. It seemed a strange thing to meet, in this little village in the interior of Yucatan, one speaking our own language, but the circuitous road by which he had reached it was not less strange.

Doctor Fasnet, or Fasnach as he was called, was a small man, considerably upward of fifty. Thirty years before he had emigrated to Jamaica, and, after wandering among the West India Islands, had gone over to the continent; and there was hardly a country in Spanish America in which he had not practised the healing art. With an uncontrollable antipathy to revolutions, it had been his lot to pass the greater part of his life in countries most rife with them. After running before them in Colombia, Peru, Chili, and Central America, where he had prescribed for Carrera when the latter was pursuing his honest calling as a pig-driver, unluckily he found himself in Salama when Carrera came upon it with twelve hundred Indians, and the cry of death to the whites. With a garrison of but thirty soldiers and sixty citizens capable of bearing arms, Doctor Fasnach was fain to undertake the defence; but, fortunately, Carrera drew off his Indians, and Doctor Fasnet drew off himself, came into Yucatan, and happened to settle in Tekax, the only town in the state that could get up a revolution. He was flying from it, and on his way to Merida, when he was arrested by the cura's illness. The doctor's long residence in tropical countries had made him familiar with their diseases, but his course of treatment would not be considered legitimate by regular practitioners. The cura's illness was cholera morbus, attended with excessive swelling and inflammation of the stomach and intestines. To reduce these, Doctor F. had a sheep killed at the door, and the stomach of the patient covered with flesh warm from the animal, which in a very few minutes became tainted and was taken off, and a new layer applied; and this was continued till eight sheep had been killed and applied, and the inflammation subsided.

From the house of Doctor Fasnet we went to the cura. The change which two weeks had made in his appearance was appalling. Naturally thin, his agonizing pains had frightfully reduced him, and as he lay extended on a cot with a sheet over him, he seemed more dead than living. He was barely able, by the feeble pressure of his shrunken hand, to show that he appreciated our visit, and to say that he had never expected to see us again; but the happy faces of those around him spoke more than words. It was actually rejoicing as over one snatched from the grave.

The next morning we visited him again. His sunken eyes lighted up as he inquired about our excavations at Uxmal, and a smile played upon his lips as he alluded to the superstition of the Indians about digging up the bones in San Francisco. Our visit seemed to give him so much satisfaction, that, though we could not talk with him, we remained at the house nearly all day, and the next day we returned to Nohcacab on horseback. Our visit to Ticul had recruited us greatly, and we found Mr. Catherwood equally improved. A few days' rest had done wonders for us all, and we determined immediately to resume our occupations.

On leaving Uxmal we had directed our steps toward Nohcacab, not from any attractions in the place itself, but on account of the ruins which we had heard of as existing in that neighbourhood; and, after ascertaining their position, we considered that they could be visited to the best advantage by making this place our head-quarters. We had the prospect of being detained there some time, and, as the casa real was low, damp, and noisy, and, moreover, our apartment was wanted for the schoolroom, by the advice of the padrecito we determined to abandon it, and take up our abode in the convent.

This was a long stone building in the rear of the church, standing on the same high table-land, overlooking the village, and removed from its annoyances and bustle. In the part immediately adjoining the church were two large and convenient apartments, except that, quick in detecting all which could bring on a recurrence of fever and ague, we noticed on one side puddles of water and green mould, from the constant shade of the great wall of the church, and on the door of one of the rooms was written, "Here died Don José Trufique: may his soul rest in peace."

In these rooms we established ouselves. On one side of us we had the padrecito, who was always gay and lively, and on the other six or eight Indian sacristans, or sextons, who were always drunk. Before the door was a broad high platform, running all round the church, and a little beyond it was a walled enclosure for our horses. Opposite the door of the sacristia was a thatched cocina, or kitchen, in which these Indian church ministers cooked and Albino and Bernaldo slept.

It is ascertained by historical accounts, that at the time of the conquest an Indian town existed in this immediate neighbourhood, bearing the name of Nohcacab. This name is compounded of three Maya words, signifying literally the great place of good land; and from the numerous and extraordinary ruins scattered around, there is reason to believe that it was the heart of a rich, and what was once an immensely populous country. In the suburbs are numerous and large mounds, grand enough to excite astonishment, but even more fallen and overgrown than those of San Francisco, and, in fact, almost inaccessible.

The village stands in the same relative position to these ruins that Ticul does to the ruins of San Francisco, and, like that, in my opinion it stands on the offskirts of the old Indian town, or rather it occupies part of the very site, for in the village itself, within the enclosures of some of the Indians, are the remains of mounds exactly like those in the suburbs. In making excavations in the plaza, vases and vessels of pottery are continually brought to light, and in the street wall of the house where the padrecito's mother lived is a sculptured head dug up fifteen years ago.

The whole of this region is retired and comparatively unknown. The village is without the line of all the present main roads; it does not lie on the way to any place of general resort, and is not worth stopping at on its own account. Notwithstanding the commencement of improvements, it was the most backward and thoroughly Indian of any village we had visited. Merida was too far off for the Indians to think of; but few of the vecinos ever reached it, and Ticul was their capital. Everything that was deficient in the village they told us was to be had at Ticul, and the sexton, who went over once a week for the holy wafer, was always charged with some errand for us.

The first place which we proposed visiting was the ruins of Xcoch, and in the very beginning of our researches in this neighbourhood we found that we were upon entirely new ground. The attention of the people had never been turned to the subject of the ruins in the neighbourhood. Xcoch was but a league distant, and, besides the ruins of buildings, it contained an ancient poso, or well, of mysterious and marvellous reputation, the fame of which was in everybody's mouth. This well was said to be a vast subterraneous structure, adorned with sculptured figures, an immense table of polished stone, and a plaza with columns supporting a vaulted roof, and it was said to have a subterraneous road, which led to the village of Mani, twenty-seven miles distant.

Notwithstanding this wondrous reputation and the publicity of the details, and although within three miles of Nohcacab, the intelligence we received was so vague and uncertain that we were at a loss how to make our arrangements for exploring the well. Not a white man in the place had ever entered it, though several had looked in at the mouth, who said that the wind had taken away their breath, and they had not ventured to go in. Its fame rested entirely upon the accounts of the Indians, which, coming to us through interpreters, were very confused. By the active kindness of the padrecito and his brother, the new alcalde Segunda, two men were brought to us who were considered most familiar with the place, and they said that it would be impossible to enter it except by employing several men one or two days in making ladders, and, at all events, they said it would be useless to attempt the descent after the sun had crossed the meridian; and to this all our friends and counsellors, who knew nothing about it, assented. Knowing, however, their dilatory manner of doing business, we engaged them to be on the ground at daylight. In the mean time we got together all the spare ropes in the village, including one from the noria, and at eight o'clock the next morning we set out.

For a league we followed the camino real, at which distance we saw a little opening on the left, where one of our Indians was waiting for us. Following him by a narrow path just opened, we again found ourselves among ruins, and soon reached the foot of the high mound which towered above the plain, itself conspicuous from the House of the Dwarf at Uxmal, and which is represented in Figure 17. The ground in this neighbourhood was open, and there were the remains of several buildings, but all prostrate and in utter ruin.

The great cerro stands alone, the only one that now rises above the plain. The sides are all fallen, though in some places

Fig. 17

the remains of steps are visible. On the south side, about half way up, there is a large tree, which facilitates the ascent to the top. The height is about eighty or ninety feet. One corner of a building is all that is left; the rest of the top is level and overgrown with grass. The view commanded an immense wooded plain, and, rising above it, toward the southeast the great church of Nohcacab, and on the west the ruined buildings of Uxmal.

Returning in the same direction, we entered a thick grove, in which we dismounted and tied our horses. It was the finest grove we had seen in the country, and within it was a great circular cavity or opening in the earth, twenty or thirty feet deep, with trees and bushes growing out of the bottom and sides, and rising above the level of the plain. It was a wild-looking place, and had a fanciful, mysterious, and almost fearful appearance; for while in the grove all was close and sultry, and without a breath of air, and every leaf was still, within this cavity the branches and leaves were violently agitated, as if shaken by an invisible hand.

This cavity was the entrance to the poso, or well, and its appearance was wild enough to bear out the wildest accounts we had heard of it. We descended to the bottom. At one corner was a rude natural opening in a great mass of limestone rock, low and narrow, through which rushed constantly a powerful current of wind, agitating the branches and leaves in the area without. This was the mouth of the well, and on our first attempting to enter it the rush of wind was so strong that it made us fall back gasping for breath, confirming the accounts we had heard in Nohcacab. Our Indians had for torches long strips of the castor-oil plant, which the wind only ignited more thoroughly, and with these they led the way. It was one of the marvels told us of this place, that it was impossible to enter after twelve o'clock. This hour was already past; we had not made the preparations which were said to be necessary, and, without knowing how far we should be able to continue, we followed our guides, other Indians coming after us with coils of rope.

The entrance was about three feet high and four or five wide. It was so low that we were obliged to crawl on our hands and feet, and descended at an angle of about fifteen degrees in a northerly direction. The wind, collecting in the recesses of the cave, rushed through this passage with such force that we could scarcely breathe; and as we all had in us the seeds of fever and ague, we very much doubted the propriety of going on, but curiosity was stronger than discretion, and we proceeded. In the floor of the passage was a single track, worn two or three inches deep by long-continued treading of feet, and the roof was incrusted with a coat of smoke from the flaring torches. The labour of crawling through this passage with the body bent, and against the rush of cold air, made a rather severe beginning, and, probably, if we had undertaken the enterprise alone we should have turned back.

At the distance of a hundred and fifty or two hundred feet the passage enlarged to an irregular cavern, forty or fifty feet wide and ten or fifteen high. We no longer felt the rush of cold wind, and the temperature was sensibly warmer. The sides and roof were of rough, broken stone, and through the centre ran the same worn path. From this passage others branched off to the right and left, and in passing along it, at one place the Indians held their torches down to a block of sculptured stone. We had, of course, already satisfied ourselves that the cave or passage, whatever it might lead to, was the work of nature, and had given up all expectation of seeing the great monuments of art which had been described to us; but the sight of this block encouraged us with the hope that the accounts might have some foundation. Very soon, however, our hopes on this head were materially abated, if not destroyed, by reaching what the Indians had described as a mesa, or table. This had been a great item in all the accounts, and was described as made by hand and highly polished. It was simply a huge block of rude stone, the top of which happened to be smooth, but entirely in a state of nature. Beyond this we passed into a large opening of an irregular circular form, being what had been described to us as a plaza. Here the Indians stopped and flared their torches. It was a great vaulted chamber of stone, with a high roof supported by enormous stalactite pillars, which were what the Indians had called the columns, and though entirely different from what we had expected, the effect under the torchlight, and heightened by the wild figures of the Indians, was grand, and almost repaid us for all our trouble. This plaza lay at one side of the regular path, and we remained in it some minutes to refresh ourselves, for the closeness of the passage and the heat and smoke were becoming almost intolerable.

Farther on we climbed up a high, broken piece of rock, and descended again by a low, narrow opening, through which we were obliged to crawl, and which, from its own closeness, and the heat and smoke of the torches, and the labour of crawling through it, was so hot that we were panting with exhaustion and thirst. This brought us to a rugged, perpendicular hole, three or four feet in diameter, with steps barely large enough for a foothold, worn in the rock. We descended with some difficulty, and at the foot came out upon a ledge of rock, which ran up on the right to a great height, while on the left was a deep, yawning chasm. A few rude logs were laid along the edge of this chasm, which, with a pole for a railing, served as a bridge, and, with the torchlight thrown into the abyss below, made a wild crossing-place; the passage then turned to the right, contracting to about three feet in height and the same in width, and descending rapidly. We were again obliged to betake ourselves to crawling, and again the heat became insufferable. Indeed, we went on with some apprehensions. To faint in one of those narrow passages, so far removed from a breath of air, would be almost to die there. As to carrying a man out, it was impossible for either of us to do more than drag himself along, and I believe that there could have been no help from the Indians.

This passage continued fifty or sixty feet, when it doubled on itself, still contracted as before, and still rapidly descending. It then enlarged to a rather spacious cavern, and took a south-west direction, after which there was another perpendicular hole, leading, by means of a rude and rickety ladder, to a steep, low, crooked, and crawling passage, descending until it opened into a large broken chamber, at one end of which was a deep hole or basin of water.

This account may not be perfectly accurate in all the details, but it is not exaggerated. Probably some of the turnings and windings, ascents and descents, are omitted; and the truest and most faithful description that could be given of it would be really the most extraordinary.

The water was in a deep, stony basin, running under a shelf of overhanging rock, with a pole laid across on one side, over which the Indians leaned to dip it up with their calabashes; and this alone, if we had wanted other proof, was confirmation that the place had been used as a well.

But at the moment it was a matter of very little consequence to us whether any living being had ever drunk from it before; the sight of it was more welcome to us than gold or rubies. We were dripping with sweat, black with smoke, and perishing with thirst. It lay before us in its stony basin, clear and inviting, but it was completely out of reach; the basin was so deep that we could not reach the water with our hands, and we had no vessel of any kind to dip it out with. In our entire ignorance of the character of the place, we had not made any provision, and the Indians had only brought what they were told to bring. I crawled down on one side, and dipped up a little with one hand; but it was a scanty supply, and with this water before us we were compelled to go away with our thirst unsatisfied. Fortunately, however, after crawling back through the first narrow passage, we found some fragments of a broken water-jar, with which the Indians returned and brought us enough to cool our tongues.

In going down we had scarcely noticed anything except the wild path before us; but, having now some knowledge of the place, the labour was not so great, and we inquired for the passage which the Indians had told us led to Mani. On reaching it, we turned off, and, after following it a short distance, found it completely stopped by a natural closing of the rock. From the best information we could get, although all said the passage led to Mani, we were satisfied that the Indians had never attempted to explore it. It did not lead to the water, nor out of the cave, and our guides had never entered it before. We advised them for the future to omit this and some other particulars in their stories about the well; but probably, except from the padrecito, and others to whom we communicated what we saw, the next travellers will hear the same accounts that we did.

As we advanced, we remained a little while in the cooler atmosphere before exposing ourselves to the rush of cold air toward the mouth, and in an hour and a half from the time of entering, we emerged into the outer air.

As a mere cave, this was extraordinary; but as a well or watering-place for an ancient city, it was past belief, except for the proofs under our own eyes. Around it were the ruins of a city without any other visible means of supply, and, what rarely happened, with the Indians it was matter of traditionary knowledge. They say that it was not discovered by them; it was used by their fathers; they did not know when it began to be used. They ascribe it to that remote people whom they refer to as the antiguos.

And a strong circumstance to induce the belief that it was once used by the inhabitants of a populous city, is the deep track worn in the rock. For ages the region around has been desolate, or occupied only by a few Indians during the time of working in the milpas. Their straggling footsteps would never have made that deep track. It could only have been made by the constant and long-continued tread of thousands. It must have been made by the population of a city.

In the grove surrounding the entrance we found some water collected in the hollow of a stone, with which we slaked our thirst and made a partial ablution; and it was somewhat extraordinary that, though we were barely recovered from illness, had exerted ourselves greatly, and been exposed to rapid alternations of heat and cold, we never experienced any bad effects from it.

On our return to the village we found that an unfortunate accident had occurred during our absence; a child had been run away with by a horse, thrown off, and killed. In the evening, in company with the alcalde, the brother of the padrecito, we went to the velorio, or watching. It was an extremely dark night, and we stumbled along a stony and broken street till we reached the house of mourning. Before the door were a crowd of people, and a large card-table, at which all who could find a place were seated playing cards. At the moment of our arrival, the whole company was convulsed with laughter at some good thing which one of them had uttered, and which was repeated for our benefit; a strange scene at the threshold of a house of mourning. We entered the house, which was crowded with women, and hammocks were vacated for our use, these being in all cases the seat of honour. The house, like most of those in the village, consisted of a single room rounded at each end. The floor was of earth, and the roof thatched with long leaves of the guano. From the cross-poles hung a few small hammocks, and in the middle of the room stood a table, on which lay the body of the child. It had on the same clothes which it wore when the accident happened, torn and stained with blood. At one side of the face the skin was scratched off from being dragged on the ground; the skull was cracked; and there was a deep gash under the ear, from which the blood was still oozing. On each side of the head was a lighted candle. It was a white child, three years old, and that morning had been playing about the house. The mother, a woman of uncommonly tall and muscular frame, was applying rags to stanch the flow of blood. She had set out that morning with all her family for Campeachy, with the intention of removing to that place. An Indian woman went before on horseback, carrying this child and another. In the suburbs of the village the horse took fright and ran away, throwing them all off; the servant and one child escaped unhurt; but this one was dragged some distance, and in two hours died of its wounds. The women were quiet and grave, but outside there was a continual laughing, jesting, and uproar, which, with the dead child before our eyes, seemed rude and heartless. While this was going on, we heard the gay voice of the padrecito, just arrived, contributing largely to the jest, and presently he came in, went up to the child, and, addressing himself to us, lifted up the head, showed us the wounds, told what he had done for it, and said that if the doctor had been there it might have been saved, or if it had been a man, but, being so young, its bones were very tender; then he lighted a straw cigar, threw himself into a hammock, and, looking around, asked us, in a tone of voice that was intended for the whole company, what we thought of the girls.

This ceremony of el velorio is always observed when there is death in a family. It is intended, as the padrecito told us, para divertirse, or to amuse and distract the family, and keep them from going to sleep. At twelve o'clock chocolate is served round, and again at daybreak; but in some respects the ceremony is different in the case of grown persons and that of children. In the latter, as they believe that a child is without sin, and that God takes it immediately to himself, the death is a subject of rejoicing, and the night is passed in card-playing, jesting, and story-telling. But in the case of grown persons, as they are not so sure what becomes of the spirit, they have no jesting or story-telling, and only play cards. All this may seem unfeeling, but we must not judge others by rules known only to ourselves. Whatever the ways of hiding or expressing it, the stream of natural affection runs deep in every bosom.

The mother of the child shed no tears, but as she stood by its head, stanching its wounds from time to time, she did not seem to be rejoicing over its death. The padrecito told us that she was poor, but a very respectable woman. We inquired about the other members of her family, and especially her husband. The padrecito said she had none, nor was she a widow; and, unfortunately for his standard of respectability, when we asked who was the father of the child, he answered laughingly, "Quien sabe?" "Who knows?" At ten o'clock he lighted a long bundle of sticks at one of the candles burning at the head of the child, and we went away.

CHAPTER XVI

The next day we set out for another ruined city. It lay on the road to Uxmal, and was the same which I had visited on my first return from Ticul, known by the name of Nohpat. At the distance of a league we turned off from the main road to the left, and, following a narrow milpa path, in fifteen minutes reached the field of ruins. One mound rose high above the rest, holding aloft a ruined building, as shown in Fig-

FIG. 18

ure 18. At the foot of this we dismounted and tied our horses. It was one hundred and fifty feet high on the slope, and about two hundred and fifty feet long at the base. At the top, the mound, with the building upon it, had separated and fallen apart, and while one side still supported part of the edifice, the other presented the appearance of a mountain slide.

234

Cocome, our guide, told us that the separation had happened only with the floods of the last rainy season. We ascended on the fallen side, and, reaching the top, found, descending on the south side, a gigantic staircase, overgrown, but with the great stone steps still in their places, and almost entire. The ruined building on the top consisted of a single corridor, but three feet five inches wide, and, with the ruins of Nohpat at our feet, we looked out upon a great desolate plain, studded with overgrown mounds, of which we took the bearings and names as known to the Indians; toward the west by north, startling by the grandeur of the buildings and their height above the plain, with no decay visible, and at this distance seeming perfect as a living city, were the ruins of Uxmal. Fronting us was the great Casa del Gobernador, apparently so near that we almost looked into its open doors, and could have distinguished a man moving on the terrace; and yet, for the first two weeks of our residence at Uxmal, we did not know of the existence of this place, and, wanting the clearings that had been made at Uxmal, no part of it was visible from the terraces or buildings there.

FIG. 19

Descending the mound, we passed around by the side of the staircase, and rose upon an elevated platform, in the centre of which was a huge and rude round stone, like that called the picote in the courtyards at Uxmal. At the base of the steps was a large flat stone, having sculptured upon it a colossal human figure in bas-relief, which is represented in Figure 19. The stone measures eleven feet four inches in length, and three feet ten in breadth, and lies on its back, broken in two in the middle. Probably it once stood erect at the base of the steps, but, thrown down and broken, has lain for ages with its face to the sky, exposed to the floods of the rainy season. The sculpture is rude and worn, and the lines were difficult to make out. The Indians said that it was the figure of a king of the antiguos, and no doubt it was intended as a portrait of some lord or cacique.

At a short distance to the southeast of the courtyard was another platform or terrace, about twenty feet high and two hundred feet square, on two sides of which were ranges of buildings standing at right angles to each other. One of them had two stories, and trees growing out of the walls and on the top, forming the most picturesque ruins we had seen in the country. As we approached it Doctor Cabot was climbing up a tree at the corner to get on the roof in pursuit of a bird, and, in doing so, started a gigantic lizard, which went bounding among the trees and along the cornice till he buried himself in a large fissure in the front.

Beyond this was another terrace, having on it ruined buildings overgrown with trees. Mr. Catherwood was tempted to sketch them merely on account of their pictureque effect, and while we were on the ground they seemed to us the most touching and interesting of any we had seen; but as they contribute nothing to illustrate the architecture and art of these unknown people, we do not present them.

Leaving this neighbourhood, and passing by many ruined buildings and mounds, at the distance of six or seven hundred feet we reached an open place, forming the most curious and interesting part of this field of ruins. It was in the vicinity of three mounds, lines drawn from which to each other would form a right angle, and in the open space were some sculptured monuments, shattered, fallen, and some of them half buried. Strange heads and bodies lay broken and scattered, so that at first we did not discover their connexion; but, by examining carefully, we found two fragments, which, from the shape of the broken surfaces, seemed to be parts of one block, one of them representing a huge head, and the other a huger body. The latter we set up in its proper position, and with some difficulty, by means of poles, and ropes which the Indians took from their sandals, we got the other part on the top, and fitted in its place, as it had once stood. Figure 20 represents this monument. It was a solid block of stone, measuring four feet three inches high,

FIG. 20

and one foot six inches thick, and represents a human figure in a crouching posture, with the face, having a hideous expression, turned over the shoulder, almost behind. The headdress is a representation of the head of a wild beast, the ears, eyes, teeth, and jaws being easily distinguishable. The sculpture is rude, and the whole appearance uncouth and ugly. Probably it was one of the idols worshipped by the people of this ancient city.

There were others of the same general character, of which the sculpture was more defaced and worn; and, besides these, there were monuments of a different character, half buried, and dispersed without apparent order, but which evidently had an

FIG. 21

adaptation to each other; after some examination, we made out what we considered the arrangement in which they had stood, and had them set up according to our combination. Figure 21 represents these stones. They vary from one foot four inches to one foot ten inches in length.

Each stone is two feet three inches high. The subject is the skull and cross-bones. The sculpture is in bas-relief, and the carving good, and still clear and distinct. Probably this was the holy place of the city, where the idols or deities were presented to the people with the emblems of death around them.

The ruins lie on the common lands of the village of Noh-cacab, at least so say the alcaldes of that place, but Don Simon Peon claims that they are within the old boundaries of the hacienda of Uxmal, and the settling of the question is not worth the expense of a survey. The name Nohpat is compounded of two Maya words, which signify a great lord or señor, and this is all the information I was able to collect about this ancient city. If we had met with it on our former journey we should have planted ourselves, and given it a thorough exploration. The mounds and vestiges of buildings were perhaps as numerous as those of Uxmal, but they were all ruined. The day was like the finest of October at home, and, as a relief from the heat of the sun, there was a constant and refreshing breeze. The country was open, or studded with trees barely enough to adorn the landscape, and give picturesque beauty to the ruins. It was cut up by numerous paths, and covered with grass like a fine piece of upland at home, and for the first and only time in the country we found pleasure in a mere ramble over fields. Bernaldo came out from the village with a loaded Indian at the precise moment when we wanted dinner, and altogether it was one of the most agreeable and satisfactory days that we passed among the relics of the antiguos.

The next day, being the eighth of January, we set out for the ruins of Kabah. Our direction was south, on the camino real to Bolonchen. The descent from the great rocky table on which the convent stands was on this side rough, broken, and precipitous. We passed through a long street having on each side thatched

Fig. 22

huts, occupied exclusively by Indians. Some had a picturesque appearance, and Figure 22 represents one of them. At the end of the street, as well as at the ends of the three other principal streets, which run toward the cardinal points, were a small chapel and altar, at which the inhabitants of the village might offer up prayers on leaving it, and thanks for their safe return. Beyond, the road was stony, bordered on both sides by scrubby trees and bushes: but as we advanced we passed through an open country, adorned with large forest trees. At the distance of two leagues we turned off by a milpa path on the left, and very soon found ourselves among trees, bushes, and a thick, overgrown foliage, which, after the fine open field of Nohpat, we regarded as among the vicissitudes of our fortunes. Beyond we saw through an opening a lofty mound, overgrown, and having upon it the ruins of a building like the House of the Dwarf, towering above every other object, and proclaiming the site of another lost and deserted city. Moving on, again, through openings in the trees, we had a glimpse of a great stone edifice, with its front apparently entire. We had hardly expressed our admiration before we saw another, and at a few horses' length a third. Three great buildings at once, with façades which, at that distance, and by the imperfect glimpses we had of them, showed no imperfection, and seemed entire. We were taken by surprise. Our astonishment and wonder were again roused; and we were almost as much excited as if this was the first ruined city we had seen.

Our guides cut a path for us, and with great difficulty we went on till we found ourselves at the foot of an overgrown terrace in front of the nearest building. Here we stopped; the Indians cleared a place for our horses, we secured them, and, climbing up a fallen wall of the terrace, out of which large trees were growing, came out upon the platform, and before us was a building with its walls entire, its front more fallen, but the remains showing that it had once been more richly decorated than any at Uxmal. We crossed the terrace, walked up the steps, and entering its open doors, ranged through every apartment. Then we descended the back terrace, and rose upon a high mound, having a great stone staircase different from anything we had seen, and, groping our way among the trees, passed on to the next; and the third presented a façade almost entire, with trees growing before it and on the top, as if nature and ruin had combined to produce their most picturesque effect. On the way we had glimpses of other buildings, separated from us by a thick growth of underwood; and after a hard but most interesting morning's work, we returned to the first building.

Since we first set out in search of ruins we had not been taken so much by surprise. During the whole time of our residence at Uxmal, and until my forced visit to Ticul, and fortunate intimacy with the cura Carillo, I had not even heard of the existence of such a place. It was absolutely unknown; and the Indians who guided us having conducted us to these buildings, of all the rest seemed as ignorant as ourselves. They told us, in fact, that these were all; but we could not believe them; we felt confident that more lay buried in the woods, and, tempted by the variety and novelty of what we saw, we determined not to go away until we had discovered all. So far, since we began at Nohcacab, we had "done up" a city a day, but we had now a great field of labour before us, and we saw at once that it was to be attended with many difficulties.

There was no rancho, and no habitation of any kind nearer than the village. The buildings themselves offered good shelter; with the necessary clearings they could be made extremely agreeable, and on many considerations it was advisable again to take up our abode among the ruins; but this arrangement was not without its dangers. The season of El Norte seemed to have no end; every day there was rain; the foliage was so thick that the hot sun could not dry the moisture before another rain came, and the whole country was enveloped in a damp, unwholesome atmosphere. Besides, unluckily for us, it was a season of great abundance in the village; the corn crop had been good; the Indians had plenty to eat, and did not care to work. Already we had found difficulty in hiring them; it would require constant urging and our continual presence to secure them from day to day. As to getting them to remain with us, it was out of the question. We determined, therefore, to continue our residence at the convent, and go out to the ruins every day.

Late in the afternoon we returned to the village, and in the evening had a levee of visiters. The sensation we had created in the village had gone on increasing, and the Indians were really indisposed to work for us at all. The arrival of a stranger even from Merida or Campeachy was an extraordinary event, and no Ingleses had ever been seen there before. The circumstance that we had come to work among the ruins was wonderful, incomprehensible. Within the memory of the oldest Indians these remains had never been disturbed. The account of the digging up of the bones in San Francisco had reached them, and they had much conversation with each other and with the padrecito about us. It was a strange thing, they said, that men with strange faces, and a language they could not understand, had come among them to disinter their ruined cities; and, simple as their ancestors when the Spaniards first came among them, they said that the end of the world was nigh.

It was late the next day when we reached the ruins. We could not set out before the Indians, for they might disappoint us altogether, and we could do nothing until they came, but, once on the ground, we soon had them at work. On both sides we watched each other closely, though from somewhat different motives: they from utter inability to comprehend our plans and purposes, and we from the fear that we should get no work out of them. If one of us spoke, they all stopped to listen; if we moved, they stopped to gaze upon us. Mr. Catherwood's drawing materials, tripod, sextant, and compass were very suspicious, and occasionally Doctor Cabot filled up the measure of their astonishment by bringing down a bird as it flew through the air. By the time they were fairly broken in to know what they had to do, it was necessary to return to the village.

The same labour was repeated the next day with a new set of men; but, by continual supervision and urging, we managed to get considerable work done. Albino was a valuable auxiliary; indeed, without him I could hardly have got on at all. We had not fairly discovered his intelligence until we left Uxmal. There all had a beaten track to move in, but on the road little things were constantly occurring in which he showed an ingenuity and a fertility of resource that saved us from many annoyances. He had been a soldier, and at the siege of Campeachy had received a sabre-cut in a fleshy part of the body, which rather intimated that he was moving in an opposite direction when the sabre overtook him. Having received neither pay for his services nor pension for his wound, he was a little disgusted with patriotism and fighting for his country. He was by trade a blacksmith, which business, on the recommendation of Doña Joaquina Peon, he had given up to enter our service. His usefulness and capacity were first clearly brought out at Kabah. Knowing the character of the Indians, speaking their language, and being but a few degrees removed from them by blood, he could get out of them twice as much work as I could. Him, too, they could ask questions about us, and lighten labour by the indulgence of social humour, and very soon I had only to give instructions as to what work was to be done, and leave the whole management of it to him. This doubled our effective force, as we could work with two sets of Indians in different places at the same time, and gave Albino a much greater value than that of a common servant. He had one bad habit, which was that of getting the fever and ague. This he was constantly falling into, and, with all our efforts, we could never break him of it, but, unluckily, we never set him a good example. In the mean time Bernaldo sustained his culinary reputation; and, avoiding the bad habit of Albino and his masters, while all the rest of us were lank as the village dogs of that country, his cheeks seemed always ready to burst open.

While we were working at the ruins, the people in the village were losing no time. On the eleventh began the fiesta of Corpus Alma, a festival of nine days' observance in honour of Santo Cristo del Amor. Its opening was announced by the ringing of church bells and firing of rockets, which, fortunately, as we were away at the ruins, we avoided hearing; but in the evening came the procession and the baile, to which we were formally invited by a committee, consisting of the padrecito, the alcalde, and a much more important person than either, styled El Patron del Santo, or the Patron of the Saint.

I have mentioned that Nohcacab was the most backward and thoroughly Indian of any village we had visited. With this strongly-marked Indian character, its church government is somewhat peculiar, and differs, I believe, from that of all the other villages. Besides smaller saints, the favourites of individuals, it has nine principal ones, who have been selected as special objects of veneration: San Mateo, the patron, and Santa Barbara, the patroness of the village; Nuestra Señora de la Concepcion; Nuestra Señora del Rosario; El Señor del Transfigùracion; El Señor de Misericordia; San Antonio, the patron of souls, and El Santo Cristo del Amor. Each of these saints, while acting as patron in general, is also under the special care of a patron in particular.

The process of putting a saint under patronage is peculiar. Among the images distributed around the walls of the church, whenever one is observed to attract particular attention, as, for instance, if Indians are found frequently kneeling before it, and making offerings, the padre requires of the cacique twelve Indians to serve and take care of the saint, who are called mayoles. These are furnished according to the requisition, and they elect a head, but not from their own number, who is called the patron, and to them is intrusted the guardianship of the saint. The padre, in his robes of office, administers an oath, which is sanctified by sprinkling them with holy water. The patron is sworn to watch over the interests of the saint, to take care of all the candles and other offerings presented to him, and to see that his fête is properly observed; and the mayoles are sworn to obey the orders of the patron in all things touching the custody and service of the saint. One of these saints, to whom a patron had been assigned, was called El Santo Cristo del Amor, the addition having reference to the love of the Saviour in laying down his life for man. The circumstance of the Saviour being reverenced as a saint was as new to us as that of a saint having a patron. It was the fiesta of this saint which was now celebrated, and to which we were formally invited. We accepted the invitation, but, having had a hard day's work, we were taking supper rather leisurely, when the patron came in a hurry to tell us that the procession was ready, and the saint was only waiting for us. Not wishing to put him to this inconvenience, we hurried through our meal, and proceeded to the church.

The procession had formed in the body of the church, and at the head of it, in the doorway, were Indians bearing the cross. Upon our arrival it began to move with a loud chant, and under the direction of the patron. Next to the cross were four Indians, bearing on a barrow the figure of the saint, being that of the Saviour on the cross, about a foot high, and fastened against a broad wooden back with a canopy overhead, and a small looking-glass on each side. This was followed by the patron and his mayoles, the padrecito and ourselves, the vecinos, or white people of the village, and a long train of Indian men and women, bareheaded, in white dresses, and all bearing long lighted candles. Moving down the great steps of the church with a loud chant, and the cross and the figure of the saint conspicuous under the light of hundreds of candles, the coup d'œil of the procession was solemn and imposing. Its march was toward the house of the patron, and, on turning up the street that led to it, we noticed a rope stretched along it for perhaps a hundred yards, and presently a piece of fireworks was set off, called by them the idas, or goers, and known by pyrotechnists among us as flying pigeons. The flaming ball whizzed along the rope backward and forward, scattering fire on the heads of the people underneath, and threw the whole procession into confusion and laughter. The saint was hurried into a place of security, and the people filed off on each side of the rope, out of reach of the sparks. The idas went off with universal applause, and showed that the custody of the saint had not been placed in unworthy hands. This over, the chant was resumed, and the procession moved on till it reached the house of the patron, at the door of which the padrecito chanted a salve, and then the saint was borne within. The house consisted of a single long room, having at one end a temporary altar, adorned with flowers, and at the other a table, on which were spread dulces, bread, cheese, and various compound mixtures both for eating and drinking.

The saint was set up on the altar, and in a few minutes the patron led the way, through a door opposite that by which we had entered, into an oblong enclosure about one hundred feet long and forty wide, having an arbour of palm leaves overhead. The floor was of hard earth, and seats were arranged around the sides. All the vecinos followed, and we, as strangers and attendants of the padrecito and his family, were conducted to the principal places, being a row of large wooden arm-chairs, two of which were occupied by the padrecito's mother and sister. Very soon all the seats were occupied by whites and Mestiza women, and the whole enclosure, with the exception of a small space for dancing, was filled up with Indian servants and children sitting on the ground.

Preparations were immediately made for dancing, and the ball was opened by the patron of the saint. This patron was not very saintly in his appearance, but really a most respectable man in his deportment and character, and in his youth had been the best bull-fighter the village had ever produced.

He began with the dance called the toros. The brother of the padrecito acted as master of the ceremonies, and with a pocket-handkerchief called out the ladies one after the other, until every dancing lady present had had her turn.

He then took the patron's place, the patron acting as Bastonero in his stead, and called out again every lady who chose to dance. It was a *bal champêtre,* in which no costume was required, and the brother of the padrecito, who had opened upon us, as alcalde elect, with a black dress-coat, white pantaloons, and fur hat, danced in shirt, drawers, straw hat, and sandals, pieces of leather on the soles of his feet, with cords wound round nearly up to the calf of the leg.

When he had finished we were solicited to take his place, which, however, though with some difficulty, we avoided.

I have not yet mentioned, what is a subject of remark throughout Yucatan, and was particularly manifest at this ball, the great apparent excess of female population. This excess was said to be estimated at the rate of two to one; but although it was an interesting subject, and I was seeking for statistical information which was said to exist, I could not obtain any authentic information in regard to it. I have no doubt, however, that there are many more than one woman to one man, which the men say makes Yucatan a great country to live in. Perhaps this is one reason why the standard of morality is not very high, and without wishing to reflect upon our friends in Nohcacab, as this was a public ball, I cannot help mentioning that one of the most personally attractive and lady-like looking women at the ball was the amiga of a married man, whose wife had left him; the best dressed and most distinguished young lady was the daughter of the padre who died in one of our rooms, and who, strictly speaking, ought never to have had any daughters; and in instances so numerous as not to be noticed by the people, husbands without wives and wives without husbands were mingling unrestrainedly together. Many of the white people could not speak Spanish, and the conversation was almost exclusively in the Maya language.

It was the first time we had appeared in society, and we were really great lions—in fact, equal to an entire menagerie. Whenever we moved, all eyes were turned upon us; when we spoke, all were silent; and when we spoke with each other in English, all laughed. In the interlude for refreshments, they had seen us eat, and all that they wanted was to see us dance. The padrecito told us we should be obliged to come out. A dance was introduced called Saca el suyo, or "take out your own," which brought us all out. The patron then called out the mother of the padrecito, a heavy old lady, whose dancing days were long since over, but she went through her part convulsed with laughter, and then called out her son, the padrecito, who, to the great merriment of the whole company, tried to avoid the challenge, but, once started, showed himself decidedly the best dancer at the ball. At eleven o'clock the ball broke up with great good humour; the vecinos lighted their torches, and all went home in a body, filing off at different streets. The Indians remained to take their places, and pass the night in the ball-room, dancing in honour of the saint.

Every evening, besides numerous visiters, we had the baile for recreation. When we did not go, Albino did. His intelligence and position as our head man gave him a degree of consequence, and admitted him within the arbour, where he completely eclipsed his masters, and was considered the best dancer in the place except the padrecito.

CHAPTER XVII

In the mean time we continued our work at Kabah, and, during all our intercourse with the Indians, we were constantly inquiring for other places of ruins. In this we were greatly assisted by the padrecito; indeed, but for him, and the channels of information opened to us through him, some places which are presented in these pages would perhaps never have been discovered. He had always eight Indian sextons, selected from the most respectable of the inhabitants, to take care of the church, who, when not wanted to assist at masses, salves, or funerals, were constantly lounging about our door, always tipsy, and glad to be called in. These sextons knew every Indian in the village, and the region in which he had his milpa, or cornfield; and through them we were continually making inquiries. All the ruins scattered about the country are known to the Indians under the general name of "Xlap-pahk," which means in Spanish "paredes viejas," and in English "old walls." The information we obtained was in general so confused that we were unable to form any idea of the extent or character of the ruins. We could establish no standard of comparison, as those who told us of one place were, perhaps, not familiar with any other, so that it was necessary to see all; and we had one perplexity, the magnitude of which can hardly be conceived, in the extraordinary ignorance of all the people, whites and Indians, in regard to the geography of their own immediate neighbourhood. A place they had never visited, though but a few leagues distant, they knew nothing about, and, from the extreme difficulty of ascertaining the juxtaposition of places, it was hard to arrange the plan of a route so as to embrace several. To some I made preliminary visits; those from which I expected most turned out not worth the trouble of going to, while others, from which I expected but little, proved extremely interesting. Almost every evening, on returning to the convent, the padrecito hurried into our room, with the greeting, "buenas noticias! otras ruinas!" "good news! more ruins!" and at one time these noticias came in so fast that I sent Albino on a two days' excursion to "do" some preliminary visits, who returned with a report justifying my opinion of his judgment, and a bruised leg from climbing over a mound, which disabled him for some days.

As these pages will be sufficiently burdened, I shall omit all the preliminary visits, and present the long line of ruined cities in the order in which we visited them for the purposes of exploration. Chichen was the only place we heard of in Merida, and the only place we knew of with absolute certainty before we embarked for Yucatan; but we found that a vast field of research lay between us and it, and, not to delay the reader, I proceed at once to the ruins of Kabah.

Plate XIV represents the plan of the buildings of this city. It is not made from actual measurements, for this would have required clearings which, from the difficulty of procuring Indians, it would have been impossible to make; but the bearings were taken with the compass from the top of the great teocalis, and the distances are laid down according to our best judgment with the eye.

On this plan the reader will see a road marked "Camino Real to Bolonchen," and on the left a path marked "Path to Milpa." Following this path toward the field of ruins, the teocalis is the first object that meets his eye, grand, picturesque, ruined, and covered with trees, like the House of the Dwarf at Uxmal, towering above every other object on the plain. It is about one hundred and eighty feet square at the base, and rises in a pyramidal form to the height of eighty feet. At the foot is a range of ruined apartments. The steps are all fallen, and the sides present a surface of loose stones, difficult to climb, except on one side, where the ascent is rendered practicable by the aid

247

Plate XIV

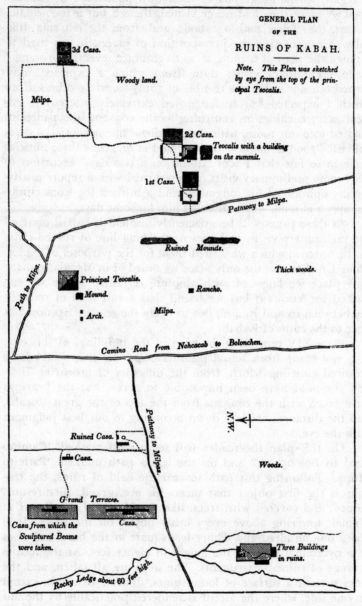

GENERAL PLAN
OF THE
RUINS OF KABAH.

Note. This Plan was sketched by eye from the top of the principal Teocalis.

3d Casa.

Woody land.

Milpa.

2d Casa.

Teocalis with a building on the summit.

1st Casa.

Pathway to Milpa.

Ruined Mounds.

Thick woods.

Principal Teocalis.

Mound.

Rancho.

Arch.

Milpa.

Path to Milpa.

Camino Real from Nohcacab to Bolonchen.

N.W.

Pathway to Milpa.

Ruined Casa.

Casa.

Woods.

Grand Terraces.

Casa.

Casa from which the Sculptured Beams were taken.

Three Buildings in ruins.

Rocky Ledge about 60 feet high.

of trees. The top presents a grand view. I ascended it for the first time toward evening, when the sun was about setting, and the ruined buildings were casting lengthened shadows over the plain. At the north, south, and east the view was bounded by a range of hills. In part of the field of ruins was a clearing, in which stood a deserted rancho, and the only indication that we were in the vicinity of man was the distant church in the village of Nohcacab.

Leaving this mound, again taking the milpa path, and following it to the distance of three or four hundred yards, we reach the foot of a terrace twenty feet high, the edge of which is overgrown with trees; ascending this, we stand on a platform two hundred feet in width by one hundred and forty-two feet deep, and facing us is the building represented in Plate XV. On the right of the platform, as we approach this building, is a high range of structures, ruined and overgrown with trees, with an immense back wall built on the outer line of the platform, perpendicular to the bottom of the terrace. On the left is another range of ruined buildings, not so grand as those on the right, and in the centre of the platform is a stone enclosure twenty-seven feet square and seven feet high, like that surrounding the picote at Uxmal; but the layer of stones around the base was sculptured, and, on examination, we found a continuous line of hieroglyphics. Mr. Catherwood made drawings of these as they lay scattered about, but, as I cannot present them in the order in which they stood, they are omitted altogether.

In the centre of the platform is a range of stone steps forty feet wide and twenty in number, leading to an upper terrace, on which stands the building. This building is one hundred and fifty-one feet in front, and the moment we saw it we were struck with the extraordinary richness and ornament of its façade. In all the buildings of Uxmal, without a single exception, up to the cornice which runs over the doorway the façades are of plain stone; but this was ornamented from the very foundation, two layers under the lower cornice, to the top.

The reader will observe that a great part of this façade has fallen; toward the north end, however, a portion of about twenty-five feet remains, which, though not itself entire, shows the gorgeousness of decoration with which this façade was once adorned. Plate XVI represents this part, exactly as it stands, with the cornice over the top fallen.

The ornaments are of the same character with those at Uxmal, alike complicated and incomprehensible, and from the

Plate XV

KABAH.
Front of the 1st Casa.

fact that every part of the façade was ornamented with sculpture, even to the portion now buried under the lower cornice, the whole must have presented a greater appearance of richness than any building at Uxmal. The cornice running over the doorways, tried by the severest rules of art recognised among us, would embellish the architecture of any known era, and, amid a mass of barbarism, of rude and uncouth conceptions, it stands as an offering by American builders worthy of the acceptance of a polished people.

The lintels of the doorways were of wood; these are all fallen, and of all the ornaments which decorated them not one now remains. No doubt they corresponded in beauty of sculpture with the rest of the façade. The whole now lies a mass of rubbish and ruin at the foot of the wall.

On the top is a structure which, at a distance, as seen indistinctly through the trees, had the appearance of a second story, and, as we approached, it reminded us of the towering structures on the top of some of the ruined buildings at Palenque.

The access to this structure was by no means easy. There was no staircase or other visible means of communication, either within or without the building, but in the rear the wall and roof had fallen, and made in some places high mounds reaching nearly to the top. Climbing up these tottering fabrics was not free from danger. Parts which appeared substantial had not the security of buildings constructed according to true principles of art; at times it was impossible to discover the supporting power, and the disorderly masses seemed held up by an invisible hand. While we were clearing off the trees upon the roof, a shower came up suddenly, and, as we were hurrying to descend and take refuge in one of the apartments below, a stone on the edge of the cornice gave way and carried me down with it. By great good fortune, underneath was a mound of ruins which reached nearly to the roof, and saved me from a fall that would have been most serious, if not fatal, in its consequences. The expression on the face of an Indian attendant as he saw me going was probably a faint reflection of my own.

The structure on the top of this building is about fifteen feet high and four feet thick, and extends over the back wall of the front range of apartments, the whole length of the edifice. In many places it has fallen, but we were now more struck than when at a distance with its general resemblance to the ruined structures on the top of some of the buildings at Palenque. The

Plate XVI

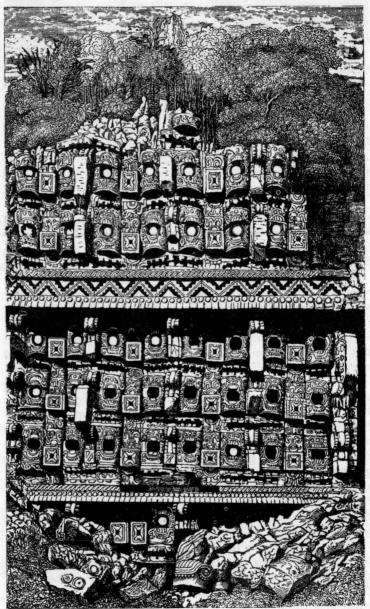

KABAH
Detail of Ornament 1st Casa

Plate XVII

KABAH.

Interior of Centre Room 1ˢᵗ Casa.

latter were stuccoed; this was of cut stone, and more chaste and simple. It could not have been intended for any use as part of the edifice; the only purpose we could ascribe to it was that of *ornament,* as it improved the appearance of the building seen from a distance, and set it off with great effect on near approach.

I have said that we were somewhat excited by the first view of the façade of this building. Ascending the steps and standing in the doorway of the centre apartment, we broke out into an exclamation of surprise and admiration. At Uxmal there was no variety; the interiors of all the apartments were the same. Here we were presented with a scene entirely new. Plate XVII represents the interior of this apartment. It consists of two parallel chambers, the one in front being twenty-seven feet long and ten feet six inches wide, and the other of the same length, but a few inches narrower, communicating by a door in the centre. The inner room is raised two feet eight inches higher than the front, and the ascent is by two stone steps carved out of a single block of stone, the lower one being in the form of a scroll. The sides of the steps are ornamented with sculpture, as is also the wall under the doorway. The whole design is graceful and pretty, and, as a mere matter of taste, the effect is extremely good. Here, on the first day of our arrival, we spread out our provisions, and ate to the memory of the former tenant. His own domains could not furnish us with water, and we were supplied from the wells of Nohcacab.

In the engraving but one doorway appears on each side of the centre, the front wall at the two ends having fallen. On both sides of this centre doorway were two other doorways opening into apartments. Each apartment contains two chambers, with the back one raised, but there are no steps, and the only ornament is a row of small pilasters about two feet high under the door, and running the whole length of the room.

Such is a brief description of the façade and front apartments, and these formed not more than one third of the building. At the rear and under the same roof were two ranges of apartments of the same dimensions with those just described, and having a rectangular area in front. The whole edifice formed nearly a square, and though having less front, with a great solic mass, nearly as thick as one of the corridors, for the centre wall, it covered nearly as many square feet as the Casa del Gobernador, and probably, from its lavishness of ornament, contained more sculptured stone. The rest of the building, however, was in a much more ruinous condition than that presented.

Plate XVIII

At both ends the wall had fallen, and the whole of the other front, with the roof, and the ruins filled up the apartments so that it was extremely difficult to make out the plan.

The whole of the terrace on this latter side is overgrown with trees, some of which have taken root among the fragments, and are growing out of the interior of the chambers.

Plate XVIII will give some idea of the manner in which the rankness of tropical vegetation is hurrying to destruction these interesting remains. The tree is called the alamo, or elm, the leaves of which, with those of the ramon, form in that country the principal fodder for horses. Springing up beside the front wall, its fibres crept into cracks and crevices, and became shoots and branches, which, as the trunk rose, in struggling to rise with it, unsettled and overturned the wall, and still grew, carrying up large stones fast locked in their embraces, which they now hold aloft in the air. At the same time, its roots have girded the foundation wall, and form the only support of what is left. The great branches overshadowing the whole cannot be exhibited in the plate, and no sketch can convey a true idea of the ruthless gripe in which these gnarled and twisted roots encircle sculptured stones.

Such is a brief description of the first building at Kabah. To many of these structures the Indians have given names stupid, senseless, and unmeaning, having no reference to history or tradition. This one they call Xcocpoop, which means in Spanish petato doblado, or a straw hat doubled up; the name having reference to the crushed and flattened condition of the façade and the prostration of the rear wall of the building.

Descending the corner of the back terrace, at the distance of a few paces rises a broken and overgrown mound, on which stands a ruined building, called by the Indians the cocina, or kitchen, because, as they said, it had chimneys to let out smoke. According to their accounts, it must have contained something curious; and it was peculiarly unfortunate that we had not reached it one year sooner, for then it stood entire. During the last rainy season some muleteers from Merida, scouring the country in search of maize, were overtaken by the afternoon's rain, and took shelter under its roof, turning their mules out to graze among the ruins. During the night the building fell, but, fortunately, the muleteers escaped unhurt, and, leaving their mules behind them, in the darkness and rain made the best of their way to Nohcacab, reporting that El Demonio was among the ruins of Kabah.

On the left of this mound is a staircase leading down to the area of Casa No. 2, and on the right is a grand and majestic pile of buildings, having no name assigned to it, and which, perhaps, when entire, was the most imposing structure at Kabah. It measured at the base one hundred and forty-seven feet on one side and one hundred and six on the other, and consisted of three distinct stories or ranges, one on the roof of the other, the second smaller than the first, and the third smaller than the second, having on each side a broad platform in front. Along the base on all four of the sides was a continuous range of apartments, with the doorways supported by pillars, and on the side fronting the rear of Casa No. 1 was another new and interesting feature.

This was a gigantic stone staircase, rising to the roof, on which stood the second range of apartments. This staircase was not a solid mass, resting against the wall of the mound, but was supported by the half of a triangular arch springing from the ground, and resting against the wall so as to leave a passage under the staircase. This staircase was interesting not only for its own grandeur and the novelty of its construction, but as explaining what had before been unintelligible in regard to the principal staircase in the House of the Dwarf at Uxmal.

The steps of this staircase are nearly all fallen, and the ascent is as on an inclined plane. The buildings on the top are ruined, and many of the doorways so encumbered that there was barely room to crawl into them. On one occasion, while clearing around this so as to make a plan, rain came on, and I was obliged to crawl into one with all the Indians, and remain in the dark, breathing a damp and unwholesome atmosphere, pent up and almost stifled, for more than an hour.

The doorways of the ranges on the north side of this mound opened upon the area of Casa No. 2. The platform of this area is one hundred and seventy feet long, one hundred and ten broad, and is elevated ten feet from the ground. It had been planted with corn, and required little clearing. Plate XIX represents the front of this building, and the picote, or great stone found thrown down in all the courtyards and areas, is exhibited on one side in the engraving. The edifice stands upon an upper terrace; forming a breastwork for which, and running the whole length, one hundred and sixty-four feet, is a range of apartments, with their doors opening upon the area. The front wall and the roof of this range have nearly all fallen.

A ruined staircase rises from the centre of the platform to

257

Plate XIX

KABAH.
Front of Casa Nº 2.

Plate XX

J. Catherwood

H Cobourne

KABAH.
3rd Casa.

the roof of this range, which forms the platform in front of the principal building.

This staircase, like that last mentioned, is supported by the half of a triangular arch, precisely like the other already mentioned. The whole front was ornamented with sculpture, and the ornaments best preserved are over the doorway of the centre apartment, which, being underneath the staircase, cannot be exhibited in the engraving.

The principal building, it will be seen, has pillars in two of its doorways. At this place, for the first time, we met with pillars used legitimately, according to the rules of known architecture, as a support, and they added greatly to the interest which the other novelties here disclosed to us presented. These pillars, however, were but six feet high, rude and unpolished, with square blocks of stone for capitals and pedestals. They wanted the architectural majesty and grandeur which in other styles is always connected with the presence of pillars, but they were not out of proportion, and, in fact, were adapted to the lowness of the building. The lintels over the doors are of stone.

Leaving this building, and crossing an overgrown and wooded plain, at the distance of about three hundred and fifty yards we reach the terrace of Casa No. 3. The platform of this terrace, too, had been planted with corn, and was easily cleared. Plate XX represents the front of the edifice, which, when we first came upon it, was so beautifully shrouded by trees that it was painful to be obliged to disturb them, and we spared every branch that did not obstruct the view. While Mr. Catherwood was making his drawing, rain came on, and, as he might not be able to get his camera lucida in position again, he continued his work, with the protection of an India-rubber cloak and an Indian holding an umbrella over the stand. The rain was of that sudden and violent character often met with in tropical climates, and in a few minutes flooded the whole ground. The washing of the water from the upper terrace appears in the engraving.

This building is called by the Indians la Casa de la Justicia. It is one hundred and thirteen feet long. There are five apartments, each twenty feet long and nine wide, and all perfectly plain. The front is plain, except the pillars in the wall between the doorways indicated in the engraving; and above, in front, at the end, and on the back are rows of small pillars, forming a simple and not inelegant ornament.

Besides these, there are on this side of the camino real the remains of other buildings, but all in a ruinous condition, and

FIG. 23

there is one monument, perhaps more curious and interesting than any that has been presented. It is a lonely arch, of the same form with all the rest, having a span of fourteen feet. It stands on a ruined mound, disconnected from every other structure, in solitary grandeur. Darkness rests upon its history, but in that desolation and solitude, among the ruins around, it stood like the proud memorial of a Roman triumph. Perhaps, like the arch of Titus, which at this day spans the Sacred Way at Rome, it was erected to commemorate a victory over enemies.

These were all the principal remains on this side of the camino real; they were all to which our Indian guides conducted us, and, excepting two mentioned hereafter, they were all of which, up to that time, any knowledge existed; but on the other side of the camino real, shrouded by trees, were the trembling and tottering skeletons of buildings which had once been grander than these.

From the top of the great teocalis we had our first glimpses of these edifices. Following the camino real to a point about in

261

a range with the triumphal arch, there is a narrow path which leads to two buildings enclosed by a fence for a milpa. They are small, and but little ornamented. They stand at right angles to each other, and in front of them is a patio, in which is a large broken orifice, like the mouth of a cave, with a tree growing near the edge of it. My first visit to this place was marked by a brilliant exploit on the part of my horse. On dismounting, Mr. Catherwood found shade for his horse, Doctor Cabot got his into one of the buildings, and I tied mine to this tree, giving him fifteen or twenty feet of halter as a range for pasture. Here we left them, but on our return in the evening my horse was missing, and, as we supposed, stolen; but before we reached the tree I saw the halter still attached to it, and knew that an Indian would be much more likely to steal the halter and leave the horse than *vice versa*. The halter was drawn down into the mouth of the cave, and looking over the edge, I saw the horse hanging at the other end, with just rope enough, by stretching his head and neck, to keep a foothold at one side of the cave. One of his sides was scratched and grimed with dirt, and it seemed as if every bone in his body must be broken, but on getting him out we found that, except some scarifications of the skin, he was not at all hurt; in fact, he was quite the reverse, and never moved better than on our return to the village.

Beyond these buildings, none of the Indians knew of any ruins. Striking directly from them in a westerly direction through a thick piece of woods, without being able to see anything, but from observation taken from the top of the teocalis, and passing a small ruined building with a staircase leading to the roof, we reached a great terrace, perhaps eight hundred feet long and one hundred feet wide. This terrace, besides being overgrown with trees, was covered with thorn-bushes, and the maguey plant, or Agave Americana, with points as sharp as needles, which made it impossible to move without cutting the way at every step.

Two buildings stood upon this overgrown terrace. The first was two hundred and seventeen feet long, having seven doorways in front, all opening to single apartments except the centre one, which had two apartments, each thirty feet long. In the rear were other apartments, with doorways opening upon a court-yard, and from the centre a range of buildings ran at right angles, terminating in a large ruined mound. The wall of the whole of this great pile had been more ornamented than either of the buildings before presented except the first, but, unfortunately, it was more dilapidated. The doorways had wooden lintels, most of which have fallen.

To the north of this building is another, one hundred and forty-two feet in front and thirty-one feet deep, with double corridors communicating, and a gigantic staircase in the centre leading to the roof, on which are the ruins of another building. The doors of two centre apartments open under the arch of this great staircase. In that on the right we again found the prints of the red hand; not a single print, or two, or three, as in other places, but the whole wall was covered with them, bright and distinct as if but newly made.

All the lintels over the doorways are of wood, and all are still in their places, mostly sound and solid. The doorways were encumbered with rubbish and ruins. That nearest the staircase was filled up to within three feet of the lintel; and, in crawling under on his back, to measure the apartment, Mr. Catherwood's eye was arrested by a sculptured lintel, which, on examination, he considered the most interesting memorial we had found in Yucatan. On my return that day from a visit to three more ruined cities entirely unknown before, he claimed this lintel as equal in interest and value to all of them together. The next day I saw them, and determined immediately, at any trouble or cost, to carry them home with me; but this was no easy matter. Our operations created much discussion in the village. The general belief was that we were searching for gold. No one could believe that we were expending money in such a business without being sure of getting it back again; and remembering the fate of my castings at Palenque, I was afraid to have it known that there was anything worth carrying away.

To get them out by our own efforts, however, was impossible; and, after conferring with the padrecito, we procured a good set of men, and went down with crowbars for the purpose of working them out of the wall. Doctor Cabot, who had been confined to the village for several days by illness, turned out on this great occasion.

The lintel consisted of two beams, and the outer one was split in two lengthwise. They lapped over the doorway about a foot at each end, and were as firmly secured as any stones in the building, having been built in when the wall was constructed. Fortunately, we had two crowbars, and the doorway being filled up with earth both inside and out, the men were enabled to stand above the beam, and use the crowbars to advantage. They began inside, and in about two hours cleared the lintel directly over the doorway, but the ends were still firmly secured. The beams were about ten feet long, and to keep the whole wall from falling and crushing them, it was necessary to knock away the stones over the centre, and make an arch in proportion to the base. The wall was four feet thick over the doorway, increasing in thickness with the receding of the inner arch, and the whole was a solid mass, the mortar being nearly as hard as the stone. As the breach was enlarged it became dangerous to stand near it; the crowbar had to be thrown aside, and the men cut down small trees, which they used as a sort of battering-ram, striking at the mortar and small stones used for filling up, on loosening which the larger stones fell. To save the beams, we constructed an inclined plane two or three feet above them, resting against the inner wall, which caught the stones and carried them off. As the breach increased it became really dangerous to work under it, and one of the men refused to do so any longer. The beams were almost within my grasp, but if the ragged mass above should fall, it would certainly bury the beams and the men too, either of which would be disagreeable. Fortunately, we had the best set of assistants that ever came out to us from Nohcacab, and their pride was enlisted in the cause. At length, almost against hope, having broken a rude arch almost to the roof, the inner beam was got out uninjured. Still the others were not safe, but, with great labour, anxiety, and good fortune, the whole three at length lay before us, with their sculptured faces uppermost. We did no more work that day; we had hardly changed our positions, but, from the excitement and anxiety, it was one of the most trying times we had in the country.

The next day, knowing the difficulty and risk that must attend their transportation, we had the beams set up for Mr. Catherwood to draw.

Plate XXI represents this lintel, indicated in the engraving as three pieces of wood, but originally consisting of only two, that on which the figure is carved being split through the middle by some unequal pressure of the great superincumbent wall. The top of the outer part was worm-eaten and decayed, probably from the trickling of water, which, following some channel in the ornaments, touched only this part; all the rest was sound and solid.

The subject is a human figure standing upon a serpent. The face was scratched, worn, and obliterated, the headdress was a plume of feathers, and the general character of the figure and ornaments was the same with that of the figures found on the

Plate XXI

F Catherwood.

KABAH
Carved Beam of Sapote Wood

walls at Palenque. It was the first subject we had discovered bearing such a striking resemblance in details, and connecting so closely together the builders of these distant cities.

But the great interest of this lintel was the carving. The beam covered with hieroglyphics at Uxmal was faded and worn. This was still in excellent preservation; the lines were clear and distinct; and the cutting, under any test, and without any reference to the people by whom it was executed, would be considered as indicating great skill and proficiency in the art of carving on wood. The consciousness that the only way to give a true idea of the character of this carving was the production of the beams themselves, determined me to spare neither labour nor expense to have them transported to this city; and when we had finished our whole exploration, we were satisfied that these were the most interesting specimens the country afforded. I had the sculptured sides packed in dry grass and covered with hemp bagging, and intended to pass them through the village without stopping, but the Indians engaged for that purpose left them two days on the ground exposed to heavy rain, and I was obliged to have them brought to the convent, where the grass was taken out and dried. The first morning one or two hundred Indians at work at the noria came up in a body to look at them. It was several days before I could get them away, but, to my great relief, they at length left the village on the shoulders of Indians, and I brought them with me safely to this city. The reader anticipates my conclusion, and if he have but a shade of sympathy with the writer, he mourns over the melancholy fate that overtook them but a short time after their arrival.

The accidental discovery of these sculptured beams, and in a position where we had no reason to look for such things, induced us to be more careful than ever in our examination of every part of the building. The lintel over the corresponding doorway on the other side of the staircase was still in its place, and in good condition, but perfectly plain, and there was no other sculptured lintel among all the ruins of Kabah. Why this particular doorway was so distinguished it is impossible to say. The character of this sculpture added to the interest and wonder of all that was connected with the exploration of these American ruins. There is no account of the existence of iron or steel among the aborigines on this continent. The general and well-grounded belief is, that the inhabitants had no knowledge whatever of these metals. How, then, could they carve wood, and that of the hardest kind?

In that large canoe which first made known to Columbus the existence of this great continent, among other fabrics of the country from which they came, the Spaniards remarked hatchets of copper, as it is expressed, for "hewing wood." Bernal Dias, in his account of the first voyage of the Spaniards along the coast of Guacaulco, in the Empire of Mexico, says, "It was a Custom of the Indians of this Province *invariably* to carry small Hatchets of Copper, very bright, and the wooden Handles of which were highly painted, as intended both for Defence and Ornament. These were supposed by us to be Gold, and were, of Course, eagerly purchased, *insomuch that within three days we had amongst us procured above six hundred,* and were, while under the Mistake, as well pleased with our Bargain as the Indians with their green Beads." And in that collection of interesting relics from Peru before referred to, in the possession of Mr. Blake of Boston—the existence of which, by-the-way, from the unobtrusive character of its owner, is hardly known to his neighbours in his own city—in that collection are several copper knives, one of which is alloyed with a small portion of tin, and sufficiently hard to cut wood. In other cemeteries in the same district, Mr. Blake found several copper instruments resembling modern chisels, which, it is not improbable, were designed for carving wood. In my opinion, the carving of these beams was done with the copper instruments known to have existed among the aboriginal inhabitants, and it is not necessary to suppose, without and even against all evidence, that at some remote period of time the use of iron and steel was known on this continent, and that the knowledge had become lost among the latter inhabitants.

From the great terrace a large structure is seen at a distance indistinctly through the trees, and, pointing it out to an Indian, I set out with him to examine it. Descending among the trees, we soon lost sight of it entirely, but, pursuing the direction, the Indian cutting a way with his machete, we came upon a building, which, however, I discovered, was not the one we were in search of. It was about ninety feet in front, the walls were cracked, and all along the base the ground was strewed with sculptured stones, the carving of which was equal to any we had seen. Before reaching the door I crawled through a fissure in the wall into an apartment, at one end of which, in the arch, I saw an enormous hornet's nest; and in turning to take a hasty leave, saw at the opposite end a large ornament in stucco, having also a hornet's nest attached to it, painted, the colours being still bright and vivid, and surprising me as much as the sculptured beams. A great part had fallen, and it had the appearance of having been wantonly destroyed. Figure 24 represents this fragment. The ornament, when entire, appears to have been intended to represent two large eagles facing each other; on each side are seen drooping plumes of feathers. The opposite end of the arch, where hung the hornet's nest, had marks of stucco in the same form, and probably once contained a corresponding ornament.

FIG. 24

Beyond this was the great building which we had set out to find. The front was still standing, in some places, particularly on the corner, richly ornamented; but the back part was a heap of ruins. In the centre was a gigantic staircase leading to the top, on which there was another building with two ranges of apartments, the outer one fallen, the inner one entire.

In descending on the other side over a mass of ruins, I found at one corner a deep hole, which apparently led into a cave, but, crawling down, I found that it conducted to the buried door of a chamber on a new and curious plan. It had a raised platform about four feet high, and in each of the inner corners was a rounded vacant place, about large enough for a man to stand in; part of the back wall was covered with prints of the red hand. They seemed so fresh, and the seams and creases were so distinct, that I made several attempts with the machete to get one print off entire, but the plaster was so hard that every effort failed.

Beyond this was another building, so unpretending in its appearance compared with the first, that, but for the uncertainty in regard to what might be found in every part of these ruins, I should hardly have noticed it. This building had but one doorway, which was nearly choked up; but on passing into it I noticed sculptured on the jambs, nearly buried, a protruding corner of a plume of feathers. This I immediately supposed to be a headdress, and that below was a sculptured human figure. This, again, was entirely new. The jambs of all the doors we had hitherto seen were plain. By closer inspection I found on the opposite jamb a corresponding stone, but entirely buried. The top stone of both was missing, but I found them near by, and determined immediately to excavate the parts that were buried, and carry the whole away; but it was a more difficult business than that of getting out the beams. A solid mound of earth descended from the outside to the back wall of the apartment, choking the doorway to within a few feet of the top. To clear the whole doorway was out of the question, for the Indians had only their hands with which to scoop out the accumulated mass. The only way was to dig down beside each stone, then separate it from the wall with the crowbar, and pry it out. I was engaged in this work two entire days, and on the second the Indians wanted to abandon it. They had dug down nearly to the bottom, and one man in the hole refused to work any longer. To keep them together and not lose another day, I was obliged to labour myself; and late in the afternoon we got out the stones, with poles for levers, lifted them over the mound, and set them up against the back wall.

Plates XXII and XXIII represent these two jambs as they stood facing each other in the doorway. Each consists of two separate stones, as indicated in the engravings. In each the upper stone is one foot five inches high, and the lower one four feet six inches, and both are two feet three inches wide. The subject consists of two figures, one standing, and the other kneeling before him. Both have unnatural and grotesque faces, probably containing some symbolical meaning. The headdress is a lofty plume of feathers, falling to the heels of the standing figure; and under his feet is a row of hieroglyphics.

While toiling to bring to light these buried stones, I little thought that I was raising up another witness to speak for the builders of these ruined cities. The reader will notice in Plate

Plate XXII

F.Catherwood.   A.Jones.

KABAH.
Figure on jamb of Doorway.

Plate XXIII

F.Catherwood.   A.Jones.

KABAH.

Figure on jamb of Doorway

271

XXII a weapon in the hands of the kneeling figure. In that same large canoe before referred to, Herrera says, the Indians had "Swords made of Wood, having a Gutter in the fore Part, in which were sharp-edged Flints, strongly fixed with a sort of Bitumen and Thread." The same weapon is described in every account of the aboriginal weapons; it is seen in every museum of Indian curiosities, and it is in use at this day among the Indians of the South Sea Islands. The sword borne by the figure represented in the engraving is precisely of the kind described by Herrera. I was not searching for testimony to establish any opinion or theory. There was interest enough in exploring these ruins without attempting to do so, and this witness rose unbidden.

In lifting these stones out of the holes and setting them up against the walls, I had been obliged to assist myself, and almost the moment it was finished I found that the fatigue and excitement had been too much for me. My bones ached; a chill crept over me; I looked around for a soft stone to lie down upon; but the place was cold and damp, and rain was threatening. I saddled my horse, and when I mounted I could barely keep my seat. I had no spurs; my horse seemed to know my condition, and went on a slow walk, nibbling at every bush. The fever came on, and I was obliged to dismount and lie down under a bush; but the garrapatas drove me away. At length I reached the village, and this was my last visit to Kabah; but I have already finished a description of its ruins. Doubtless more lie buried in the woods, and the next visiter, beginning where we left off, if he be at all imbued with interest in this subject, will push his investigations much farther. We were groping in the dark. Since the hour of their desolation and wo came upon them, these buildings had remained unknown. Except the cura Carillo, who first informed us of them, perhaps no white man had wandered through their silent chambers. We were the first to throw open the portals of their grave, and they are now for the first time presented to the public.

But I can do little more than state the naked fact of their existence. The cloud which hangs over their history is much darker than that resting over the ruins of Uxmal. I can only say of them that they lie on the common lands of the village of Nohcacab. Perhaps they have been known to the Indians from time immemorial; but, as the padrecito told us, until the opening of the camino real to Bolonchen they were utterly unknown to the white inhabitants. This road passed through the ancient city, and discovered the great buildings, overgrown, and in some places towering above the tops of the trees. The discovery, however, created not the slightest sensation; the intelligence of it had never reached the capital; and though, ever since the discovery, the great edifices were visible to all who passed along the road, not a white man in the village had ever turned aside to look at them, except the padrecito, who, on the first day of our visit, rode in, but without dismounting, in order to make a report to us. The Indians say of them, as of all the other ruins, that they are the works of the antiguos; but the traditionary character of the city is that of a great place, superior to the other Xlap-pahk scattered over the country, coequal and coexistent with Uxmal; and there is a tradition of a great paved way, made of pure white stone, called in the Maya language Sacbé, leading from Kabah to Uxmal, on which the lords of those places sent messengers to and fro, bearing letters written on the leaves and bark of trees.

At the time of my attack, Mr. Catherwood, Doctor Cabot, and Albino were all down with fever. I had a recurrence the next day, but on the third I was able to move about. The spectacle around was gloomy for sick men. From the long continuance of the rainy season our rooms in the convent were damp, and corn which we kept in one corner for the horses had swelled and sprouted.

Death was all around us. Anciently this country was so healthy that Torquemada says, "Men die of pure old age, for there are none of those infirmities that exist in other lands; and if there are slight infirmities, the heat destroys them, and so there is no need of a physician there;" but the times are much better for physicians now, and Doctor Cabot, if he had been able to attend to it, might have entered into an extensive gratuitous practice. Adjoining the front of the church, and connecting with the convent, was a great charnel-house, along the wall of which was a row of skulls. At the top of a pillar forming the abutment of the wall of the staircase was a large vase piled full, and the cross was surmounted with them. Within the enclosure was a promiscuous assemblage of skulls and bones several feet deep. Along the wall, hanging by cords, were the bones and skulls of individuals in boxes and baskets, or tied up in cloths, with names written upon them, and, as at Ticul, there were the fragments of dresses, while some of the skulls had still adhering to them the long black hair of women.

The floor of the church was interspersed with long patches

FIG. 25

of cement, which covered graves, and near one of the altars was a box with a glass case, within which were the bones of a woman, the wife of a lively old gentleman whom we were in the habit of seeing every day. They were clean and bright as if polished, with the skull and cross-bones in front, the legs and arms laid on the bottom, and the ribs disposed regularly in order, one above the other, as in life, having been so arranged by the husband himself; a strange attention, as it seemed, to a deceased wife. At the side of the case was a black board, containing a poetical inscription (in Spanish) written by him.

> "Stop, mortal!
> Look at yourself in this mirror,
> And in its pale reflection
> Behold your end!
> This eclipsed crystal
> Had splendour and brilliancy;
> But the dreadful blow
> Of a fatal destiny
> Fell upon Manuela Carillo.

274

Born in Nohcacab in the year 1789, married at the same village to Victor-
iano Machado in 1808, and died on the first of August, 1833, after a union
of 25 years, and in the forty-fourth of her age.
    He implores your pious prayers."

The widowed husband wrote several stanzas more, but could
not get them on the black board; and made copies for private
distribution, one of which is in my hands.

Near this were the bones of a brother of our friend the cura
of Ticul and those of a child, and in the choir of the church,
in the embrazure of a large window, were rows of skulls, all
labelled on the forehead, and containing startling inscriptions.
I took up one, and staring me in the face were the words, "Soy
Pedro Moreno: un Ave Maria y un Padre nuestro por Dios, her-
mano." "I am Peter Moreno: an Ave Maria and Paternoster for
God's sake, brother." Another said, "I am Apolono Balche: a
Paternoster and an Ave Maria for God's sake, brother." This
was an old schoolmaster of the padrecito, who had died but two
years before.

FIG. 26

The padrecito handed me another, which said, "I am Bartola
Arana: a Paternoster," &c. This was the skull of a Spanish lady
whom he had known, young and beautiful, but it could not be
distinguished from that of the oldest and ugliest Indian woman.
"I am Anizetta Bib," was that of a pretty young Indian girl
whom he had married, and who died but a year afterward. I
took them all up one by one; the padrecito knew them all; one

was young, another old; one rich, another poor; one ugly, and another beautiful; but here they were all alike. Every skull bore the name of its owner, and all begged a prayer.

One said, "I am Richard Joseph de la Merced Truxeque and Arana, who died the twenty-ninth of April of the year 1838, and I am enjoying the kingdom of God forever." This was the skull of a child, which, dying without sin, had ascended to heaven, and needed not the prayers of man.

In one corner was a mourning box, painted black, with a white border, containing the skull of an uncle of the padrecito. On it was written in Spanish, "In this box is enclosed the skull of Friar Vicente Ortigon, who died in the village of Cuhul in the year 1820. I beseech thee, pious and charitable reader, to intercede with God for his soul, repeating an Ave Maria and a Paternoster, that he may be released from purgatory, if he should be there, and may go to enjoy the kingdom of heaven. Whoever the reader may be, God will reward his charity. 26th of July, 1837." The writing bore the name of Juana Hernandez, the mother of the deceased, an old lady then living in the house of the mother of the padrecito.

Accustomed as we were to hold sacred the bones of the dead, the slightest memorial of a departed friend accidentally presented to view bringing with it a shade of sadness, such an exhibition grated harshly upon the feelings. I asked the padrecito why these skulls were not permitted to rest in peace, and he answered, what is perhaps but too true, that in the grave they are forgotten; but when dug up and placed in sight with labels on them, they remind the living of their former existence, of their uncertain state—that their souls may be in purgatory—and appeal to their friends, as with voices from the grave, to pray for them, and have masses said for their souls. It is for this reason, and not from any feeling of wantonness or disrespect, that the skulls of the dead are thus exposed all over the country. On the second of November, at the celebration of the fête in commemoration *de los fieles difuntos*, all these skulls are brought together and put into the túmulo, a sort of bier hung with black and lighted by blessed candles, and grand mass is said for their souls.

In the afternoon the padrecito passed our door in his robes, and, looking in, as he usually did, said, "Voy á buscar un muerto," "I am going for a corpse." The platform of the church was the campo santo; every day the grave-digger was at his work, and soon after the padrecito left us we heard the chant heralding the funeral procession. I went out, and saw it coming up the steps, the padrecito leading it and chanting the funeral service. The corpse was brought into the church, and, the service over, it was borne to the grave. The sacristans were so intoxicated that they let it fall in with its neck twisted. The padrecito sprinkled it with holy water, and, the chant over, went away. The Indians around the grave looked at me with an expression of face I could not understand. They had told the padrecito that we had brought death into the village. In a spirit of conciliation I smiled at a woman near me, and she answered with a laugh. I carried my smile slowly around the whole circle; as my eyes met theirs, all burst into a laugh, and while the body lay uncovered and distorted in the grave I went away. With these people death is merely one of the accidents of life. "Voy á descansar," "I am going to rest," "Mis trabajos son acabados," "My labours are ended," are the words of the Indian as he lies down to die; but to the stranger in that country death is the king of terrors.

In the mean time pleasure was treading lightly upon the heels of death. The fiesta of Santo Cristo del Amor was still going on, and it was to conclude the next day with a baile de dia, or ball by daylight, at the place where it began, in the house of the patron. We were busy in making preparations for our departure from Nohcacab, and, though strongly solicited, I was the only one of our party able to attend. Early in the morning the saint was in its place at one end of the room, the altar was adorned with fresh flowers, and the arbour for dancing was covered with palm leaves to protect it from the sun. Under a shed in the yard was a crowd of Indian women making tortillas, and preparing dishes of various kinds for a general village feast. At twelve o'clock the ball began, a little before two the padrecito disappeared from my side, and soon after the ball broke up, and all moved toward the house. When I entered, the padrecito was in his robes before the image of the saint, singing a salve. The Indian sexton was perfuming it with incense, and the dancers were all on their knees before it, each with a lighted candle in her hand. This over, came the procession de las velas, or of the candles. The cross led the way; then the figure of the saint, a drunken Indian sexton perfuming it with incense. The padrecito, in taking his place behind it, took my arm and carried me along; the patron of the saint supported me on the other side. We were the only men in the procession. An irregular troop of women followed, all in their ball dresses, and bearing long lighted candles. Moving on to the church, we restored the saint to his altar, and set up the candles in rough wooden tripods, to be ready for grand mass the next morning. At this time a discharge of rockets was heard without, and going out, I saw another strange procession. We had all the women; this was composed entirely of men, and might have passed for a jubilee over the downfall of temperance. Nearly all were more than half intoxicated; and I noticed that some who had kept sober during the whole of the fiesta were overtaken at last. The procession was preceded by files of them in couples, each carrying two plates, for the purpose of receiving some of the dishes provided by the bounty of the patron. Next came, borne on barrows on the shoulders of Indians, two long, ugly boxes, the emblems of the custody and property of the saint, one of them being filled with wax received as offerings, ropes for the fireworks, and other property belonging to the saint, which were about being carried to the house of the person now entitled to their custody; and the other had contained these things, and was to remain with its present keeper as a sort of holy heirloom. Behind these, also on the shoulders of Indians, were two men, sitting side by side in large arm-chairs, with scarfs around their necks, and holding on desperately to the arms of the chairs, with an expression of face that seemed to indicate a consciousness that their elevation above their fellow-citizens was precarious, and of uncertain duration, for their Indian carriers were reeling and staggering under their load and agua ardiente. These were the hermanos de la misa, or brothers of the mass, the last incumbent of the office of the keeper of the box and his successor, to whom it was to be delivered over. Moving on with uproarious noise and confusion, they were set down under the corridor of the quartel.

In the mean time our procession of women from the church had arrived, the musicians took their places under the corridor, and preparations were immediately made for another dance. Cocom, who had acted as our guide to Nohpat, and had repaired the locks and keys of our boxes, was master of ceremonies; and the first dance over, two Mestiza girls commenced a song. The whole village seemed given up to the pleasure of the moment; there were features to offend the sight and taste, but there were pretty women prettily dressed; in all there was an air of abandonment and freedom from care that enlisted sympathetic feelings; and as the padrecito and myself returned to the convent, the chorus reached us on the steps, soft and sweet from the blending of women's voices, and seeming to spring from the bottom of every heart,

A Song

"Que bonito es el mundo;
  Lastima es que yo me muera."

"How beautiful is the world;
  It is a pity that I must die."

APPENDIX

THERMOMETRICAL OBSERVATIONS.

Temperature of Merida, according to observations taken by the cura Don Eusebio Villamil, for one year, beginning on the 1st of September, 1841, and ending on the 31st of August, 1842. The observations were taken with a Fahrenheit thermometer at six in the morning, midday, and six in the evening. The thermometer stood in the shade, in an apartment well ventilated.

SEPTEMBER, 1842.

Days.	Morn.	Noon.	Even.
1,	80°	84°	84°
2,	80	84	83
3,	80	84	83
4,	80	84	82
5,	80	84	83
6,	81	85	84
7,	81	84	82
8,	81	86	85
9,	81	85	84
10,	82	85	85
11,	83	85	84
12,	82	85	84
13,	82	85	85
14,	82	86	85
15,	82	86	85
16,	83	86	85
17,	83	85	84
18,	83	85	84
19,	83	85	84
20,	84	86	85
21,	84	86	86
22,	84	86	84
23,	84	86	86
24,	84	85	83
25,	80	84	83
26,	80	85	83
27,	81	85	83
28,	82	85	84
29,	82	86	86
30,	83	86	85

OCTOBER.

Days.	Morn.	Noon.	Even.
1,	83°	86°	85°
2,	83	86	85
3,	83	85	83
4,	81	84	82
5,	81	84	83
6,	81	84	82
7,	81	84	82
8,	81	84	82
9,	80	84	82
10,	80	84	83
11,	80	85	84
12,	82	85	84
13,	80	84	84
14,	80	84	84
15,	81	84	84
16,	81	84	83
17,	80	83	83
18,	81	83	83
19,	81	84	84
20,	82	83	81
21,	80	81	80
22,	78	80	78
23,	76	78	78
24,	76	78	78
25,	76	76	76
26,	74	76	76
27,	74	78	78
28,	76	80	79
29,	77	81	80
30,	78	81	81
31,	81	82	82

NOVEMBER.

Days.	Morn.	Noon.	Even.
1,	82°	83°	82°
2,	80	82	81
3,	78	80	80
4,	80	77	77
5,	77	78	78
6,	74	77	76
7,	74	76	76
8,	75	78	78
9,	75	78	78
10,	74	79	79
11,	76	79	79
12,	77	80	80
13,	77°	80°	80°
14,	80	80	80
15,	78	79	79
16,	74	78	78
17,	74	78	78
18,	72	77	77
19,	73	79	79
20,	75	79	79
21,	78	82	82
22,	80	83	82
23,	80	84	83
24,	79	82	82
25,	80	83	83
26,	79	82	80
27,	79	78	78
28,	78	76	75
29,	73	73	74
30,	73	74	74

DECEMBER.

Days.	Morn.	Noon.	Even.
1,	72°	74°	74°
2,	73	77	77
3,	73	79	79
4,	78	79	79
5,	75	76	75
6,	72	74	74
7,	72	74	74
8,	71	74	74
9,	70	74	74
10,	74	78	78
11,	76	78	78
12,	74	77	77
13,	74	78	77
14,	73	78	78
15,	75	79	79
16,	76	78	77
17,	75	75	75
18,	71	74	74
19,	65	73	75

Days.	Morn.	Noon.	Even.
20,	68°	74°	74°
21,	70	76	76
22,	72	88	78
23,	74	78	78
24,	76	77	77
25,	75	77	76
26,	75	78	77
27,	74	79	78
28,	76	79	78
29,	76	78	78
30,	76	77	76
31,	76	78	78

JANUARY, 1842.

Days.	Morn.	Noon.	Even.
1,	75°	78°	77°
2,	75	77	77
3,	76	76	76
4,	74	78	77
5,	74	78	78
6,	74	78	78
7,	74	78	78
8,	74	78	77
9,	74	77	76
10,	74	77	76
11,	73	78	77
12,	74	78	77
13,	74	77	76
14,	73	78	77
15,	74	77	76
16,	74	76	76
17,	73	76	75
18,	73	76	75
19,	70	76	76
20,	73	76	76
21,	72	72	72
22,	70	72	72
23,	68	72	72
24,	68	73	72
25,	69	74	74
26,	72	78	77
27,	73	76	76
28,	73	76	77
29,	74	78	78
30,	74	79	79
31,	74	80	80

FEBRUARY.

Days.	Morn.	Noon.	Even.
1,	75°	78°	78°
2,	74	80	80
3,	76	81	81
4,	76	80	79
5,	77	80	79
6,	76	80	80
7,	76	80	80
8,	76	74	74
9,	73	74	74
10,	71°	76°	76°
11,	74	79	78
12,	74	80	79
13,	76	80	79
14,	77	80	79
15,	77	80	80
16,	78	76	76
17,	72	76	76
18,	75	79	79
19,	76	79	78
20,	77	80	80
21,	78	76	75
22,	73	74	74
23,	70	74	72
24,	69	78	76
25,	71	77	77
26,	74	78	78
27,	76	81	81
28,	77	81	81

MARCH.

Days.	Morn.	Noon.	Even.
1,	78°	82°	82°
2,	78	83	82
3,	78	83	82
4,	78	83	82
5,	78	84	84
6,	78	84	84
7,	78	85	84
8,	78	84	82
9,	77	82	84
10,	76	84	84
11,	78	84	84
12,	78	84	83
13,	76	84	83
14,	79	84	81
15,	78	84	81
16,	78	81	80
17,	77	82	80
18,	76	83	82
19,	76	81	81
20,	76	81	80
21,	75	80	80
22,	76	81	80
23,	76	82	81
24,	74	82	81
25,	76	82	81
26,	76	84	80
27,	76	80	75
28,	76	82	80
29,	76	82	82
30,	78	83	82
31,	78	83	82

APRIL.

Days.	Morn.	Noon.	Even.
1,	78°	83°	80°
2,	76	80	82
3,	77°	83°	82°
4,	78	84	84
5,	78	84	84
6,	79	86	84
7,	79	84	84
8,	79	84	84
9,	81	85	84
10,	77	84	83
11,	79	85	84
12,	78	85	83
13,	78	84	83
14,	77	84	83
15,	79	84	83
16,	80	85	84
17,	81	84	84
18,	80	84	84
19,	79	83	82
20,	78	84	82
21,	78	84	83
22,	79	83	82
23,	77	83	82
24,	78	84	84
25,	80	85	85
26,	81	86	85
27,	84	83	82
28,	80	83	82
29,	78	84	84
30,	78	83	83

MAY.

Days.	Morn.	Noon.	Even.
1,	79°	84°	84°
2,	81	86	86
3,	82	87	86
4,	83	86	83
5,	82	84	84
6,	80	82	82
7,	79	81	80
8,	78	81	80
9,	78	81	81
10,	76	83	81
11,	78	84	82
12,	78	84	83
13,	80	85	83
14,	80	85	83
15,	79	85	84
16,	79	84	84
17,	79	85	85
18,	79	86	86
19,	80	86	86
20,	81	86	85
21,	82	86	85
22,	82	86	85
23,	82	86	86
24,	81	86	86
25,	82	86	85
26,	82	84	82

Thermometrical Observations

Days.	Morn.	Noon.	Even.	Days.	Morn.	Noon.	Even.	Days.	Morn.	Noon.	Even.
27,	82°	83°	81°	28,	82°	88°	85°	30,	83°	88°	86°
28,	80	84	80	29,	82	86	85	31,	83	87	86
29,	80	83	80	30,	82	88	85				
30,	80	83	81					AUGUST.			
31,	80	84	83					1,	83°	88°	86°
				JULY.				2,	82	87	86
				1,	83°	86°	84°	3,	84	87	86
JUNE.				2,	83	86	84	4,	84	87	86
1,	79°	84°	84°	3,	82	86	84	5,	83	87	86
2,	80	86	85	4,	82	86	85	6,	82	86	85
3,	81	86	85	5,	82	86	83	7,	82	86	86
4,	82	86	85	6,	81	86	86	8,	82	87	86
5,	83	86	86	7,	82	88	86	9,	83	88	86
6,	84	87	85	8,	82	86	85	10,	83	88	87
7,	82	86	85	9,	81	86	85	11,	84	88	82
8,	83	87	85	10,	81	84	82	12,	82	86	86
9,	83	86	85	11,	80	82	81	13,	83	86	86
10,	83	86	83	12,	78	82	82	14,	82	87	85
11,	81	86	85	13,	80	84	83	15,	83	86	83
12,	82	86	85	14,	79	86	85	16,	82	86	83
13,	84	86	86	15,	82	87	85	17,	81	85	84
14,	84	87	86	16,	82	86	86	18,	81	86	85
15,	85	88	88	17,	82	86	86	19,	80	86	84
16,	85	88	84	18,	81	85	83	20,	82	86	86
17,	84	87	86	19,	81	85	83	21,	82	86	86
18,	84	88	88	20,	81	85	82	22,	82	86	84
19,	84	88	88	21,	80	85	82	23,	81	86	86
20,	84	88	87	22,	80	85	82	24,	82	86	86
21,	84	88	87	23,	80	85	82	25,	83	87	86
22,	83	88	88	24,	81	86	85	26,	84	87	86
23,	82	88	86	25,	82	87	85	27,	82	87	86
24,	82	89	86	26,	81	86	84	28,	80	85	85
25,	83	88	86	27,	82	87	86	29,	80	85	85
26,	82	88	86	28,	83	87	86	30,	81	86	86
27,	82	88	86	29,	83	86	86	31,	82	86	86

TABLE OF STATISTICS OF YUCATAN.

Districts.	Principal Places.	Parishes.	Villages annexed.	Distance from the Capital.—Leagues.	Population.	PRODUCTIONS.
Capital	Mérida	4	5		37,801	Horned cattle, horses, mules, tallow, jerked beef, leather, salt, gypsum, hemp, raw and manufactured, straw hats, guitars, cigars, and extract of logwood.
Campeachy	City of Campeachy	2	"	36	19,600	Salt, logwood, rice, sugar, and marble of good quality.
Lerma	Village of Lerma	3	8	37	10,567	Logwood, timber, rice, and fish oil.
Valladolid	City of Valladolid	11	17	36	63,161	Cotton, sugar, starch, gum copal, tobacco, cochineal, saffron, vanilla, cotton fabrics, yarns, &c., wax, honey, castor oil, horned cattle, hogs, and skins.
Coast	City of Izamal	16	27	15	78,846	Horned cattle, horses, mules, tallow, jerked beef, castor oil, hides, wax, honey, timber, indigo, hemp, raw and manufactured, straw cigars, barilla, and salt.
The Upper Highlands	City of Tekax	9	7	25	60,776	Horned cattle, horses, mules, hogs, sheep, skins, sugar, molasses, timber, rice, tobacco, in the leaf and manufactured, spirits, arrow-root, straw hats, cotton lace, ochre, flints, and grindstones.
The Lower Highlands	Village of Teabo	8	5	17	42,188	Horned cattle, horses, mules, hogs, sheep, skins, tallow, dried beef, hemp, raw and manufactured, and cotton lace.
The Upper Royal Road	Town of Jequelchakan	6	11	26	54,447	Cattle, horses, mules, skins, tallow, dried beef, logwood, tobacco, sugar, and rum.
The Lower Royal Road	Village of Maxcanú	5	7	14	41,726	Horned cattle, horses, mules, oil of palma Cristi, tobacco, hemp, and fine straw hats.
The Upper "Beneficios"	Village of Ichmul	7	15	39	66,680	Sugar, molasses, rum, tobacco of good quality, rice, laces, pepper, gum copal, sarsaparilla, hats, hammocks, ebony, barilla, gypsum, and skins.
The Lower "Beneficios"	Village of Sotuta	6	16	22	49,443	Horned cattle, horses, mules, hogs, skins, tallow, and dried beef.
Tizimin	Village of Tizimin	7	18	41	37,168	Tortoise-shell, skins, timber, logwood, India-rubber, incense, tobacco, achiote (a substitute for saffron, and a very rich dye), starch from the yuca, cotton, wax, honey, molasses, sugar, rum, castor oil, salt, amber, vanilla, hogs, cochineal.
Island of Cármen	Town of Cármen	2	1	80	4,364	Logwood.
Sciba-playa	Village of Seiba-playa	3	6	42	8,183	Timber, rice, logwood, and salt.
Bacalar	Town of Bacalar	2	"	88	3,986	Logwood, valuable timber, sugar of inferior quality, tobacco of the best description, rum, a fine species of hemp, known under the name of *pita*, resin, India-rubber, gum copal, pimento, sarsaparilla, vanilla, and gypsum.
Total	15	91	143		578,939	

POPULATION OF YUCATAN.

STATEMENT showing the number of inhabitants in the five departments into which the state is divided, distinguishing the sexes; taken from the census made by order of the government on the 8th of April, 1841.

Departments.	Men.	Women.	Total.
Merida . .	48,606	58,663	107,269
Izamal . .	32,915	37,933	70,848
Tekax . .	58,127	64,697	122,824
Valladolid .	45,353	46,926	92,279
Campeachy	39,017	40,639	79,656
			472,876

NOTE.—"This census is probably not very exact, because, having continually the fear of new contributions, and detesting military service, every one reduces as far as possible the number of his family in the lists prepared for the census. It appears to me that the total population of Yucatan may be fixed at 525,000 souls."—P. DE R.

"The best information I have been enabled to obtain goes to show that the population of the state cannot fall short of 600,000 souls."—J. B. JR.

SYSTEM ADOPTED BY THE ANCIENT BUILDERS OF YUCATAN IN COVERING THEIR ROOMS WITH STONE ROOFS.

THE engraving No. 1 represents the arch referred to in the description of the Monjas at Uxmal; and as the stones are not quite horizontal, but stand nearly at right angles to the line of the arch, it shows how near an approach was made to the real principle on which the arch is constructed.

Throughout every part of Central America, Chiapas, and Yucatan, the same method is to be traced with slight modifications. The stones forming the side walls are made to overlap each other until the walls almost meet above, and then the narrow ceilings are covered with a layer of flat stones. In every case the stones were laid in horizontal layers, the principle of constructing arches, as understood by us, being unknown to the aboriginal builders. This readily accounts for the extreme narrowness of all their rooms, the widest not exceeding twenty feet, and the width more frequently being only from six to ten feet. In a few cases the covering stone is wanting, and the two sides meet so as to form a sharp angle. At Palenque the builders did not cut the edges of the stones, so as to form an even surface, their practice differing in this respect from that adopted in Yucatan, where in every instance the sides of the arch are made perfectly straight, or have a slight curve, with the inner surfaces smooth.

It may now be interesting to inquire if any similarity exists between the American method and those observed among the nations of antiquity in

No. 1.

Europe and Asia. A true arch is formed of a series of wedge-like stones or of bricks, supporting each other, and all bound firmly together by the pressure of the centre one upon them, which latter is therefore distinguished by the name of keystone.

It would seem that the arch, as thus defined, and as used by the Romans, was not known to the Greeks in the early periods of their history, otherwise a language so copious as theirs, and of such ready application, would not have wanted a name properly Greek by which to distinguish it. The use of both arches and vaults appears, however, to have existed in Greece previous to the Roman conquest, though not to have been in general practice. And the former made use of a contrivance, even before the Trojan war, by which they were enabled to gain all the advantages of our archway in making corridors or hollow galleries, and which, in appearance, resembled the pointed arch, such as is now termed Gothic. This was effected by cutting away the superincumbent stones at an angle of about 45° with the horizon.

Of the different forms and curves of arches now in use, the only one adopted by the Romans was the semicircle; and the use of this constitutes one leading distinction between Greek and Roman architecture, for by its application the Romans were enabled to execute works of far bolder construction than those of the Greeks: to erect bridges and aquæducts, and the most durable and massive structures of brick. On the antiquity of the arch among the Egyptians, Mr. Wilkinson has the following remarks: "There is reason to believe that some of the chambers in the pavilion of Remeses III., at Medeenet Haboo, were arched with stone, since the devices on the upper part of their walls show that the fallen roofs had this form. At Saggara, a stone arch still exists of the time of the second Psamaticus, and, consequently, erected six hundred years before our era; nor can any one, who sees the style of its construction, for one moment doubt that the Egyptians had been long accustomed to the erection of stone vaults. It is highly probable that the small quantity of wood in Egypt, and the consequent expense of this kind of roofing, led to the invention of the arch. It was evidently used in their tombs as early as the commencement of the eighteenth dynasty, or about the year 1540 B.C.; and, judging from some of the drawings at Beni Hassan, it seems to have been known in the time of the first Osirtasen, whom I suppose to have been contemporary with Joseph."—*Manners and Customs of the Anc. Egyptians*, vol. ii., p. 116, 117, 1st series.

The entrance to the great Pyramid at Gizeh is somewhat similar in form to the arches found in Yucatan; it consists of two immense granite stones of immense size, meeting in a point and forming a sharp angle.

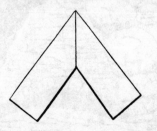

Of the accompanying plates, No. 2 represents the arches in the walls of Tiryns, copied from Sir W. Gell's Argolis; No. 3, an arch (called Cyclo-

No. 2.

No. 3.

CATHERWOOD.

pean) at Arpino, in the Neapolitan Territory; No. 4, the most common

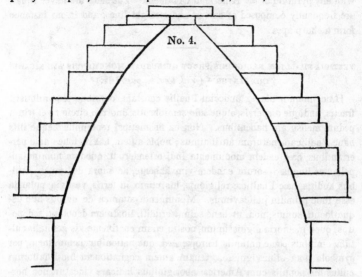

No. 4.

form of arch used by the ancient American builders. A striking resemblance will doubtless be observed, indeed, they may almost be considered identical; and it may be added, that at Medeenet Haboo, which forms a part of the ancient Egyptian Thebes, a similar contrivance was observed by Mr. Catherwood. From this it will appear that the true principles of the arch were not understood by the ancient Egyptians, Greeks, or Etruscans, or by the American builders. It might be supposed that a coincidence of this strongly-marked character would go far to establish an ancient connexion between all these people; but, without denying that such may have been the case, the probabilities are greatly the other way.

This most simple mode of covering over a void space with stone, when single blocks of sufficient size could not be employed, would suggest itself to the most barbarous as well as to the most refined people. Indeed, in a mound lately opened in the Ohio Valley, two circular chambers were discovered, and are still preserved, the walls being made of logs, and the roofs formed by overlapping stones rising to a point, on precisely the same plan as the Treasury of Atreus at Mycenæ, and the chamber at Orchomenus, built by Minyas, king of Bœotia. No inference as to common origin or international communication can with safety be drawn from such coincidences, or from any supposed coincidence between the pyramidal structures of this Continent and those of Egypt, for no agreement exists, except that both are called pyramids.

In the Egyptian Pyramids the sides are of equal lengths, and, with one exception (Saccara), composed of straight lines, which is not the case

291

with any pyramid of the American Continent. The sides are never equal, are frequently composed of curves and straight lines, and in no instance form a sharp apex.

VESTIGIA PHALLICÆ RELIGIONIS PROUT QUIBUSDAM MONUMENTIS AMERICANIS INDICANTUR.—(*Vid. tom.* i., *pag.* 181.)

Hæc monumenta ex undecim Phallis constant, omnibus plus minusve fractis, undique dispersis, atque solo semiobrutis, duorum circiter vel trium pedum mensuram habentibus. Non ea nosmetipsi reperimus neque illis hanc Phallicam naturam attribuimus; nobis autem, has regiones ante pererrantibus, hæc eadem monumenta Indi ostenderunt, quodam nomine appellantes lingua ipsorum eandem vim habente, ac supra dedimus. Quibus auditis, hæc Phallicæ religionis, his etiam in terris, vestigia putanda esse tunc primum judicavimus. Monumenta attamen de quibus huc usque locuti sumus, non, ut bene sciunt eruditi, libidinem denotant, sed potius, quod memoria dignissimum, nostra etiam continente vis genitalis cultum, omnibus pæne antiquis Europæ Asiæque nationibus communem, per symbola nota olim viguisse. Quam autem cognationem hic Phallorum cultus his populis cum Americæ aboriginibus indicare videatur, non nostrum est, qui visa tantum vel audita litteris mandamus, his paginis exponere.

ANCIENT CHRONOLOGY OF YUCATAN; OR, A TRUE EXPOSITION OF THE METHOD USED BY THE INDIANS FOR COMPUTING TIME.—*Translated from the Manuscript of Don Juan Pio Perez, Gefe Politico of Peto, Yucatan.*

1°. *Origin of the Period of* 13 *Days* (triadecateridas).

THE inhabitants of this peninsula, which, at the time of the arrival of the Spaniards, was called *Mayapan*, and by its first inhabitants or settlers *Chacnouitan*, divided time by calculating it almost in the same manner as their ancestors the Tulteques, differing only in the particular arrangement of their great ages (siglos).

The period of 13 days, resulting from their first chronological combinations, afterward became their sacred number, to which, introducing it ingeniously in their reckonings, they made all those divisions subordinate which they devised to adjust their calendar to the solar course; so that the days, years, and ages were counted by periods of thirteen numbers.

It is very probable that the Indians, before they had corrected their computation, used the lunations (neomenias) to regulate the annual course of the sun, counting (señalando) 26 days for each lunation; which is a little more or less than the time during which the moon is seen above the horizon in each of its revolutions; dividing this period into two of 13 days, which served them as weeks, giving to the first the first 13 days during which the new moon is seen till it is full; and to the second, the other thirteen, during which the moon is decreasing until it cannot be seen by the naked eye.

In the lapse of time, and by constant observations, they obtained a better knowledge of the solar course, perceiving that the 26 days, or two periods of 13 days, did not give a complete lunation, and that the year could not be regulated exactly by lunations, inasmuch as the solar revolutions do not coincide with those of the moon, except at long intervals. Adding this knowledge to more correct principles and data, they finally constructed their calendar in accordance with the course of the principal luminary, preserving always their periods of 13 days, not in order to make them agree with the apparent course of the moon, but to use them as weeks, and for their chronological divisions.

2°. *The Weeks.*

It must not be supposed that the weeks of the ancient Indians were similar to ours, that is to say, that they were the revolution of a period of days, each having a particular name: they were only the revolution or successive repetition of thirteen numbers applied in arithmetical progression to the twenty days of the month. The year being composed of 28 weeks and one additional day or number, the course of the years, on account of that excess, followed the arithmetical progression of the thirteen weekly numbers; so that if a year commenced with the number 1, the next would commence with number 2, and so on to the close of the 13 years, which formed an indiction, or week of years, as will be explained hereafter.

3°. *The Month.*

"Month" is called in the Yucateco language "U," which means also "the moon;" and this corroborates the presumption that the Indians went on from the computation of lunations to determine the course of the sun, calling the months "moons." But in some manuscripts, the name of *Uinal* in the singular and *Uinalob* in the plural is given to the eighteen months which compose the year; applying this comprehensive term to the series, and to each one of the particular names assigned to the twenty days that composed the month.

The day was called *Kin*, "the sun;" and the particular names by which the 20 days composing the month were designated are stated in the following table, in which they are divided into sets of five, for the better understanding of the subsequent explanations.

1st.	2d.	3d.	4th.
Kan.	Muluc.	Gix (Hix).	Ca-uac.
Chicchan.	Oc.	Men.	Ajau (Ahau).
Quimí (Cimí).	Chuen.	Quib (Cib).	Ymix.
Manik.	Eb.	Caban.	Yk.
Lamat.	Been.	Edznab.	Akbal.

293

As those names corresponded in number with the days of the month, it followed that, the name of the first day of the year being known, the names
of the first days of all the successive months were equally known; and
they were distinguished from each other only by adding the number of the
week to which they respectively belonged. But the week consisting of
thirteen days, the month necessarily consisted of a week and seven days;
so that if the month began with the first number of a week, it ended with
the seventh number of the week ensuing.

[In order to know the number of the week corresponding with the first
day of each month respectively, it is necessary only to know the number
of the week with which the year begins, and to add successively seven, but
subtracting thirteen whenever the sum of this addition exceeds thirteen,
which gives the following series for the first days of the eighteen months:
1, 8, 2 (15–13), 9, 3 (16–13), 10, 4, 11, 5, 12, 6, 13, 7, 1, 8, 2, 9, 3, supposing
the first day of the year to be the first day of the week, and generally taking
for the first number of the series the number of the week by which the year
begins.]

4°. *The Year.*

To this day the Indians call the year *Jaab* or *Haab*, and, while heathens,
they commenced it on the 16th of July. It is worthy of notice that their
progenitors, having sought to make it begin from the precise day on which
the sun returns to the zenith of this peninsula on his way to the southern
regions, but being destitute of instruments for their astronomical observations, and guided only by the naked eye, erred only forty-eight hours in advance. That small difference proves that they endeavoured to determine,
with the utmost attainable correctness, the day on which the luminary passed
the most culminating point of our sphere, and that they were not ignorant
of the use of the gnomon in the most tempestuous days of the rainy season.

They divided the year into 18 months, as follows:

1st, Pop, beginning on the 16th of July.

2d, U66, beginning on the 5th of August.

3d, Zip, beginning on the 25th of August.

4th, Zodz, beginning on the 14th of September.

5th, Zeec, beginning on the 4th of October.

6th, Xul, beginning on the 24th of October.

7th, Dze-yaxkin, beginning on the 13th of November.

8th, Mol, beginning on the 3d of December.

9th, Dchen, beginning on the 23d of December.

10th, Yaax, beginning on the 12th of January.

11th, Zac, beginning on the 1st of February.

12th, Quej, beginning on the 21st of February.

13th, Mac, beginning on the 13th of March.

14th, Kankin, beginning on the 2d of April.

15th, Moan, beginning on the 22d of April.

16th, Pax, beginning on the 12th of May.

17th, Kayab, beginning on the 1st of June.

18th, Cumkú, beginning on the 21st of June.

As the 18 months of 20 days each contained but 360 days, and the common year consists of 365, five supplementary days were added at the end of each year, which made part of no month, and which, for that reason, they called "days without name," *xona kaba kin.* They called them also *uayab* or *uayeb Jaab;* which may be interpreted two different ways. The word *uayab* may be derived from *uay,* which means "bed" or "chamber," presuming that the Indians believed the year to rest during those days; or *uayab* may equally be derived from another signification of *uay,* viz., to be destroyed, wounded, corroded by the caustic juice of plants, or with ley and other strong liquids. And on this account the Indians feared those days, believing them to be unfortunate, and to carry danger of sudden deaths, plagues, and other misfortunes. For this reason these five days were assigned for the celebration of the feast of the god *Mam,* "grandfather." On the first day they carried him about, and feasted him with great magnificence; on the second they diminished the solemnity; on the third they brought him down from the altar and placed him in the middle of the temple; on the fourth they put him at the threshold or door; and on the fifth, or last day, the ceremony of taking leave (or dismissal) took place, that the new year might commence on the following day, which is the first of the month *Pop,* corresponding with the 16th of July, as appears by the preceding table. The description of the god *Mam* may be seen in Cogolludo.

The division of the year into 18 months of 20 days would have given only the sum of 360 days; and the first day of the year falling on *Kan,* the last would have fallen on *Akbal,* so as to begin again the next year with the same *Kan,* making all the years alike. But as, in order to complete the year, they added five days, the result was that the year which commenced in *Kan* ended in *Lamat,* the last of the first series of five days; the ensuing year commenced in *Muluc,* the first of the second series of five days; the third commenced in *Gix,* the first of the third series; and the fourth in Cauac (the first ending in *Akbal*), the last of the fourth series of five days; so that the fifth year again began with *Kan.* It has also been stated that the year consisted of 28 weeks of 13 days each, and of one additional day; so that, if the year commenced with the number one of the week, it ended with the same number, and the ensuing year began with number two; and so on through the thirteen numbers of the week, thus forming, with the four initial days, the week of years, or indiction, of which we shall speak hereafter.

The following is the order of the twenty days in each of the 18 months composing the years formed by the four initial days, together with the intercalary or complementary days.

Year beginning with the day *Kan.*	Year beginning with the day *Muluc.*	Year of Gix.	Year of Cauac.
Kan.	Muluc.	Gix.	Cauac.
Chicchan.	Oc.	Men.	Ajau.
Quimí.	Chuen.	Quib.	Ymix.
Manik.	Eb.	Caban.	Yk.
Lamat.	Ben.	Edznab.	Akbal.
Muluc.	Gix.	Cauac.	Kan.
Oc.	Men.	Ajau.	Chicchan.
Chuen.	Quib.	Ymix.	Quimí.
Eb.	Caban.	Yk.	Manik.
Ben.	Edznab.	Akbal.	Lamat.
Gix.	Cauac.	Kan.	Muluc.
Men.	Ajau.	Chicchan.	Oc.
Quib.	Ymix.	Quimí.	Chuen.
Caban.	Yk.	Manik.	Eb.
Edznab.	Akbal.	Lamat.	Ben.
Cauac.	Kan.	Muluc.	Gix.
Ajau.	Chicchan.	Oc.	Men.
Ymix.	Quimí.	Chuen.	Quib.
Yk.	Manik.	Eb.	Caban.
Akbal.	Lamat.	Ben.	Edznab.
Intercalary days.	*Intercalary days.*	*Intercalary days.*	*Intercalary days.*
Kan.	Muluc.	Gix.	Cauac.
Chicchan.	Oc.	Men.	Ajau.
Quimí.	Chuen.	Quib.	Ymix.
Manik.	Eb.	Caban.	Yk.
Lamat.	Ben.	Edznab.	Akbal.

5°. *The Bissextile.*

The connexion between the days or numbers of the week which designate the beginning of the year, and the four initial or first days of the series of five, is so intimate that it is very difficult to intercalate an additional day for the bissextile, without disturbing that correlative order of the initials which is constantly followed in the denomination of the years, and forms their indictions, or weeks. But as the bissextile is necessary to complete the solar course, and as I have not any certain knowledge of the manner in which the Indians effected that addition, I will exhibit the method adopted by the Mexicans, their computation being very analogous to that of Yucatan, which in its origin probably emanated from Mexico.

Veyta asserts, in ch. x. of his "Historia Antigua de Mexico," that the bissextile was made by adding at the end either of the 18 months or of the five supplementary days, a day which was marked with the same hieroglyphic as the one preceding, but with a different number of the week, viz., with the succeeding number. But in each way that numerical order by which the years follow each other till they form the week of years, is disturbed; since the fifth year would thus be designated by the number 6 instead of 5, and the regular order of the years 4 to 6 be thereby interrupted. These interruptions, recurring every fourth year, would render it impossible to preserve that continuous harmony (on which rests the whole system of the Indian computation) between the numbers of the week which designate the ending year and its successor, as shown in the uniform succession of the four initial days.

In order to prevent that inconvenience, it is necessary to suppose that the Indians, whether they intercalated the additional day at the end of the 18 months or after the five supplementary days, did not only give to it the same number and hieroglyphic as to the day immediately preceding, but also designated it by some peculiar sign or number, in order that it might not be confounded with any other.

In a treatise published by Akerman, the opinion is expressed that the Indians, at the end of their cycle of 52 years, added a week of days in lieu of the bissextile days which had been neglected. This method has not the defect of disturbing the numerical order of the years, but that of deranging the series of the four initial days, which, as has been stated, gives designation to the years. It will be seen by the table of indictions, that each cycle consists of four complete weeks of years, formed by series of each one of the four initial signs, each week of years commencing with number one and ending with number thirteen; consequently, if, at the end of each cycle, a week of days be added, the first day of the ensuing year would be the 14th in the series of the 20 days of the month (instead of being the 1st, 6th, 11th, or 16th), thus abandoning the regular series of the four initial days, and substituting others, changing them again at each new cycle.

6°. *Katun, or Cycle.*

The Indians made (painted) a small wheel, in which they placed the four hieroglyphics of the initial days, *Kan* in the east, *Muluc* in the north, *Gix* in the west, and *Cauac* in the south, to be counted in that order. Some suppose that when the fourth year was accomplished, and *Kan* was again in order, a *Katun*, or lustre of four years, was completed; others, that three revolutions of the wheel, with its four signs, were reckoned, with one (sign) more, which made 13 years, and that this completed the *Katun*; others, again, that the four complete weeks of years, or indictions, constituted the *Katun*; and this is probable. Besides the small wheel aforesaid, they made another great wheel, which they also called *buk xoc*, and in which they placed three revolutions of the four signs of the small wheel, making 12 signs; beginning to count by the first *Kan*, and continuing to reckon all until the fourth naming of the same Kan, which was included, thus making thirteen years, and forming one indiction, or week (of years); the second reckoning began with *Muluc*, ending in the same, which formed the next thirteen; and so on, till they came to Cauac, which formed a Katun.

7°. *Of the Indiction and Cycle of 52 Years, or Katun.*

As in the preceding explanations sufficient idea has been given of what constituted the indiction and the cycle of 52 years, called by the Indians *Katun*, the facts are briefly recapitulated here, that the reader may not be fatigued hereafter with new explanations.

1st. The name of indiction is given to each one of the four weeks of years composing the cycle of 52 years.

2d. The American week was formed by the course of 13 numbers, applied indiscriminately to the 20 days of the month.

3d. It has been explained, that as the year was formed of 28 weeks and one day, by this overplus the years succeeded each other, following the correlative order of their numbers up to 13, in order to form a week, or indiction; for if the year had been composed of exactly 28 weeks, the numbers of the new years would never have formed a correlative week, because they would have commenced with the number 1, and finished with 13; by the other method, one year begins with the first, and terminates in the same; the second year commences with the number 2, and also finishes with it; and so on successively, until the 13 are completed.

4th. It has also been explained that the Indians, seeing that 18 months of 20 days did not make up the sum of 365, in order to complete them added five days more; resulting from this, the 20 days were divided into four portions, and the first of each of these, being *Kan*, *Muluc*, *Gix*, and *Cauac*, became initials, forming in turn the beginning of the years by courses of four years, every fifth year commencing again with Kan. But as the weeks were composed of 13 numbers, there were in each week three revolutions of the four initials and one initial more, by this excess of one causing each initial to have its own week: thus the indiction, or week, which began with *Kan* concluded also with the same *Kan*; so that the next indiction might commence with *Muluc*, the second initial, and in its turn conclude with the same *Muluc*; and so on continually, until each one of the initials had formed its own indiction, or week, and given to it its name, the whole composing 52 years, which is the sum of the four weeks of 13 years each, as may be seen in the following table.

Order of the years in the cycle of 52, *divided into four indictions, or weeks of years; and as the year* 1841 *happens to be the first of one of these cycles, it is taken as the starting-point.*

1st Indiction.		2d Indiction.		3d Indiction.		4th Indiction.	
1841,	1. Kan.	1854,	1. Muluc.	1867,	1. Gix.	1880,	1. Cauac.
1842,	2. Muluc.	1855,	2. Gix.	1868,	2. Cauac.	1881,	2. Kan.
&c.	3. Gix.	&c.	3. Cauac.	&c.	3. Kan.	&c.	3. Muluc.
	4. Cauac.		4. Kan.		4. Muluc.		4. Gix.
	5. Kan.		5. Muluc.		5. Gix.		5. Cauac.
	6. Muluc.		6. Gix.		6. Cauac.		6. Kan.
	7. Gix.		7. Cauac.		7. Kan.		7. Muluc.
	8. Cauac.		8. Kan.		8. Muluc.		8. Gix.
	9. Kan.		9. Muluc.		9. Gix.		9. Cauac.
	10. Muluc.		10. Gix.		10. Cauac.		10. Kan.
	11. Gix.		11. Cauac.		11. Kan.		11. Muluc.
	12. Cauac.		12. Kan.		12. Muluc.		12. Gix.
	13. Kan.		13. Muluc.		13. Gix.	1892,	13. Cauac.

This period of 52 years was called by the Indians *Katun,* and at its conclusion great feasts were celebrated, and a monument was raised, on which a large stone was placed crosswise, as is signified by the word *Kat-tun,* for a memento and record of the cycles, or *Katunes,* that had elapsed. It should be observed, that until the completion of this period, the initial days of the years did not again fall upon the same numbers of the week; for which reason, by merely citing them, it was at once known what year of that cycle was arrived at; being aided in this by the wheel or table on which the years were engraved in hieroglyphics.

8°. *Of the great Cycle of* 312 *Years, or Aiau Katunes.*

Besides the cycle of 52 years, or *Katun,* there was another great cycle peculiar to the Yucatecos, who referred to its periods for dating their principal epochs and the most notable events of their history. It contained 13 periods of 24 years each, making together 312 years. Each period, or *Ajau Katun,* was divided into two parts; the first of 20 years, which was included in a square, and therefore called *amaytun, lamayte,* or *lamaytun;* and the other of four years, which formed, as it were, a pedestal for the first, and was called *chek oc Katun,* or *lath oc Katun,* which means "stool" or "pedestal." They considered those four years as intercalated; therefore believed them to be unfortunate, and called them *u yail Jaab,* as they did the five supplementary days of the year, to which they likened them.

From this separation of the first 20 years from the last four, arose the erroneous belief that the *Ajaus* consisted only of 20 years, an error into which almost all have fallen who have written on the subject; but if they had counted the years which compose a period, and noted the positive declarations of the manuscripts that the *Ajaues* consisted of 24 years divided as above stated, they would not have misled their readers on this point.

It is incontrovertible that those periods, epochs, or ages, took the name of *Ajau Katun,* because they began to be counted from the day *Ajau,* which was the second day of those years that began in Cauac; but as these days and numbers were taken from years which had run their course, the periods of 24 years could never have an arithmetical order, but succeeded each other according to the numbers 13, 11, 9, 7, 5, 3, 1, 12, 10, 8, 6, 4, 2. As the Indians established the number 13 as the first, it is probable that some remarkable event had happened in that year, because, when the Spaniards came to this peninsula, the Indians reckoned then the 8th as the 1st, that being the date at which their ancestors came to settle it; and an Indian writer proposed that they should abandon that order also, and begin counting from the 11th, solely because the conquest had happened in that. Now if the 13 *Ajau Katun* began on a second day of the year, it must be that year which began on 12 *Cauac,* and the 12th of the indiction. The 11 *Ajau* would commence in the year of 10 *Cauac,* which happens after a period of 24 years, and so on with the rest; taking notice that after that lapse of years we come to the respective number marked in the course of the Ajaues, which is placed first; proving that they consist of 24, and not, as some have believed, of 20 years.

Series of the years completed in two Ajau Katunes, having their beginning in the year of our Lord 1488, *in which the* 13th *Ajau commences on the* 2d *day of the year* 12 *Cauac, being the* 12th *of the first indiction.*

A.D.	13th Ajau.	A.D.	13th Ajau.	A.D.	11th Ajau.	A.D.	11th Ajau.
1488	12. Cauac	1500	11. Cauac	1512	10. Cauac	1524	9. Cauac
1489	13. Kan	1501	12. Kan	1513	11. Kan	1525	10. Kan
1490	1. Muluc	1502	13. Muluc	1514	12. Muluc	1526	11. Muluc
1491	2. Gix	1503	1. Gix	1515	13. Gix	1527	12. Gix
1492	3. Cauac	1504	2. Cauac	1516	1. Cauac	1528	13. Cauac
1493	4. Kan	1505	3. Kan	1517	2. Kan	1529	1. Kan
1494	5. Muluc	1506	4. Muluc	1518	3. Muluc	1530	2. Muluc
1495	6. Gix	1507	5. Gix	1519	4. Gix	1531	3. Gix
1496	7. Cauac	1508	6. Cauac	1520	5. Cauac	1532	4. Cauac
1497	8. Kan	1509	7. Kan	1521	6. Kan.	1533	5. Kan
1498	9. Muluc	1510	8. Muluc	1522	7. Muluc	1534	6. Muluc
1499	10. Gix	1511	9. Gix	1523	8. Gix	1535	7. Gix

The fundamental point of departure from which to adjust the Ajaus with the years of the Christian era, to count the periods or cycles which have elapsed, and to make the years quoted by the Indians in their histories agree with the same era, is the year of our Lord 1392, which, according to all sources of information, confirmed by the testimony of Don Cosme de Burgos, one of the conquerors, and a writer (but whose observations have been lost), was the year in which fell the 7 *Cauac,* giving in its second day the commencement of 8 Ajau; and from this, as from a root, all that preceded and have followed it are adjusted according to the table of them which has been given; and as this agrees with all the series that have been found, it is highly probable that it is the correct one.

"At the end of each Ajau Katun, or period of 24 years," says a manuscript, "great feasts were celebrated in honour of the god thereof, and a statue of the god was put up, with letters and inscriptions." It must be supposed that these were expressed by means of signs or hieroglyphics.

The use of this cycle was of very great advantage and importance, because when, for example, the 8th Ajau was referred to in their histories in describing some event which it was necessary to distinguish from others, the 8th Ajau was established as a distinct date, and it was understood that the 312 years had elapsed, which made up the whole Katun, in order to return to the same number; this was more clear, if the writer explained that a *uudz Katun* had elapsed, which is the sum total of the thirteen Katunes, or the great cycle. They had various modes of quoting the *Ajaues*, as by saying generally the beginning, middle, or end of such an Ajau, or by mentioning the years of the Katun which had elapsed, without stating the month or day of the year, or by specifying all the particulars of the epoch, the year, month, and day. Such is the passage in which is noticed the death of a certain, without doubt very notable, *Ajpula*. It is said that he died in the 6th year of 13 Ajau, when the first day of the year was 4 Kan at the east end of the wheel, in the day of 9 Ymix, 18th of the month Zip. This date being so circumstantial, we will trace it out, that it may serve as an example.

Looking at the series of years which belong to the 13 Ajau, and which we have given above, it will be seen that 12 Cauac falls in the year 1488, the second day of that year being, therefore, the beginning of the 13th Ajau; that the year 1493 is the sixth from the beginning of the said Ajau, and that its first day is designated as 4 Kan, which is the title of that year, "18th of the month Zip." As this month begins on the 25th of August, the 18th corresponds with the 11th of September. Let us see now whether this 18th day falls on 9 Ymix. The first month of that year commenced with 4 Kan, since 4 Kan designates that year (see the rule given in treating of the months). We find the numbers (of the week) annexed to the first days of the following months by successively adding 7 to each month, &c. (or, which is the same thing, by the rule *buk xoc*). The number of the 1st day of the 1st month being in this case 4, the number of the 1st day of the 2d month will be 4+7=11, and that of the 1st day of the 3d month, viz., of Zip, will be 11+7—13=5. That month begins, therefore, in that year, with 5 Kan, and the following days are,

Days of Aug.	Zip.	Days of the Week.	Days of Sept.	Zip.	Days of the Week.	Days of Sept.	Zip.	Days of the Week.
25	1	5. Kan.	1	8	12. Chuen.	8	15	6. Edznab.
26	2	6. Chicchan.	2	9	13. Eb.	9	16	7. Cauac.
27	3	7. Quimí.	3	10	1. Ben.	10	17	8. Ajau.
28	4	8. Manik.	4	11	2. Gix.	11	18	9. Ymix.
29	5	9. Lamac.	5	12	3. Men.			
30	6	10. Muluc.	6	13	4. Quin.			
31	7	11. Oc.	7	14	5. Caban.			

Thus the 11th of September was the 18th of Zip, which does fall on 9 Ymix, and accords with the date given in the MS. This date appears, therefore, to have been very correct.

Of the Origin of this Cycle.

The origin and use of this species of age, epoch, or cycle, and (the time) when it commenced, are not known. Neither the Mexican nor Toltecan authors, nor those who corrected the chronological system for the computation of time, ever used it, nor had their writers any knowledge of its existence. The few and incomplete manuscripts which exist in this peninsula make no mention of it; so that there is neither record nor even conjecture to guide us, unless there be something on the subject in the work written by Don Cristobal Antonio Xiu, son of the King of Mani, by order of the then government, which, according to the padre Cogolludo, existed in his time, and some allege to be even yet extant.

It appears only that the Chevalier Boturini had some knowledge, though imperfect, of that mode of reckoning time; inasmuch as Don Mariano Veytia, in the second chapter of his "Historia Antigua de Mexico," transcribes literally the explanation which Boturini gives at page 122 of the work which he published under the title of "Idea of a New History of North America," and says, "that the Mexican Indians, when they reckoned in their calendar the first sign of their indiction under number 1, as, for instance, Ce Tecpatl (1 Tecpatl), it was understood that it was (so placed) only one time in every four cycles, because they spoke then of the initial characters of each cycle; and thus, according to the contrivance of their painted wheels, Ce Tecpatl was but once the commencement of the four cycles" [meaning—began a cycle but once in four cycles. But the fact is not so: both in the Mexican and the Yucatec calendar, every cycle of 52 years begins with the same initial character of the year]; "for which reason, any character of those initial signs placed in their history means that four Indian cycles of 52 years each have elapsed, which makes 208 years before they can again occur as initial, because, in this way, no account is taken of characters which are in the body of the four cycles; and though the same characters are found there, they have not the same value."

Veytia affirms that he did not find any similar explanation, or anything alluding to the system of Boturini, in any of the ancient monuments which he had collected or examined, or mentioned by any Indian historian, not even in order to designate the epochs of the most remarkable events. But I believe that, in answer to this remark of Veytia, it may be said that Boturini, as Veytia states elsewhere, had examined the calendars used in old times by the Indians of Oaxacac, Chiapas, and Soconusco, and these being similar to that of the Yucatecos, it is not unreasonable to suppose that they, like the Yucatecos, computed by cycles greater than the Mexicans employed; and that Boturini took from them the idea, though confused and incorrect, of our Ajaus, or great cycles. This incorrectness might arise either from his not understanding the mechanism of their mode of computing, owing to the defective explanation given by the Indians, or from the manuscripts which Boturini had before him being mutilated, or, finally, from the possible fact that the Indians in those provinces had a particular custom of counting by cycles of four indictions, or of 208 years, which, notwithstanding the difference observed in their calculation, and the number of years which it produces, have a great analogy with the Yucateco cycles of 312 years. The only thing for which Boturini may be censured, if the Mexicans had no knowledge of that cycle, and did not use it, was the ascribing of it to them as being in common use for the computation of the greater periods of time.

The great similarity between the names of the days in the calendar of Oajaca, Chiapas, and Soconusco, and those of the Yucatecos, has been mentioned, and appears clearly by comparing the latter with those of the said provinces, which Veytia has transcribed in his history, chap. xi., at the end.

Days of the Oajaquian Month.		Days of the Yucateco Month.	
1. Votan.	11. Ben.	1. Kan.	11. Hix or Gix.
2. Ghanan.	12. Hix.	2. Chicchan.	12. Men.
3. Abagh.	13. Tzinkin.	3. Quimí.	13. Quib.
4. Tox.	14. Chabin.	4. Manik.	14. Caban.
5. Moxic.	15. Chue or Chic.	5. Lamat.	15. Edznab.
6. Lambat.	16. Chinax.	6. Muluc.	16. Cauac.
7. Molo or Mulu.	17. Cahogh.	7. Oc.	17. Ajau.
8. Elah or Elab.	18. Aghual.	8. Chuen.	18. Ymix.
9. Batz.	19. Mox.	9. Eb.	19. Yk.
10. Enoh or Enob.	20. Ygh.	10. Ben.	20. Akbal.

Oajacan Ghanan, *gh* being pronounced as *k*, is the same with the Yucateco *Kan* or *Kanan* (yellow); Molo or Mulu, *Muluc;* Chue, *Chuen;* Aghual, *Akbal* or *Akual;* Ygk, *Yk;* Lambat, *Lamat;* Ben and Hix, *Be-en* and *Gix* or *Hix.* These analogies, and the fact that some of the Yucateco names have no known signification, induce the belief that both calendars had a common origin, with only such alterations as the priests made on account of particular events or for other reasons; which alterations our Indians adopted, leaving the other signs unchanged, either because they were accustomed to them, or because their signification, now forgotten, was then known.

The Indians of Yucatan had yet another species of cycle; but as the method followed by them in using it cannot be found, nor any example by which an idea of its nature might be imagined, I shall only copy what is literally said of it in a manuscript, viz.: "There was another number, which they called *Ua Katun*, and which served them as a key to find the Katunes. According to the order of its march, it falls on the days of the *Uayeb jaab*, and revolves to the end of certain years: Katunes 13, 9, 5, 1, 10, 6, 2, 11, 7, 3, 12, 8, 4."

[N.B. Uayeb jaab is one of the names given to the five supplementary days of the year, and also to the last four years of the Ajau of 24 years.]

Series of Ajaues, from the beginning of the vulgar era to the present year, and those following until the end of the cycle. It is formed of three columns: the first containing the years of the Christian era; the second, the years of the indiction in which the Ajaues commenced, on their second day; and the third, the succession of these Ajaues. (The vulgar era began in the year 7 Kan, which was the 2d of 7 Ajau, that commenced the second day of the year of the indiction 6 Cauac).

Years of our Lord.	Years of the Indiction.	Ajaues that began in them.	Years of our Lord.	Years of the Indiction.	Ajaues that began in them.
24	4. Cauac.	5. Ajau.	984	2. Cauac.	3. Ajau.
48	2. Cauac.	3. Ajau.	1008	13. Cauac.	1. Ajau.
72	13. Cauac.	1. Ajau.	1032	11. Cauac.	12. Ajau.
96	11. Cauac.	12. Ajau.	1056	9. Cauac.	10. Ajau.
120	9. Cauac.	10. Ajau.	1080	7. Cauac.	8. Ajau.
144	7. Cauac.	8. Ajau.	1104	5. Cauac.	6. Ajau.
168	5. Cauac.	6. Ajau.	1128	3. Cauac.	4. Ajau.
192	3. Cauac.	4. Ajau.	1152	1. Cauac.	2. Ajau.
216	1. Cauac.	2. Ajau.	*1176	*12. Cauac.	*13. Ajau.
*240	*12. Cauac.	*13. Ajau.	1200	10. Cauac.	11. Ajau.
264	10. Cauac.	11. Ajau.	1224	8. Cauac.	9. Ajau.
288	8. Cauac.	9. Ajau.	1248	6. Cauac.	7. Ajau.
312	6. Cauac.	7. Ajau.	1272	4. Cauac.	5. Ajau.
336	4. Cauac.	5. Ajau.	1296	2. Cauac.	3. Ajau.
360	2. Cauac.	3. Ajau.	1320	13. Cauac.	1. Ajau.
384	13. Cauac.	1. Ajau.	1344	11. Cauac.	12. Ajau.
408	11. Cauac.	12. Ajau.	1368	9. Cauac.	10. Ajau.
432	9. Cauac.	10. Ajau.	1392	7. Cauac.	8. Ajau.
456	7. Cauac.	8. Ajau.	1416	5. Cauac.	6. Ajau.
480	5. Cauac.	6. Ajau.	1440	3. Cauac.	4. Ajau.
504	3. Cauac.	4. Ajau.	1464	1. Cauac.	2. Ajau.
528	1. Cauac.	2. Ajau.	*1488	*12. Cauac.	*13. Ajau.
*552	*12. Cauac.	*13. Ajau.	1512	10. Cauac.	11. Ajau.
576	10. Cauac.	11. Ajau.	1536	8. Cauac.	9. Ajau.
600	8. Cauac.	9. Ajau.	1560	6. Cauac.	7. Ajau.
624	6. Cauac.	7. Ajau.	1584	4. Cauac.	5. Ajau.
648	4. Cauac.	5. Ajau.	1608	2. Cauac.	3. Ajau.
672	2. Cauac.	3. Ajau.	1632	13. Cauac.	1. Ajau.
696	13. Cauac.	1. Ajau.	1656	11. Cauac.	12. Ajau.
720	11. Cauac.	12. Ajau.	1680	9. Cauac.	10. Ajau.
744	9. Cauac.	10. Ajau.	1704	7. Cauac.	8. Ajau.
768	7. Cauac.	8. Ajau.	1728	5. Cauac.	6. Ajau.
792	5. Cauac.	6. Ajau.	1752	3. Cauac.	4. Ajau.
816	3. Cauac.	4. Ajau.	1776	1. Cauac.	2. Ajau.
840	1. Cauac.	2. Ajau.	*1800	*12. Cauac.	*13. Ajau.
*864	*12. Cauac.	*13. Ajau.	1824	10. Cauac.	11. Ajau.
888	10. Cauac.	11. Ajau.	1848	8. Cauac.	9. Ajau.
912	8. Cauac.	9. Ajau.	1872	6. Cauac.	7. Ajau.
936	6. Cauac.	7. Ajau.	1896	4. Cauac.	5. Ajau.
960	4. Cauac.	5. Ajau.			

From the preceding series it is manifest that from the birth of Christ until the beginning of this cycle, have elapsed 6 great cycles, one epoch, and 17 (years) of another; the first epoch of the first cycle requiring a year, as has been stated.

Since this exposition was written, I have had an opportunity of seeing the work, above quoted, of Chevalier Boturini, in which, speaking of the Toltec Indians, he says:

After their peregrination through Asia, they reached the Continent (America), and penetrated to Hutchuetlapallan, the first city of New Spain, in which their wise men convened 130 and some years before the birth of Christ; and seeing that the civil did not agree with the astronomical year, and that the equinoctial days were altered, they determined to add in every four years one day, in order to recover the hours which were (annually) lost. And it is supposed that they effected it by counting one of the symbols of the last month of the year twice (as the Romans did with their bissextile days), without disturbing their order, because adding or taking away (a symbol) would destroy their perpetual system; and thus they made the commencement of the civil year to agree with the vernal equinox, which was the principal and governing part of the year.

He adds, that although the intercalated day had not a place in the order of the symbols of the days of the year, but was thrust in, as it were, like an interloper, still it gave a name (or character) to the bissextile year, having most solemn feasts reserved to it, which, even in the third age, were sanctioned by the emperor or king of those provinces; and they were held in honour of the god *Xinteuctli*, "lord of the year," with great preparation of viands and sumptuous dances, in which the lords alone danced and sang; and for this reason they were called "the songs and dances of the lords." In the same bissextile year was held the solemn ceremony of piercing the ears of the girls and young men, it being reserved for the high-priest to execute that function, assisted by godfathers and godmothers.

In the 27th paragraph of the observations he says, that there was in the third age another mode of intercalating, applied only to the ritual calendar, and that, in order not to disturb either the perpetual order of the fixed feasts, or of the sixteen movable feasts, which circulated among the symbols of the days of the year, by (or for the sake of) counting twice the symbol of the last month of the bissextile year, which caused them much anxiety on account of the displeasure of their gods, it was held better to reserve the 13 bissextile days for the end of the cycle of 52 years; which (days) are distinguished in their wheels or tables by thirteen ciphers, (painted) blue or of some other colour; and they belonged neither to any month nor any year, nor had they particular or individual symbols, like the other days. It was with them as if there were no such days, nor were they dedicated to any of their gods, on which account they were reputed "unfortunate." The whole of those 13 days was a time of penitence and fasting, for fear that the world should come to an end; nor did they eat any warm food, as the fire was extinguished through the whole land till the new cycle began, when the ceremony of the new fire was celebrated.

But as all these were matters relating only to rites and sacrifices (not to the true computation of time), this mode of intercalating had no application to the natural year, because it would have greatly deranged the solstices, equinoxes, and beginnings of the years; and the fact is abundantly proved by the circumstance that the days thus intercalated (at the end of the cycle) had none of the symbols belonging to the days of the year, and the ritual calendar accounted them bissextiles at the end of each cycle, in imitation, though by a different order, of the civil bissextiles, which (as being more accurate) were more proper for the regulation of public affairs.

AN ALMANAC, ADJUSTED ACCORDING TO THE CHRONOLOGICAL CALCULATION OF THE ANCIENT INDIANS OF YUCATAN, FOR THE YEARS 1841 AND 1842, BY DON JUAN PIO PEREZ.

Observations.—The notes or remarks *utz, yutz kin,* a lucky day, *lob, u lob kin,* an unlucky day, signify that the Indians had their days of good and of ill fortune, like some of the nations of ancient Europe; although it is easily perceived that the number of their days of ill fortune is excessive, still they are the same found by me in three ancient almanacs which I have examined, and found to agree very nearly. I have applied them to the number, not the name, of the day, because the announcements of rain, of planting, &c., must, in my opinion, belong to the fixed days of the month, and not to the names of particular days; as these each year are changed, and turn upon the four primaries, *Kan, Muluc, Gix,* and *Cauac,* chiefs of the year. In another place, however, I have seen it laid down as a rule that the days *Chicchan, Cimí* or *Kimí, Oc, Men, Ahau,* and *Akbal,* are the days of rest in the month; and this appears probable, as I see no reason why there should be so great an excess of days of ill fortune. In the almanacs cited above, this order was not observed, either from ignorance or excessive superstition.

Thus the days on which the burner takes his fire, kindles it, gives it free scope, and extinguishes it, are subject to the 3d, 4th, 10th, and 11th of the days *Chicchan, Oc, Men,* and *Ahau;* as they say, for example, that on the 3d Chicchan the burner takes his fire, on the 10th Chicchan he begins, the 4th Chicchan he gives it scope, and the 11th Chicchan he extinguishes it; the same may be said of Oc, Men, and Ahau; from which we see that these epochs are movable, as the days 3, 4, 10, and 11 do not always fall on the same days of the month, but only according to the combination of the weekly numbers with the days referred to.

306

It may be asked, who is this burner that takes his fire, kindles it, permits it to destroy, and extinguishes it? To this I cannot reply, as I have been unable to find an explanation of the mystery; perhaps the days specified might be days of sacrifice, or some other act of superstition.

1ST INDIAN MONTH, "POP," OF THE YEAR 1 KAN.

	Pop.		July.
1. Kan.	1	Hun Kan, utz licil u cutal, Pop (good, as the beginning of Pop).	16
2. Chicchan.	2	Ca Chicchan, utz u tial pakal (good for planting).	17
3. Quimí.	3	Ox Quimí, lob kin (an unlucky day).	18
4. Manik.	4	Can Manik, utz u tial pakal (good for planting).	19
5. Lamat.	5	Ho Lamat, utz kin (a good day).	20
6. Muluc.	6	Uac Muluc, utz kin (6 Muluc; a good day).	21
7. Oc.	7	Uuc Oc, utz u tial ahguehob (good for hunting; for the settlers).	22
8. Chuen.	8	Uaxxac Chuen, yutz kin, kal ikal u chibal tok (good day; without wind).	23
9. Eb.	9	Bolon Eb, u lob kin (9 Eb; a bad day).	24
10. Been.	10	Lahun Been, yutz kin (10 Been; a good day).	25
11. Hix.	11	Buluc Hix, yutz kin (11 Hix; a good day).	26
12. Men.	12	Lahca Men, yutz kin (12 Men; a good day).	27
13. Quib.	13	Oxlahun Quib, u lob kin (13 Quib; an unlucky day).	28
1. Caban.	14	Hun Caban, u lob kin (1 Caban; an unlucky day).	29
2. Edznab.	15	Ca Edznab, yutz kin, licil u zihil ahmiatz yetel ahdzib hunob (good day; in which are born writers and wise men).	30
3. Cauac.	16	Ox Cauac, yutz kin (a good day).	31
4. Ahau.	17	Can Ahau, yutz kin ti almehenob; yalcab u kak ahtoc (a good day for the nobles; the burner gives the fire scope).	Aug. 1
5. Ymix.	18	Ho Ymix, u lob kin (a bad day).	2
6. Yk.	19	Uac Yk, u lob kin (an unlucky day).	3
7. Akbal.	20	Uuc Akbal, yutz kin (a good day).	4

UO, 2D INDIAN MONTH.

	Uo.		August.
8. Kan.	1	Uaxxac Kan, u lob kin licil u cutal Uo (a bad day, as the root of Uo).	5
9. Chicchan.	2	Bolon Chicchan, u lob kin (an unlucky day).	6
10. Quimí.	3	Lahun Quimí, u lob kin (an unlucky day).	7
11. Manik.	4	Buluc Manik, u lob kin (an unlucky day).	8
12. Lamat.	5	Lahca Lamat, u lob kin (an unlucky day).	9
13. Muluc.	6	Oxlahun Muluc, u lob kin (an unlucky day).	10

uo, 2d INDIAN MONTH (Continued).

Uo.		August.
7	1, Oc, u lob kin, cimil hoppol kin (a bad day; death in the five following).	11
8	2, Chuen, u lob kin (an unlucky day).	12
9	3, Eb, u lob kin, chetun cimil yani (a bad day; sudden deaths).	13
10	4, Been, u lob kin, u ɔoc cimil (an unlucky day; sudden deaths).	14
11	5, Hix, u lob kin (an unfortunate day).	15
12	6, Men, u lob kin (an unfortunate day).	16
13	7, Quib, u lob kin (an unfortunate day).	17
14	8. Caban, u lob kin (an unfortunate day).	18
15	9, Edznab, u lob kin, cimil yani (a bad day; death is here).	19
16	10, Cauac, u lob kin (an unlucky day).	20
17	11, Ahau, lob, u tup kak ahtoc (bad; the burner puts out the fire).	21
18	12, Ymix, u lob kin (an unfortunate day).	22
19	13, Yk, u lob kin (an unfortunate day).	23
20	1, Akbal, au yutz kin (a lucky day).	24

ZIP, 3D INDIAN MONTH.

Zip.		August.
1	2, Kan, yutz kin, licil u cutal Zip (a good day; the root of Zip).	25
2	3, Chicchan, lob, u cha kak ahtoc (bad; the burner takes the fire).	26
3	4, Quimí, yutz kin, u kin takal u kab balam (a good day; one in which the hands are laid on the tiger).	27
4	5, Manik, u lob kin (an unlucky day).	28
5	6, Lamat, u lob kin.	29
6	7, Muluc, u lob kin.	30
7	8, Oc, u lob kin.	31
8	9, Chuen, u lob kin.	Sept. 1
9	10, Eb, u lob kin.	2
10	11, Ben, u lob kin.	3
11	12, Hix, utz kin (a good day).	4
12	13, Men, utz u zihíl ahau (good; the king is born).	5
13	1, Quib, utz kin.	6
14	2, Caban, yutz kin.	7
15	3, Edznab, yutz kin.	8
16	4, Cauac, yutz kin.	9
17	5, Ahau, yutz kin.	10
18	6, Ymix, yutz kin, haahal telá (a good day; there is rain).	11
19	7, Yk, yutz kin, haahal telá (a good day; there is rain).	12
20	8, Akbal, yutz.	13

ZODZ, 4TH INDIAN MONTH.

Zodz.		Sept.
1	9, Kan, utz u zian ku, u kin chac licil u cutal zoɔ (good; church day, of rain, &c.).	14
2	10, Chicchan, u lob kin, u hoppol u kak ahtoc (a bad day; the fire begins).	15

ZODZ, 4TH INDIAN MONTH (Continued).

Zodz.		Sept.
3	11, Quimí, u lob kin, u kin u nichco hun ahau, coh u nich (a bad day).	16
4	12, Manik, u lob kin (a bad day).	17
5	13, Lamat, yutz kin.	18
6	1, Muluc, yutz kin.	19
7	2, Oc, yutz kin.	20
8	3, Chuen, yutz kin.	21
9	4, Eb, lob kin, licil u zihil ahau (bad; the king is born).	22
10	5, Ben, lob kin.	23
11	6, Hix, utz u tial Ahcabnalob licil u pakal cab (good for the bee-hunters; in it the swarms are hived).	24
12	7, Men, utz.	25
13	8, Quib, yutz kin.	26
14	9, Caban, u yutz kin.	27
15	10, Edznab, u yutz kin.	28
16	11, Cauac, u yutz kin.	29
17	12, Ahau, lob u kukumtok chapahal yani (bad; the plume of infirmities).	30
18	13, Ymix, lob kin.	Oct. 1
19	1, Yk, utz kin, u zian chac (good; a day of rain).	2
20	2, Akbal, u lob kin.	3

ZEC, 5TH INDIAN MONTH.

Zec.		October.
1	3, Kan, utz u zian chac licil u cutal zec (good; beginning of Zec; rain).	4
2	4, Chicchan, lob u yalcab u kak ahtoc (bad; the burner gives the fire scope).	5
3	5, Quimí, lob u lubul u koch mehen palalob; chapahal yani (bad; the tax on children falls due; there is sickness).	6
4	6, Manik, lob.	7
5	7, Lamat, u lob kin.	8
6	8, Muluc, u lob kin.	9
7	9, Oc, u yutz kin, zut ti kaax xinxinbal (good for walking, &c.).	10
8	10, Chuen, u lob kin.	11
9	11, Eb, u lob kin.	12
10	12, Been, u lob kin.	13
11	13, Hix, u lob kin.	14
12	1, Men, u lob kin.	15
13	2, Quib, u lob kin, kalal hub, cinil yani (an unlucky day; the snail retreats to his shell, or is sawn open; death is in the day).	16
14	3, Caban, yutz kin.	17
15	4, Edznab, lob, u hokol chacmitan tac metnal ti kin ti akab (bad; hunger is loosed from hell by day and night).	18
16	5, Cauac, u lob kin.	19
17	6, Ahau, u lob kin.	20
18	7, Ymix, u lob kin.	21
19	8, Yk, u lob kin.	22
20	9, Akbal, u lob kin.	23

XUL, 6TH INDIAN MONTH.

Xul.		October.
1	10, Kan, lob, u zian chac licil u cutal Xul (bad; rain; beginning of Xul).	24
2	11, Chicchan, utz u tup kak ahtoc, u ca kin haí (good; second day of rain; the burner extinguishes the fire).	25
3	12, Quimí, lob kin.	26
4	13, Manik, u lob kin.	27
5	1, Lamat, utz u yalcab muyal (good; the clouds fly).	28
6	2, Muluc, lob u lubul u koch mehenob yetel akkinob licil u ppixichob (bad; day of watching; the tax of the sons and priests falls due).	29
7	3, Oc, lob u cha kak ahtoc (bad; the burner takes fire).	30
8	4, Chuen, lob kin.	31
9	5, Eb, u lob kin.	Nov. 1
10	6, Been, u lob kin.	2
11	7, Hix, lob kin, u lubul u koch almehenob ppixich yani (bad; a day of watching; of taxes from the nobles).	3
12	8, Men, u lob kin.	4
13	9, Quib, u lob kin.	5
14	10, Caban, u lob kin.	6
15	11, Edznab, u lob kin.	7
16	12, Cauac, u lob kin, u mupptun cizin lae (a bad day, and of attacks from the devil).	8
17	13, Ahau, u lob kin.	9
18	1, Ymix, u lob kin.	10
19	2, Yk, u lob kin.	11
20	3, Akbal, u lob kin.	12

DZEYAXKIN, 7TH INDIAN MONTH.

Dzeyaxkin.		Nov.
1	4, Kan, u lob kin, licil u cutal Teyaxkin (bad day; beginning of Dzeyaxkin).	13
2	5, Chicchan, u lob kin.	14
3	6, Quimí, u lob kin.	15
4	7, Manik, lob, utz u pec chaci u kin haí, u zut muyal nocoycaan chalbaku (bad; thunder, rain, clouds, &c.)	16
5	8, Lamat, u lob kin.	17
6	9, Muluc, lob u kaalal hub u yail kin, u chibal, hub yani (bad; the snail's horn is closed; a bad day on it, a snail will bite).	18
7	10, Oc, lob kin, u hoppol u kak ahtoc (bad; the burner begins).	19
8	11, Chuen, u lob kin.	20
9	12, Eb, u lob kin.	21
10	13, Been, u lob kin.	22
11	1, Hix, yutz kin.	23
12	2, Men, yutz kin.	24
13	3, Quib, u lob kin, yoc uah payambe (bad; beginning of bread).	25
14	4, Caban, u lob kin, ceel yani (bad; there are agues).	26
15	5, Edznab, u lob kin.	27
16	6, Cauac, u lob kin.	28
17	7, Ahau, u lob kin.	29
18	8, Ymix, u lob kin.	30
19	9, Yk, utz u hoppol haí (good; the rain begins).	Dec. 1
20	10, Akbal, utz kin.	2

310

MOL, 8TH INDIAN MONTH.

Mol.		Dec.
1	11, Kan, u lob kin, licil u cutal Mol (a bad day; the beginning of Mol).	3
2	12, Chicchan, u lob kin.	4
3	13, Quimí, u lob kin.	5
4	1, Manik, utz.	6
5	2, Lamat, u lob kin.	7
6	3, Muluc, u lob kin.	8
7	4, Oc, yutz kin u yalcab u kak ahtoc (a good day; the burner gives scope to the fire).	9
8	5, Chuen, yutz kin.	10
9	6, Eb, u lob kin.	11
10	7, Been, yutz kin.	12
11	8, Hix, u lob kin.	13
12	9, Men, u lob kin.	14
13	10, Quib, yutz kin u kin noh uah (a day of abundance).	15
14	11, Caban, yutz kin.	16
15	12, Edznab, u lob kin, u Chaalba ku (a bad day for the church).	17
16	13, Cauac, yutz kin licil, u kokol u yik hub u kin ha (good; the horn sounds well; rain).	18
17	1, Ahau, u lob kin.	19
18	2, Ymix, u lob kin, u coi kinal ahau ku (bad; a day lessened by the King of the Temple, God).	20
19	3, Yk, u lob kin.	21
20	4, Akbal, u lob kin, u coi kinal ahau ku (an unlucky day; lessened by the King God, or King of the Temple).	22

CHEN, 9TH INDIAN MONTH.

Chen.		Dec.
1	5, Kan, lob (utz) licil u cutal Chen (bad or good; beginning of Chen).	23
2	6, Chicchan, u lob kin (utz).	24
3	7, Quimí, yutz kin.	25
4	8, Manik, lob kin.	26
5	9, Lamat, u lob kin.	27
6	10, Muluc, u lob kin.	28
7	11, Oc, utz, u tup kak ahtoc (good; the burner puts out the fire).	29
8	12, Chuen, yutz kin.	30
9	13, Eb, yutz kin.	31
10	1, Been, yutz kin. 1842	Jan. 1
11	2, Hix, yutz kin.	2
12	3, Men, utz u cha kak ahtoc (good; the burner takes his fire).	3
13	4, Quib utz.	4
14	5, Caban, lob licil u cimil uinicob u xulti (bad; the end of man).	5
15	6, Edznab, u lob kin.	6
16	7, Cauac, utz kin, u tial kabnal (good for the bee-hunter).	7
17	8, Ahau, yutz kin.	8
18	9, Ymix, yutz kin.	9
19	10, Yk, yutz kin.	10
20	11, Akbal, yutz kin.	11

YAX, 10TH INDIAN MONTH.

Yax.		January.
1	12, Kan, lob licil u cutal Yax (bad; beginning of Yax).	12
2	13, Chicchan, lob u kukumtok chapahal yani (an unfortunate day; plume of maladies).	13
3	1, Quimí, lob kin.	14
4	2, Manik, utz u xul kaxal haí (end of rains).	15
5	3, Lamat, u lob kin.	16
8	4, Muluc, utz u zian chaac (day of rain).	17
7	5, Oc, licil u kalal u koch mehen palal (the taxing of children is ended).	18
8	6, Chuen, u lob kin.	19
9	7, Eb, yutz kin.	20
10	8, Been, yutz kin.	21
11	9, Hix, u lob kin.	22
12	10, Men, utz u hoppol u kak ahtoc, utz ti cucut, ti kaax u tial ahcehob (a good day; the fire of the burner begins; good for the body, for the forests, and the deer).	23
13	11, Quib, u lob kin.	24
14	12, Caban, u lob kin.	25
15	13, Edznab, u lob kin.	26
16	1, Cauac, u lob kin.	27
17	2, Ahau, u lob kin.	28
18	3, Ymix, u lob kin, u kin kal be hub (bad; the horn does not sound).	29
19	4, Yk, yutz kin.	30
20	5, Akbal, lob u kin, u hokol chacmitan choctal metnal chetun cimil yani (bad; hunger stalks abroad; death is here).	31

ZAC, 11TH INDIAN MONTH.

Zac.		February
1	6, Kan, lob licil u cutal Zac (bad; the commencement of Zac).	1
2	7, Chicchan, lob kin.	2
3	8, Quimí, u lob kin.	3
4	9, Manik, u lob kin.	4
5	10, Lamat, u lob kin.	5
6	11, Muluc, utz cu pec chaaci, hâ yani (good; thunder and rain).	6
7	12, Oc, yutz kin.	7
8	13, Chuen, u lob kin.	8
9	1, Eb, lob kin.	9
10	2, Been, yutz kin.	10
11	3, Hix, u lob kin.	11
12	4, Men, u lob kin, u yalcab a kak ahtoc, u lubul u koch ahkin ppixich (a bad day; the burner gives scope to the fire; taxation of the priests).	12
13	5, Quib, u lob kin chapahal chocuil.	13
14	6, Caban, u lob kin.	14
15	7, Edznab, u lob kin.	15
16	8, Cauac, u lob kin ti ppix ich.	16
17	9, Ahau, u lob kin, u lubul u koch al mehenob (bad; the days of the contribution of the nobles are completed).	17
18	10, Ymix, u lob kin (utz).	18
19	11, Yk, u lob kin.	19
20	12, Akbal, u lob kin, u nup cizin telae (bad; insidious attacks of the arch-fiend).	20

QUEJ, 12TH INDIAN MONTH.

Quej.		February
1	13, Kan, u lob kin.	21
2	1, Chicchan, u lob kin.	22
3	2, Quimí, u lob kin u thalal u koch ahkulelob (day of lawyers).	23
4	3, Manik, yutz kin u thalal u koch ahaulil uincob (a day of service, or binding on the kings of men).	24
5	4, Lamat, u lob kin.	25
6	5, Muluc, u lob kin.	26
7	6, Oc, u lob kin.	27
8	7, Chuen, u lob kin.	28
9	8, Eb, yutz kin, u kin pec chaac (good; it thunders).	Mar. 1
10	9, Been, u lob kin.	2
11	10, Hix, lob kin u kalaal hub.	3
12	11, Men, u lob kin, u tup kak ahtoc (bad; the burner puts out the fire).	4
13	12, Quib, u lob kin.	5
14	13, Caban, u lob kin.	6
15	1, Edznab, u lob kin, uchac u pec chaaci (bad; it may thunder).	7
16	2, Cauac, u lob kin.	8
17	3, Ahau, u lob kin, u cha kak ahtoc (bad; the burner handles the fire).	9
18	4, Ymix, utz, yoc uil payambe, ti u kaxal ha: chikin chaac (good; abundance).	10
19	5, Yk, u lob kin; ceel xan u yoc uil (bad; agues; and day of plenty).	11
20	6, Akbal, lob chac ceeli (utz) (bad; fevers).	12

MAC, 13TH INDIAN MONTH.

Mac.		March.
1	7, Kan, u lob kin, licil u cutal Mac (bad; beginning of Mac).	13
2	8, Chicchan, u lob kin.	14
3	9, Quimí, u lob kin.	15
4	10, Manik, utz, u hoppol haí (good; the beginning of rain).	16
5	11, Lamat, yutz kin.	17
6	12, Muluc, yutz kin.	18
7	13, Oc, u lob kin.	19
8	1, Chuen, u lob kin.	20
9	2, Eb, yutz kin.	21
10	3, Been, u lob kin, licil u pec chikin chac (bad; westerly rains).	22
11	4, Hix, u lob kin.	23
12	5, Men, u lob kin.	24
13	6, Quib, u lob kin.	25
14	7, Caban, u lob kin.	26
15	8, Edznab, utz yoc uil (sign of abundance).	27
16	9, Cauac, utz kin.	28
17	10, Ahau, utz u hoppol u kak ahtoc, yoc uil (the burner lights his fire; harvest day).	29
18	11, Ymix, utz u yoc uil.	30
19	12, Yk, yutz kin.	31
20	13, Akbal, utz u chaalba ku (u zian ku) (church day).	Apr. 1

KANKIN, 14TH INDIAN MONTH.

Kankin.		April.
1	1, Kan, lob, licil u cutal Kankin (bad; the root of Kankin).	2
2	2, Chicchan, lob u hokol u yik hub, u kin ha (an unlucky day; day of rain; the horn sounds).	3
3	3, Quimí, yutz kin.	4
4	4, Manik, yutz kin.	5
5	5, Lamat, yutz kin.	6
6	6, Muluc, yutz kin.	7
7	7, Oc, yutz kin.	8
8	8, Chuen, utz, licil u lubul hâ hach kaam (heavy rains).	9
9	9, Eb, lob ca cha u kin haí (day of rain).	10
10	10, Been, u lob kin.	11
11	11, Hix, yutz kin.	12
12	12, Men, yutz kin.	13
13	13, Quib, yutz kin.	14
14	1, Caban, yutz kin.	15
15	2, Edznab, yutz kin.	16
16	3, Cauac, yutz kin.	17
17	4, Ahau, utz u yalcab u kak ahtoc (licil u zihil cabnal) (good; the bee-hunter is born; the burner gives scope to the fire).	18
18	5, Ymix, u lob kin.	19
19	6, Yk, u lob kin.	20
20	7, Akbal, u lob kin.	21

MOAN, 15TH INDIAN MONTH.

Moan.		April.
1	8, Kan, lob, licil u cutal Moan (bad; the root of Moan.)	22
2	9, Chicchan, u lob kin.	23
3	10, Quimí, u lob kin.	24
4	11, Manik, u lob kin.	25
5	12, Lamat, u lob kin.	26
6	13, Muluc, yutz kin, chac ikal (good; a hurricane).	27
7	1, Oc, u lob kin.	38
8	2, Chuen, u lob kin, u nuptun cizin oxppel kin ca uchuc ppixich chabtan kini (bad; a day of temptation; three days of watching).	29
9	3, Eb, lob hun chabtan oxppel akab u ppixichlae, u cappel u kinil nuptun cizin ca ppixichnac uinic baix tu yoxppel kinil xan (bad; a day of temptation; three days of watching),	30
10	4, Been, yutz u kin u haí (rain).	May 1
11	5, Hix, u lob kin.	2
12	6, Men, u lob kin.	3
13	7, Quib, u lob kin zutob ti kax (bad for travellers).	4
14	8, Caban, lob, u tabal u keban yahanlil cabob (an unlucky day; the sins of the king are proved).	5
15	9, Edznab, u lob kin.	6
16	10, Cauac, u lob kin ximxinbal ti kax (bad for those who walk).	7
17	11, Ahau, u tup kak ahtoc, lob pazal cehob (the burner puts out the fire).	8
18	12, Ymix, u lob kin ti kuku uincob (bad for the sacrificers).	9
19	13, Yk, utz ti yahanlil cabob (good for the queen bees).	10
20	1, Akbal, utz u kin haí (a good day of rain).	11

314

PAX, 16TH INDIAN MONTH.

Pax.		May.
1	2, Kan, lob, ti batabob licil u cutal Pax (bad for the caciques; the beginning of Pax).	12
2	3, Chicchan, lob u cha kak ahtoc iktan yol uinici (bad; the burner puts out the fire).	13
3	4, Quimí, u lob kin, licil u ppixichob (bad; a day of watching).	14
4	5, Manik, u lob kin, cup ikal (bad; a great and suffocating heat).	15
5	6, Lamat, u lob kin.	16
6	7, Muluc, u lob kin.	17
7	8, Oc, yutz kin.	18
8	9, Chuen, yutz kin.	19
9	10, Eb, yutz kin u xocol yoc kin (the days of the sun are reckoned).	20
10	11, Been, u lob kin.	21
11	12, Hix, u lob kin.	22
12	13, Men, yutz kin.	23
13	1, Quib, u lob kin.	24
14	2, Caban, u lob kin.	25
15	3, Edznab, lob, u lubul haí tu kuch haabil Muluc u cappel yoc uil) bad; year of Muluc; second day of planting).	26
16	4, Cauac, yutz kin.	27
17	5, Ahau, yutz kin.	28
18	6, Ymix, yutz kin.	29
19	7, Yk, yutz kin, u hoppol haí (it rains).	30
20	8, Akbal, u lob kin.	31

KAYAB, 17TH INDIAN MONTH.

Kayab.		June.
1	9, Kan, lob, licil u cutal kayab (bad; the beginning of Kayab).	1
2	10, Chicchan, lob, u hoppol u kak ahtoc (the burner begins).	2
3	11, Quimí, u lob kin.	3
4	12, Manik, u lob kin.	4
5	13, Lamat, u lob kin.	5
6	1, Muluc, yutz kin.	6
7	2, Oc, u lob kin.	7
8	3, Chuen, u lob kin.	8
9	4, Eb, yutz u kin noh haí (heavy rains).	9
10	5, Been, u lob kin.	10
11	6, Hix, u lob kin.	11
12	7, Men, u lob kin.	12
13	8, Quib, u lob kin.	13
14	9, Caban, u lob kin.	14
15	10, Edznab, u lob kin thol caan chaac (bad; from all parts).	15
16	11, Cauac, u lob kin, mankin ha (daily rains).	16
17	12, Ahau, u lob kin.	17
18	13, Ymix, yutz kin.	18
19	1, Yk, yutz kin.	19
20	2, Akbal, yutz kin.	20

CUMKU, 18TH INDIAN MONTH.

Cumkú.		June.
1	3, Kan, utz, ncil u cutal Cumkú (good; beginning of Cumkú).	21
2	4, Chicchan, lob kin, yalcab u kak ahtoc (bad; the burner gives scope to the fire).	22
3	5, Quimí, u lob kin.	23
4	6, Manik, u lob kin.	24
5	7, Lamat, u lob kin.	25
6	8, Muluc, utz u zian ku (a day to attend the temple).	26
7	9, Oc, yutz kin.	27
8	10, Chuen, u lob kin.	28
9	11, Eb, u lob kin.	29
10	12, Been, yutz kin.	30
11	13, Hix, u lob kin.	July 1
12	1, Men, u lob kin.	2
13	2, Quib, u lob kin.	3
14	3, Caban, utz u kin balam haabil.	4
15	4, Edznab, utz ppixichnebal ppolom (the traders watch).	5
16	5, Cauac, u lob kin.	6
17	6, Ahau, u lob kin.	7
18	7, Ymix, utz u payalte lae ɔac uinabal uli.	8
19	8, Yk, u lob kin.	9
20	9, Akbal, u lob kin.	10

" XMA KABA KIN," OR INTERCALARY DAYS.

		July.
1	10, Kan, yutz kin, u nay eb haab, xma kaba kin ca culac u chun haab poop (cradle of the year, &c.).	11
2	11, Chicchan, u lob kin, u tup kak ahtoc (the burner puts out the fire).	12
3	12, Quimí, u lob kin.	13
4	13, Manik, utz u tial sabal ziil (to make presents).	14
5	1, Lamat, yutz kin.	15

The next year would commence with 2 Muluc, the following one with 3 Hix, the fourth year with 4 Cauac, the fifth with 5 Kan; and so on continually, until the completion of the 13 numbers of the week of years, which commences with the day Kan; after which the weeks of Muluc, Hix, and Cauac follow, in such manner that, after the lapse of 52 years, the week of years again begins with 1 Kan, as in the preceding almanac. Respecting the bissextile, I have already manifested my opinion in the chronology of the Indians.

The translation of the names of the months and days is not as easy as it would appear, because some are not at present in use, and others, again, from the different meanings attached to them, and from the want of their true pronunciation, cannot be correctly understood; however, be this as it may, I shall endeavour to decipher them as nearly as possible, and according to the present state of the language, beginning with the months.

1. Pop, mat of cane. 2. Uo, frog. 3. Zip, a tree. 4. Zodz, a bat. 5. Zec, obsolete. 6. Xul, end or conclusion. 7. Dzeyaxkin; I know not its signification, although the meaning of *yaxkin* is summer. 8. Mol, to reunite. 9.

Chen, a well. 10. Yax, first, or Yaax, green or blue, though, as the following month is *Zac*, white, I believe this should be Yaax. 11. Zac, white. 12. Quez, a deer. 13. Mac, a lid or cover. 14. Kankin, yellow sun, perhaps because in this month of April the atmosphere is charged with smoke; owing to the woods being cut down and burned, the light of the sun is darkened, and at 5 P.M. it appears red and throws but little light. 15. Moan, antiquated, and its signification forgotten. 16. Pax, any instrument of music. 17. Kayab, singing. 18. Cumkú, a thunder-clap, or noise like the report of a cannon, which is heard in the woods while the marshes are drying, or from some other cause. Uayebhaab, Xma kaba kin, which signifies bed, or chamber of the year, or days without name, were the appellations given to the intercalary days, as they appertained to no month to which a name was given.

Translation of the 20 Days.

1. Kan, string or yarn of twisted hemp; it also means anything yellow, or fruit and timber proper for cutting. 2. Chicchan, obsolete; if it is Chichan, it signifies small or little. 3. Quimí, or Cimí, death or dead. 4. Manik, obsolete, but if the word may be divided, it would signify wind that passes; for *Man* is to pass, to buy, and *ik* is wind. 5. Lamat, obsolete, not understood. 6. Muluc, obsolete; although, should it be the primitive of *mulucbal*, it will signify reunion. 7. Oc, that which may be held in the palm of the hand. 8. Chuen, disused; some say it is equivalent to board. 9. Eb, ladder. 10. Been, obsolete. 11. Hix, not used, although, combined with others, it signifies roughness, as in Hixcay, rasp, Hihixci, rough. 12. Men, builder. 12. Quib, or Cib, wax or gum copal. 14. Caban, obsolete. 15. Edznab, obsolete. 16. Cauac, disused, although it appears to be the word *cacau*. 17. Ahau, king, or period of 24 years; the day in which this period commenced, and therefore they called it Ahau Katun. 18. Ymix, obsolete; although it appears to be the same as Yxim, corn or maize. 19. Yk, wind. 20. Akbal, word disused and unknown.

This is the signification given to those days.

Peto, 14th *April*, 1842.

END OF VOL. I.

Este libro se terminó de imprimir el día
6 de agosto de 1986 en los talleres de
Offset Marvi, Leiria núm. 72, 09440
México, D.F. Se tiraron 2 000 ejemplares

Esta obra se terminó de imprimir el día
26 de agosto de 1989 en los talleres de
Offset Alfaro Libros núm. 2, C.P 09
México, D.F. Se tiraron 2000 ejemplares.